NEIGHBOURHOOD REGENERATION

An international evaluation

NEIGHBOURHOOD
REGENERATION

An international evaluation

EDITED BY
RACHELLE ALTERMAN
GÖRAN CARS

MANSELL

LONDON AND NEW YORK

First published 1991 by Mansell Publishing Limited

A Cassell imprint

Villiers House, 41/47 Strand, London WC2N 5JE
387 Park Avenue South, New York, NY 10016-8810, USA

British Library Cataloguing in Publication Data

Neighbourhood Regeneration: An International Evaluation.
 1. Community development
 I. Alterman, Rachelle *1946*– II. Cars, Göran
 307.14

 ISBN 0–7201–2073–X

Library of Congress Cataloging-in-Publication Data

Neighbourhood regeneration: an international evaluation /
 edited by Rachelle Alterman, Göran Cars.
      p.   cm.
   Includes bibliographical references and index.
   ISBN 0–7201–2073–X
   1. Urban renewal – Evaluation. 2. Neighborhood – Government policy –
Evaluation. 3. Community development, Urban – Evaluation.
4. Planned communities – Evaluation. 5. Urban policy – Evaluation.
I. Alterman, R. II. Cars, Göran.
HT170.C28 1991   90–43173
307.3′36216 – dc20   CIP

Typeset by Colset Private Limited, Singapore
Printed and bound in Great Britain by Biddles Ltd, Guildford and King's Lynn

CONTENTS

PREFACE

This book represents the cross-national collaboration of its editors and authors. In bringing together reports from several countries on the regeneration of urban neighbourhoods, this book tries to overcome the insularity of public policy. It encourages the transfer of experience, following rigorous evaluations, from one country to the other in order to expand knowledge and the availability of policy tools.

Transnational exchange can be useful on two levels. The first level calls for systematic reports on the interrelationship of problems, policies, and manner of implementation, in order to yield an expansion in the number of policy tools available for tackling different types of neighbourhood decline. This was attempted for each of the nine countries represented in this book. Beyond this level lies the question of the evaluation of outputs and outcomes achieved. Regeneration programmes often lack evaluation mechanisms or the evaluations sometimes fail to provide a foundation for improving the programmes or assessing their transferability. Therefore, special emphasis is placed on the methodological dilemmas that researchers in some countries have faced in evaluating regeneration programmes.

We owe thanks to many people who have helped us develop this book from idea to reality. The idea for this book originated with the European Regional Science Congress in Stockholm in August 1988, where Rachelle Alterman was asked to organize a special session on the evaluation of large-scale renewal projects and Göran Cars was asked to present a paper on the Swedish experience. This session gathered participants from three of the countries included in this book. The participants shared the view that there is a need for a vehicle for international comparison and exchange.

We owe thanks to Professor Folke Snickars of the Royal Institute of Technology in Stockholm and to Björn Hårsman, planning director of the Regional Planning Office in Stockholm, who initiated the idea of the conference session as well as the book.

The road from idea to published book is long and we thank the Swedish Council for Building Research for providing essential economic support in the complex prepublication activity that this multinational book required.

Linda Mandeville of the United States is our masterful language editor.

She managed, with great skill and excellent judgment, to overcome the disparities in English of fifteen authors in nine countries who sometimes seemed to be writing in different languages.

Finally we would like to thank all the participating authors for their contributions. Without their efforts and patience when faced with repeated requests for additions and revisions, this book would not have been possible.

Rachelle Alterman
Göran Cars
Haifa and Stockholm

CONTRIBUTORS

Rachelle Alterman is Director of the Klutznick Center for Urban and Regional Studies and Associate Professor at the Faculty of Architecture and Town Planning at Technion — Israel Institute of Technology, Haifa, Israel.

Peter Birghoffer is an engineer–architect at the Hungarian Institute for Building Science, Budapest, Hungary.

Göran Carlén is a researcher and lecturer in the Department of Regional Planning of the Royal Institute of Technology, Stockholm, Sweden.

Göran Cars is a researcher and senior lecturer in the Department of Regional Planning of the Royal Institute of Technology, Stockholm, Sweden.

Tom Carter is the Director of the Institute of Urban Studies at the University of Winnipeg, Winnipeg, Manitoba, Canada.

Anna Gaspár is an engineer–architect with the Building Information Centre in Budapest, Hungary.

Rose Gilroy is a lecturer in housing policy and management in the Department of Town and Country Planning at the University of Newcastle upon Tyne, U.K.

Marshall Kaplan is Dean of the Graduate School of Public Affairs at the University of Colorado, Denver, Colorado, U.S.A.

Hugo Priemus is Managing Director of the OTB Research Institute for Policy Sciences and Technology in Delft and Professor of Housing at the Delft University of Technology, Delft, The Netherlands.

Fritz Schmoll is an independent researcher and consultant in the field of urban renewal and the economy of housing.

Shimon Spiro is Associate Professor at the Bob Schapell School of Social Work and the Department of Sociology and Anthropology at Tel Aviv University, Tel Aviv, Israel.

Jean-Paul Tricart is a sociology researcher at the National Centre for Scientific Research (CNRS), Paris, France. He is currently on secondment to the Commission of the European Communities in Brussels.

CONTRIBUTORS

Richard Williams is a lecturer in town and country planning at the University of Newcastle upon Tyne, U.K.

Colin Wood is a senior lecturer in planning and housing, in the Department of Planning and Landscape, the Faculty of the Built Environment, at Birmingham Polytechnic, Birmingham, U.K.

1 INTRODUCTION: COMPARISONS AND COUNTERPARTS

Göran Cars

In many countries the problems of declining neighbourhoods have become increasingly more critical. Policymakers in various countries have cast about for new policies and strategies for regeneration activities and have allocated more of their country's housing resources to regeneration measures. Government policies to combat neighbourhood deterioration have become more sophisticated in response to the failure of past initiatives, in recognition of the growing complexities of the problems, and in light of economic restraints faced by many countries today.

This book examines neighbourhood renewal—the problems, the policies, their successes and failures—from an international and from a multisectoral perspective. The problem of neighbourhood decay—neighbourhoods infested with vandalism, plagued with violence, blighted with crumbling structures and untended grounds—is not isolated to one country, one city, one block. Rather, neighbourhood decay has emerged internationally as an unfortunate symbol of the failure of urban life. It is a housing problem, an employment problem, a social integration problem, an education problem, an architectural problem. Analyses cannot proceed unless the full dimension of the neighbourhood decay problem is recognized.

THE DEVELOPMENT OF NEIGHBOURHOOD REGENERATION POLICIES

Neighbourhood regeneration is not new. Rather, it can be seen as a permanent phenomenon of the industrialized twentieth century. The need has emanated from two sources. As buildings grow old the need for maintenance increases. The large numbers of buildings constructed in the late nineteenth and early twentieth centuries have been the focus of regenerating measures for a long time. The other reason for regeneration efforts is the higher standard of living and the subsequent demand for larger and better-equipped flats.

Today's regeneration needs, however, diverge significantly from those of the past. Thus, in many countries, regeneration policies began to shift in the 1970s. Following the Second World War, demolition and new construction were considered the most effective way of overcoming housing problems and raising housing standards. Over the last decade the wisdom of demolition has been questioned with increased intensity. Some have claimed that demolition in conjunction with new construction is not only a very expensive improvement method, but one that usually fails to meet the most urgent needs of the neighbourhood residents. Demolition has also been criticized because it destroys the social fabric of neighbourhoods and the built heritage that gives neighbourhoods their identity.

Another condition that separates the present situation from the past is the influence that social problems and disturbances have on neighbourhood deterioration in most Western European and North American countries today. Social problems have always been present in areas needing regeneration, but today's social deficiencies and problems seem to have changed dramatically. In the past, social problems emerged from the overcrowding and substandard conditions characteristic of poverty. These factors still exist, but they are exacerbated by even more serious conditions. (To some extent this increased focus on social problems can be explained by a growing social awareness. Problems that used to be ignored are today often given high priority on the political agenda.)

In many countries, drug abuse is seen as the basic problem. It is a cause as well as a symptom of deterioration. The spread of drug abuse in a neighbourhood may be a sign of its weakened attractiveness, as expressed in low living standards, small flats, and the need for physical rehabilitation. At the same time, drug abuse can cause and accelerate decline through increased crime and social disturbances. As the neighbourhood is considered to be less safe and secure, those who are better off socially and economically move from the area. They are, to a large extent, replaced by people with less resources. The number of poor people with social problems increases. The area is caught in a vicious cycle of decline.

Another feature of today's declining neighbourhoods is the influx of immigrants to these areas. Many immigrant groups, characterized by poverty and a lack of social mobility, are strongly over-represented in areas of low and weakening attractiveness. But the concentration of immigrants in these areas has also hastened the process of decline. Social and cultural differences as well as language problems have led, in many cases, to antagonism between the native inhabitants and the immigrants, and also among various immigrant groups.

The problem that must be addressed to achieve significant change in deteriorating areas is to a large extent, social. It is more commonly recognized that demolition and new construction do not solve the problem. Unanimity has emerged among many countries: regeneration cannot be directed exclusively towards physical change. Upgrading must include social improvements.

DIFFERENCES AND SIMILARITIES AMONG COUNTRIES

As important as the social factors are, physical and functional deficiencies are also causes of deterioration. The physical deficiencies include wear and tear and inappropriate and deferred maintenance. The functional deficiencies include poor, if not declining, retail services, transportation, employment opportunities, and public services. These deficiencies can also lead an area into a vicious cycle of decline.

The precise reasons, however, for neighbourhood deterioration are unique to each country, if not each neighbourhood. Variables include different approaches to policy making and government intervention, the type of neighbourhood, its location, age, and type of construction.

In the U.S.A., Canada, and the U.K., regeneration efforts have been mainly directed towards city centres. Time seems to have passed by these once relatively well off, or even prosperous, neighbourhoods. The relocation of economic activities to the urban periphery and the flight of the middle class to the suburbs have paralleled the influx of low-income households, ethnic minorities, and people with social problems into inner city neighbourhoods. This has led to a general decline in attractiveness. The new residents do not have the economic resources to make regeneration possible or economically profitable for the landlord, nor do they have the political clout to influence government decisions on regeneration. This development has reinforced the spiral of decline in many inner city neighbourhoods.

The geography of renewal is somewhat different in many Western European countries, such as France, the F.R.G, The Netherlands, and Sweden. In these countries, regeneration efforts are often focused outside the city centre. This does not mean that inner cities are without need of regeneration. To varying degrees, regeneration policies and measures have had a very positive impact on the inner cities. These measures have included the upgrading of residential neighbourhoods and the rehabilitation of historic centres as well as the stimulation of economic development in the inner city. These strategies have, in general, preserved attractiveness, sometimes so successfully that they have often been discussed in terms of gentrification.

For financially secure households the inner city has been and still is an appealing residential environment. Meanwhile, though many suburbs have maintained their high status, some of the least attractive areas are located in the suburbs. In these countries it is obvious that poorer households have been pushed out of the city centres, mainly for economic reasons – rental or purchase price increases.

Part of the reason for these varying patterns of deterioration is the different approaches to the regeneration of city centre neighbourhoods and the rehabilitation of historic centres. But the architecture of and services to post-Second World War dwellings and their concentration in outer neighbourhoods are also part of the explanation. Those countries that are facing the most urgent needs for suburban rehabilitation are those that were struck by acute housing shortages after the Second World War because of wartime bombings and the unparalleled concentration of the work force in the cities. This led to demands for increased housing production.

During the 1950s and the 1960s urbanization accelerated in many of these countries, with the result that housing shortages increased despite relatively ambitious housing production programmes. This paved the way for the reformulation of housing policies, in terms of both quantity and quality. In many countries the major ambition was to construct large numbers of dwellings to modern standards, at reasonable prices, and in a short time. These

3

new dwellings were sited in relatively peripheral locations. The contributions in this book from France, the F.R.G., The Netherlands, and Sweden paint a fairly common picture of these areas: neighbourhoods of a thousand or more flats, constructed on virgin soil, monotonously designed, and built with prefabricated materials. These estates are characterized by inadequate public and commercial services and, despite the relative newness of the dwellings, severe maintenance problems. These deficiencies are caused by either poor or non-existing maintenance or faulty construction methods. The transportation systems serving these estates are often inefficient, which isolates these neighbourhoods from regional and city centres and work places. In combination, such conditions often gave these areas a poor reputation right from the start.

The differences among countries with regard to the location and age of the housing stock should not be exaggerated, however, for two reasons. First, the differences are not as clear cut as the general trends suggest. In most countries regeneration needs can be identified in the city centre as well as in the suburbs. This is the case in Israel, for example. Also, in the U.S.A. and the U.K., where the need for renewal is primarily an urban pehnomenon, gentrification here, too, has threatened the integrity of renewal projects. Second, and more important, the underlying problems that form the need for regeneration are, to a large extent, similar. A common feature is that social problems and disturbances constitute an important, often the most important reason, for regeneration.

A BROAD-BASED APPROACH TO NEIGHBOURHOOD RENEWAL

Many books, professional journals, and articles have been devoted to discussions of neighbourhood renewal. But these analyses tend to examine the issues from a single perspective. Technical improvements, costs, or aspects of social development are examples of starting points for such analyses. These types of analyses can, of course, be very useful for a variety of purposes. They can provide knowledge of actual changes in the regenerated neighbourhood and they can also, at least to some extent, be useful starting points for comparisons among neighbourhoods. But the one-sector analysis is restricted for many reasons. First, it ignores the interconnectedness of the various activities and measures during regeneration and the influence that initiatives from other sectors have on the sector being analysed. For example, in the course of an evaluation focused on a social programme, a significant change in the residents' social situation might be identified, but it may not be related directly to the social programme. The change might be caused by activities outside the social programme, such as the technical improvement of dwellings, general economic development measures, amelioration of transportation difficulties, or influences from adjacent areas. These factors might, to a lesser or greater extent, contribute to the change. Thus, a one-sector evaluation can make only a limited contribution to explaining the degree of success or failure in a programme.

Yet another restriction is that it is very hard — if not impossible — to draw conclusions about efficiency from a one-sector study. It precludes the ability to determine whether measures taken within other sectors could have, at the same or lower cost, provided an equal or better outcome.

In this book on neighbourhood regeneration policy, the authors have been encouraged to present a broad-based analysis. The comprehensive approach here allows for the comparison of regeneration programmes, with respect to aims, measures, and outcomes. This comprehensiveness includes an emphasis on measures taken across various sectors to establish interconnections among housing policy, social welfare, physical infrastructure, and economic development.

Secondly, the authors have also provided broad institutional and geographic perspectives in their discussions of regeneration policy. Renewal areas are not insular. Decisions made by central and regional governments can have an important influence on the health and welfare of renewal areas. They are also influenced by their immediate surroundings. Municipal decisions concerning public services and infrastructure investments are of vital importance. Population moves to and from the regeneration area can determine who benefits from renewal measures and their long-term effects. Our comprehensive approach, therefore, includes descriptions of renewal programme in various countries, issues of evaluation, and discussions of international transferability.

National descriptions of neighbourhood regeneration programmes

Contributions from nine countries, mostly Western European, are included in this book: The Netherlands, the U.K., France, the F.R.G., and Sweden. Israel, a country with some European characteristics, is also included. A Hungarian contribution is included to show an Eastern European approach to renewal problems. North America is represented by the U.S.A. and Canada.

Each author was given the same agenda of topics to be covered in their national descriptions, but because of differences among countries, the weight given to each topic varies. Our intent was two-fold: on the one hand, we wanted the descriptions to be similar in format; on the other, we did not want the contributors to be straitjacketed by the format. Therefore we asked the authors to follow a common structure, but to highlight topics that are especially relevant to their context and that address the issue of international transferability. Most of the descriptive articles cover the following:

- a history of declining neighbourhoods;
- a brief overview of the planning, housing, and land system;
- a description of policies and tools for regeneration and their institutional context for implementation;
- an evaluation of success in implementing decisions;
- an evaluation of success in achieving physical and social change; and
- an evaluation of the research.

In several descriptions, neighbourhood policy is illustrated by local case studies. In the absence of a universal classification scheme, national descriptions are presented from west to east. However, this classification is not strictly done with reference to geographic location, it also takes into account the degree of governmental intervention in rehabilitation activities.

Evaluations of regeneration programmes

The evaluations examine programme outcomes to determine what social and physical changes have been achieved. The authors address the success or failure of the programmes as well as the reasons for the outcomes. To what extent have programme goals been met? Over what time period? At what cost, in terms of funds and efficiency?

This book also attempts to assess the evaluations of neighbourhood renewal programmes. Do we really know how to evaluate the achievements and shortcomings of neighbourhood regeneration programmes? What are the weaknesses and strengths of these evaluations? What are the biases? Are they relevant to decision makers? What are the factors that inhibit scientific and thorough evaluations? To what extent can evaluations affect programme adaptability to changing circumstances or misunderstood problems? Does the institutional framework of an evaluation influence its reliability?

International comparisons and transferability

Throughout the book, authors discuss international comparisons and transferability. Yet it is important to realize that the tools for regeneration receive their definition and their strengths and weaknesses from their national context. Measures that have proved successful in one country may be difficult or impossible to undertake in other countries because of institutional differences, as well as cultural, social, and economic variables. The reader will become readily aware, however, of the factors that seem to emerge in most contexts as determinants of success or failure. Among the constant themes are the degree of local participation in the determination and implementation of renewal policy; the extent of government commitment to the programme; the degree to which the programme serves existing residents of deteriorating neighbourhoods; the balance of measures within the various sectors (physical, social, and economic); and the breadth and individualization of neighbourhood programmes.

PART I NATIONAL DESCRIPTIONS AND EVALUATIONS OF NEIGHBOURHOOD PROGRAMMES

2 NEIGHBOURHOOD IMPROVEMENT: THE CANADIAN EXPERIENCE

Tom Carter

Major policy initiatives in Canadian social housing and neighbourhood improvement originated basically with the Dominion Housing Act in 1935. Previous policy initiatives were modest and infrequent and were mainly the prerogative of philanthropists and charitable organizations. Government involvement at any level was limited to sporadic and short-term programmes. There were few integrated and long-term programmes or policies (Rose, 1980, pp. 1–13).

Since this period and the formation of the Canada Mortgage and Housing Corporation in 1945 (*Canada Statutes*, 1945), a wide variety of policy initiatives and programmes have ensued. Initially the federal government played the major role, which is still the case in terms of public expenditures. The provinces and municipalities, however, now play a more active role than they did prior to 1945 or even as late as 1970.

Until recently, public emphasis had been on increasing supply or improving household access to the market. This was done through programmes meant to stimulate the construction of new rental or ownership units and to increase the social housing portfolio and through subsidies to reduce the shelter expenditures of both owners and renters.

As Canada's demographic profile changed, concern about the overall supply of affordable housing has now been either supplemented or replaced by an emphasis on the maintenance or modernization of the existing stock and on neighbourhood improvement. Canada, like many industrialized countries, is characterized by an ageing population, low and declining fertility rates, changing household composition with less emphasis on the nuclear family, lower levels of household formation, and, of course, declining demand for housing. More of the demand can be met by the existing housing stock through initiatives not only to maintain this stock but to facilitate adjustments in its design and features that would accommodate the changing household composition. This shift in emphasis has emerged from a growing awareness of the adverse social consequences that have frequently accompanied demolition and rebuilding, especially when this has led to the destruction of established communities. The combination of these factors has prompted the pursuit of qualitative rather than quantitative strategies.

This chapter focuses on the only major public initiative in Canada that addressed not only the repair and renovation of owner-occupied housing units and rental projects but also improvements to the social and physical

9

infrastructure of the neighbourhoods in which these units are located. This initiative was the Neighbourhood Improvement Program (NIP) and its companion programme, the Residential Rehabilitation Assistance Program (RRAP). These programmes together marked the first major effort to resolve problems in the built environment rather than to increase the supply of or access to housing. The policy context under which this initiative was introduced, the programme objectives, programme implementation, and intergovernmental relationships will be analysed. The strengths and weaknesses of the initiative will be discussed, as will the policy context that saw the demise of NIP. In addition, policy and programme initiatives both pre- and post-NIP will be highlighted and case study material on more multi-sectoral approaches to neighbourhood improvement will be discussed. Comments on the scope and approaches to evaluating these initiatives will be incorporated, as well as comments on the international transferability of these approaches.

POLICY INITIATIVES PRIOR TO THE NEIGHBOURHOOD IMPROVEMENT PROGRAM

Following the Dominion Housing Act in 1935, the first nationwide government initiative even indirectly related to neighbourhood improvement was the 1937 Home Improvement Loans Guarantee Program [Canada Mortgage and Housing Corporation (CMHC), 1987, p. 24], which provided loan guarantees for improvements or extensions to dwellings. Although 126,000 loans totalling $50 million were approved from 1937 to 1940, the programme was not specifically aimed at deteriorating neighbourhoods. The adoption of the National Building Code in 1941, which prompted improved and uniform construction standards, also indirectly led to improvements in residential units in both old and new neighbourhoods (CMHC, 1987, p. 24).

The first programme with the specific objective of improving deteriorating areas of cities was the Urban Renewal Program, introduced in 1944 (CMHC; 1987, p. 25) and initiated in 1948. Through 1968 the CMHC spent approximately $125 million on 48 urban renewal projects (Filhion, 1988, p. v). These projects primarily replaced the built environment with freeways, commercial buildings, and public institutional uses. Although 18,000 new dwellings were built—two-thirds of them public housing—over 13,000 housing units were demolished. Not all 13,000 units were beyond repair nor were all the displaced residents accommodated in the new dwellings. Generally urban renewal in this period was quite disruptive for the inhabitants of affected neighbourhoods (Filhion, 1988, p. 5).

Resident protests in Toronto's Trefan Court and Vancouver's Strathcona focused national attention on the intensifying neighbourhood resistance to urban renewal. In fact, these protests were instrumental in the creation of the Hellyer Task Force in 1968, chaired by Paul Hellyer, the federal minister responsible for CMHC. The task force identified urban renewal as a main concern, questioning not its necessity, but the practices and principles of the approach (Axworthy, 1971, pp. 137–145). Consequently, in November 1969 the federal government discontinued its support of urban renewal, though it maintained its financing of ongoing projects. The freeze was intended to buy time to devise a new urban renewal policy. Simultaneously the government was developing the Ministry of State for Urban Affairs to co-ordinate its urban initiatives and to play a role in federal urban planning and policy making. This transition period in federal interdepartmental relations and the ensuing examination of the relationship of the new department to the constitutional role of provinces in urban affairs – the provinces being very sensitive to perceived encroachments on their jurisdiction by the federal government – provided time for reflection on alternative approaches to urban renewal.

Taking into consideration past mistakes, policy makers adopted several key objectives in an effort to reorient federal urban renewal policy:

- preserving, to the greatest extent possible, the built environment and social fabric of each neighbourhood in an effort to minimize social costs and conflicts involved in urban revitalization;
- developing a programme sensitive to the political reality of the time, particularly the constitutional relationship among the three levels of government with respect to urban affairs;
- targeting assistance to low-income groups and individuals in the inner city least able to bear the pressures of urban change, especially the competition for housing in the private market;
- making a transition from the single function approach that was so characteristic of earlier urban renewal to a form of neighbourhood development that integrates housing with social, recreational, and infrastructure improvements; and
- more community involvement in planning as opposed to the top-down approach so characteristic of earlier urban renewal efforts (Young, 1979, pp. 55–70).

THE NEIGHBOURHOOD IMPROVEMENT PROGRAM: A NEW APPROACH

Programme objectives and funding levels

Within this general context NIP was passed in Parliament in June 1973. The programme sought to distance the federal government, provinces, and municipalities from the urban renewal experience of the late 1950s and early 1960s by formalizing a role for resident participation, placing an emphasis on selective clearance and repair of existing structures, providing funds for social and community purposes and improvements to public infrastructure, and providing protection for displaced persons (Government of Canada, 1985, p. 12). More specifically, the programme objectives encompassed a desire to conserve and rehabilitate the housing stock (through the companion RRAP), to add or rehabilitate required social and recreational amenities and municipal services, to remove blighted land use, to promote the maintenance of neighbourhoods after the NIP project was terminated, and to increase the effect of related programmes (CMHC and United States Department of Housing and Urban Development, 1979, p. 2).

11

Federal funding in the form of grants varied with the type of activity. Grants were available for 50% of the costs of selecting neighbourhoods; developing neighbourhood plans; acquiring or clearing land for open space, community facilities, and low- and moderate-income housing; developing social and recreational facilities; hiring administrators and project implementers; and relocating displaced persons. For more expensive projects, such as improving municipal and public utility services, only 25% of the cost was provided (CMHC, Neighbourhood and Residential Improvement Division, 1979, pp. 108–109). Provincial contributions varied from as little as 2.5% in Nova Scotia to 25% depending on the province and the level of federal funding, while residual municipal contributions ranged from 25 to 72.5% depending on the type of project and the level of provincial funding.

The NIP legislation, one of the first federal pieces to employ a sunset clause, stated that no applications for loans or grants would be approved after 31 March 1978. The aggregate federal contribution to NIP was set at $300 million ($200 million in grants and $100 million in loans) subject to any additional funds authorized by Parliament (Lyon and Newman, 1986, p. 7). The provinces and municipalities were expected to secure other resources to supplement NIP funding; some projects drew on provincial programmes that provided grants for infrastructure. To ensure that meaningful improvements were carried out the minimum federal contribution was set at $100 per resident in designated areas and $150,000 per NIP project (CMHC, Neighbourhood and Residential Improvement Division, 1977, pp. 19–20).

Amendments in 1973 to the National Housing Act introduced two programmes to complement the NIP initiative: the Site Clearance Program (SCP) and the Residential Rehabilitation Assistance Program (RRAP). SCP was used by municipalities to purchase and clear property for low- and moderate-income housing and community facilities. RRAP, however, was the most integral component of the NIP initiative as it provided financial assistance to lower income homeowners and landlords for the upgrading of residential property. Homeowners were eligible for loans to a maximum of $10,000. Up to $5,000 of the loan was forgivable, if the homeowner continued to own and occupy the dwelling for 5 years. Owners of older rental apartments were also eligible for loans up to $10,000 per unit with a non-repayable portion of up to $3,500 (Canada, Minister of Supply and Services, 1986, p. 73). NIP funding addressed the community component of the neighbourhood, while RRAP addressed the deteriorating housing stock. In addition to the two complementary programmes, federal designers hoped to leverage capital from a variety of other federal and provincial programmes, as well as private funds to be spent on residential property and commercial ventures.

Neighbourhood selection, delivery roles, and responsibilities

There were no federal criteria for the designation of municipalities under NIP but there were for the selection of neighbourhoods. NIP areas had to be identifiable neighbourhoods defined by existing geographic, social, physical, or functional features where residential land uses constituted 50% or more of the built-up gross land area and no more than 20% was unserviced vacant land. In addition, more than 25% of the residential units, as determined by available statistics or a visual survey, had to be in need of rehabilitation. Deterioration or deficiencies in physical aspects of the neighbourhood (sewer and water services, paving, street lighting, local utilities, and non-residential buildings) had to be evident, as did the deterioration or lack of social and recreational facilities (community centres, libraries, clinics, sports facilities, and public open space). Areas had to be occupied by low- and moderate-income people with an average household income below the municipal average, or, in very small municipalities, below the provincial average. Areas had to have potentially stable residential land uses, with no plans for major construction or redevelopment other than those changes outlined in the project objectives, and with no conditions within or immediately adjacent to the area that could not be ameliorated by government action. Selection of an area also depended on the municipality's intent to adopt and enforce a property maintenance and occupancy standard by-law to reinforce stability and improvement after the NIP project terminated (CMHC and Province of Ontario, 1975, p. 6).

The federal government's role was to initiate NIP; design the programme's overall framework, features, and criteria; and undertake the necessary fine tuning. CMHC kept a very low profile in the implementation process, only co-ordinating and evaluating projects and providing the necessary technical and financial resources.

The provinces' responsibilities were much broader with a more active role in delivery. Provinces were responsible for negotiating annual agreements with CMHC; designating eligible municipalities; determining the extent of provincial contributions; and setting objectives and criteria for the selection, planning, and implementation stages of NIP. The provinces also handled administration at the municipal level, co-ordinated the relationship between CMHC and the municipalities, provided technical assistance and training for municipal officials, monitored and evaluated programme activity, and encouraged municipal action on occupancy and maintenance by-laws (Lyon and Newman, 1986, pp. 11–12).

Municipal officials and NIP area residents undertook the primary planning and implementation functions associated with designating NIP areas, problem assessment, developing project plans, priority setting, and programme delivery. Resident involvement was a legislative requirement but because the precise nature and form of such participation were not defined by programme criteria, municipalities and residents worked out the level of involvement. The result was extreme variation from one area to another. The senior governments tended not to intervene except to suggest guidelines and alternative models (Guerrette, 1980, pp. 56–57).

Implementation experience

The effectiveness and success of the initiatives, like many of the characteristics of NIP, varied substantially among areas and depended on timing, the interpretation of programme objectives and criteria, intergovernmental

13

co-ordination, staff levels and expertise, resident participation, and municipal commitment. In all, 322 municipalities containing 479 NIP areas were approved for funding (Lyon and Newman, 1986, p. 22). It is not clear what, if any, criteria were used to select particular municipalities and it appears that the provinces tended to identify municipalities on an *ad hoc* basis. Over 60% of the designated municipalities were relatively small centres with populations of 10,000 or less (over half of these involved centres of less than 2,500 people, Table 1). Small centres accounted for 43% of all NIP areas, receiving 23% of the federal funds allocated under the programme (CMHC, 1979b, p. 17). Some provinces chose to disperse the programme's resources over a large number of small centres while others concentrated on a few large municipalities. Despite the considerable emphasis on small centres, over 70% of Canada's urban municipalities with populations exceeding 100,000 did receive NIP funding and 36% of the federal funding went to these major centres (Table 2). Generally municipalities of 100,000 or more were underfunded, while small and particularly mid-sized municipalities were overfunded. Evidence suggests, however, that small municipalities contributed far more per capita than large municipalities (Table 1), raising the possibility that the programme presented a financial burden for centres with a small tax base.

Table 1. Designated municipalities and NIP areas by population size: 1974–78

Population class	Number of municipalities	Percent of total	Number of NIP areas	Percent of total	Per capita municipal expenditure $
>2,500	100	31	100	21	118
2,500–10,000	97	30	107	22	63
10,000–30,000	58	18	86	18	29
30,000–100,000	45	14	91	19	12
Over 100,000	22	7	95	20	5
Total	322	100	479	100	12

Source: CMHC, Neighbourhood and Residential Improvement Division (August 1979) *Evaluation of the Neighbourhood Improvement Program, National Housing Act – Main Report*, Table 7, p. 17. Ottawa.

Although no federal criteria were established for the designation of municipalities, CMHC could have exerted considerable pressure on the actual selection of NIP areas on the basis of the neighbourhood criteria. It appears, however, that this process was also often compromised. A federal evaluation of 20 NIP areas found that only nine satisfied all criteria, nine were deficient in one, and two deficient in more than one criteria. In Toronto only two of eleven areas met all criteria (CMHC, 1979a, p. 23).

Data on municipalities with designated NIP areas suggest that generally they were the higher priority areas but the differences between municipalities with designated NIP areas and all municipalities were not substantial (Table 3). Designated municipalities illustrated greater stability since a lower percentage of their population had moved over the previous 10 years

14

Table 2. NIP municipalities as a proportion of all municipalities by population size class

All	NIP municipalities	NIP/all municipalities	NIP/all %	Percentage of federal funding
Under 10,000	1,049	83	8	23.5
10,000–30,000	151	40	26	17.2
30,000–100,000	65	33	51	23.3
100,000 plus	25	18	72	36.0

Source: CMHC (1979) *Evaluation of the Neighbourhood Improvement Program, National Housing Act – Analysis of Program and Case Study Data*, p. 45.

in all population size classes. The percentage of owner-occupied dwellings was also higher in both the smaller and larger municipalities and a much higher percentage of owners had no mortgages. The housing stock in municipalities containing NIP areas was older and a higher proportion lacked adequate facilities. The per capita income, however, was lower only for centres of 10,000 to 100,000 and actually higher in both smaller and larger centres. Therefore, although areas met the criterion of older stock in need of upgrading and illustrated considerable stability, there was little evidence to suggest that funds were directed to lower income areas.

Many observers believe that the flexibility and ambiguity of NIP's federal objectives, criteria, and guidelines resulted in conflicting interpretation at the local level, which led to implementation and delivery variation and, of course, affected which areas were designated as well as the success and effectiveness of the NIP projects (Detomasi, 1979, pp. 56–73). Flexibility is required to make a national programme work effectively at the regional and provincial levels where circumstances can deviate substantially from the national average. Such flexibility, however, if not monitored closely, can result in poorly targeted programmes and expenditures on non-priority items.

One of NIP's inherent ambiguities was the 'viable neighbourhood' requirement in the objectives. This complicated and confused the selection process as many 'unstable' neighbourhoods most in need of assistance did not meet the viability criterion. Thus NIP went to older residential areas with less need or to smaller municipalities that were designated in their entirety as neighbourhoods (Saskatchewan Department of Urban Affairs, 1978, p. 34).

The ambiguity in objectives also led to problems in assessing a community's need for NIP. There were no federal or provincial standards for assessing the physical environment and the suitability of community services and facilities beyond the specific criteria built into RRAP that related to dwelling conditions. Also, there was no method for determining priorities among such diverse needs as a skating rink, the removal of incompatible land uses, or the provision of land for social housing. This lack of standards and priorities biased the delivery of NIP towards those neighbourhoods with a primary need for RRAP (Saskatchewan Department of Urban Affairs, 1978, pp. 35–36). There were also no consistent guidelines for allocating NIP funds among municipalities. The policy of selecting communities that displayed

15

Table 3. Comparative characteristics – NIP municipalities and all urban municipalities

	Municipal population size class											
	Under 10,000			10,000–30,000			30,000–100,000			Over 100,000		
	All	NIP	% Diff	All	NIP	% Diff	All	NIP	% Diff	All	NIP	% Diff
No. of municipalities	1,049	83	N.A.	151	40	N.A.	65	33	N.A.	25	18	N.A.
% Population with no moves, 1966–71	54.1	53.3	-1	49.9	51.6	3	48.7	50.6	4	48.3	48.8	1
% Dwellings built before 1951	54.2	61.9	14	42.3	55.5	31	39.7	47.1	19	43.5	48.6	12
% Dwellings no exclusive use toilet	5.5	8.1	47	1.8	2.6	44	1.6	1.9	19	2.1	2.7	28
% Owner-occupied dwellings	67.6	69.9	3	64.1	60.6	-5	56.9	52.9	-7	49.5	51.2	3
% Homeowners with no mortgage	35.4	39.8	12	19.4	23.1	19	15.6	17.1	10	17.1	17.9	5
Per capita income	3,339	3,652	9	4,278	3,984	-7	4,279	4,065	-5	4,421	4,444	1

Source: CMHC (1979) *Evaluation of the Neighbourhood Improvement Program, National Housing Act – Analysis of Program and Case Study Data*, p. 45.

need according to the RRAP indicators pre-empted the possibility of giving priority to intercommunity projects, thus further diluting the NIP objectives. The provinces were powerless to hold back grants for frivolous projects even when other communities may have had projects more relevant to NIP.

Differences in staff expertise and the number of staff dedicated to delivery also resulted in considerable variation in the success of projects across the country. Many municipalities were too understaffed to administer the programme effectively. In Saskatchewan, for example, each NIP co-ordinator had responsibility for 15 to 20 NIP communities. The co-ordinator was responsible for the overall administration of the programme, including visits to NIP communities, book-keeping, policy evaluation and monitoring, and intergovernmental relations. The co-ordinator had no research or support staff other than a typist. Because daily book-keeping, co-ordination, and liaison consumed most of the co-ordinator's time, policy review, evaluation, and monitoring were not given appropriate attention. Programmes had to operate on a day-to-day basis, leaving little time for planned development of the programme (Saskatchewan Department of Urban Affairs, 1978, p. 51).

Generally NIP projects were completed within allocated budgets but implementation often took longer than programme designers had anticipated. These projects became less viable over time because of inflation and the increasing restraints on government programming. At least 1 year of the 5-year implementation period was required for negotiating the federal/provincial agreements (CMHC, 1979a, p. 22). Lack of forward budgeting also created short-term planning problems as annual allocations always had to await parliamentary approval of that year's CMHC budget.

With three levels of government involved there were also the inevitable co-ordination problems. The absence of an intergovernmental co-ordinating committee, which had been a feature of the earlier urban renewal programme, often meant slow, circuitous communication and a pass-the-buck approach to decision making. This not only slowed delivery but had a negative effect on planning and development (CMHC, 1979a, pp. 66–67).

The degree of municipal commitment to resident participation and maintenance and occupancy by-laws also affected project success. NIP objectives encouraged residents to be given an advisory role during the selection and planning phases with more limited involvement in implementation. The federal government, however, did not ensure that this happened. Each municipality, therefore, interpreted this requirement differently and the provinces, in the absence of a set procedure, were obliged to accept this interpretation. Actual project participation ran from nil to extensive. In some cases the involvement was controversial, but overall the level of involvement was low (Lyon and Newman, 1986, p. 45). Municipalities often found expedient ways around citizen participation to obtain a level that was the least disruptive to the current local administration. In one community, which wanted a citizen vote on a skating rink, the notices of a public meeting were posted in obscure places and in other skating facilities so that hockey fans were the ones who mainly turned out (Saskatchewan Department of Urban Affairs, 1978, p. 54). NIP, however, did encourage the formation of many new resident groups that continued to play a grass-roots planning role even after the programme ended.

Municipal maintenance and occupancy standards were mandatory for NIP designations. The purpose of the standards was two-fold: to provide a means to deal with substandard units and recalcitrant owners within NIP areas, and to encourage continued maintenance and upgrading, thus protecting investments made under NIP (Lyon and Newman, 1986, pp. 46–47). In general, municipal enforcement of such by-laws was lacklustre. Many areas applied by-laws only to owners eligible for RRAP or in reaction to complaints about the worst cases of dereliction. Little effort was made to apply the standards to an entire area or municipality. Larger municipalities with trained staff and other resources were more aggressive but they were cautious about the possible displacement of residents, particularly if enforcement prompted landlords to close or demolish properties.

Each NIP area had its own mix of needs, project types, and funding priorities. Some concentrated on major community facilities, others emphasized capital works, while several merely acquired and cleared land for social housing. Data illustrate that nationally 45% of the budget was allocated to social and recreational facilities (Table 4). Spending in this category was more prominent in small centres. Only 12% of the budget was allocated to acquiring land for social housing and larger municipalities placed greater priority on this item. Municipal services accounted for 23% of the allocated budget. This was a relatively important component of NIP in all municipalities, but particularly so in smaller municipalities. Approximately 7% of the allocated budget went to planning and administration and not surprisingly expenditures on this item were higher in larger centres. Very little money was allocated to relocation, indicating an expectation of modest displacement activity. Minimal amounts of money were allocated to land uses other than social housing and 11% to reserves. If information were available on

17

Table 4. Allocations by activity type and municipal population size class of Neighbourhood Improvement Program

Budgetary items	Canada	Municipal population class				
		Under 2,500	2,500– 10,000	10,000– 30,000	30,000 100,000	Over 100,000
Social/recreation (%)	45.3	62.3	43.6	40.4	39.3	46.3
Land for social housing	12.2	7.7	7.7	6.0	19.4	14.1
Participation planning and admin.	6.8	4.7	6.7	7.6	5.5	7.8
Relocation	0.6	0.3	0.5	0.9	0.5	0.6
Municipal services	23.1	18.5	33.5	33.6	22.1	16.5
Land for other uses	1.2	0.8	0.5	0.5	0.3	2.3
Reserve	11.3	6.0	9.2	11.3	13.0	12.5

Source: CMHC (1979) *Evaluation of the Neighbourhood Improvement Program, National Housing Act – Main Report,* Table 19, p. 38.

the ultimate distribution of reserve funds, this would affect the final distribution in other categories.

The federal government committed $201.9 million in grants and $64.4 million in loans or 89% of the legislated maximum. Total contributions from all three levels of government were estimated at $500 million including $109.7 million from the provinces and $186.7 million from the municipalities (CMHC, Statistical Services Division, 1979, p. 66; CMHC, 1979a, pp. 8–9). One of the stated objectives of NIP was to increase the effectiveness of related programmes. No estimates are available, however, to suggest how much funding from other government programmes or, for that matter, private capital was leveraged by NIP funding. RRAP, Canada Works, New Horizons, Municipal Infrastructure, and Culture and Youth Facilities grants were used by NIP communities. There was little evidence, however, of a co-ordinated or integrated approach. Because of the lack of co-ordination and communication, particularly among provincial government departments, the potential for integrated development offered by NIP was lost.

In general, however, implementation was not considered to be overly problematic and project success was probably affected most by the number and skill of staff that municipalities could devote to the programme. More improvements would have been possible had the commitment to the programme been longer with an assured level of funding, which would have allowed the provinces and particularly the municipalities to make the appropriate organizational and staffing changes that they were not prepared to take for a short-term programme.

Policy implications

NIP also raised some broader and more general policy issues than those discussed above. NIP was judged by most of its active participants as a qualified and, in some cases, astonishing success that led the way in sensitive

18

revitalization and conservation of older neighbourhoods. Evaluations under-taken by the Ontario Ministry of Municipal Affairs and Housing cited positive community impact, the accommodation of defined community needs, and the arresting of neighbourhood deterioration before it became irreparable (Ontario Ministry of Municipal Affairs and Housing Project Planning Branch, 1981). Other evaluations were not as enthusiastic: the Canadian Council on Social Development stated that the programme required a refinement of objectives, design, and delivery mechanisms and that NIP in many instances failed as a viable effective tool for neighbourhood revitalization (Lyon and Newman, 1986, p. 53).

Nearly all participants, evaluators, and federal and provincial officials agree, however, that NIP resulted in positive physical changes in designated neighbourhoods. The addition of social and recreational amenities, the rehabilitation of existing housing and construction of new social housing, infrastructure improvements, and down-zoning were all considered positive aspects of the programme. The verdict was not as positive on issues such as citizen participation, by-law enforcement, community planning, and the continued ability of municipalities and provinces to bear the cost of neigh-bourhood improvement without continual federal assistance. One very obvious conclusion about the programme was its tremendous variability among provinces and among municipalities. Because this variability sur-faced in all aspects of policy and programme implementation, it is difficult to consider NIP a 'national' programme.

The substantial number of small municipalities designated under NIP was of considerable concern from a policy point of view. The issue was not one of need but really a deviation from the primary intent of NIP. Smaller municipalities were less likely to enforce maintenance and occupancy standards, involve residents in planning and implementation, or pursue social housing projects. There was concern that small municipalities used NIP too extensively to provide social and recreational facilities at the expense of other items funded under the programme. Many smaller muni-cipalities in some provinces were able to stack NIP funding with grants from such departments as Culture and Recreation to help cover capital and operating costs. It is not surprising, therefore, that smaller municipalities concentrated on activities such as skating rinks rather than social housing; improvement of infrastructure, utilities, and streetscape; or removal of incompatible land uses for which there were no other sources of funding (Saskatchewan Department of Urban Affairs, 1978, pp. 40–42). Federal cost sharing also helped bias projects towards social and recreational facilities even in larger municipalities, since the federal grant for recreation projects was higher (50%) than for the more expensive projects involving local improvements or utilities (25%).

The ability of smaller municipalities to deliver NIP effectively was also open to question given the number and expertise of staff. There was also the question of the smaller municipalities' ability to afford NIP, particularly over the longer term if the operating costs of social and recreational facilities climbed and funding from other departments was discontinued. Given these policy issues in the small municipalities, what should have been considered was a two-tier structure, one for larger and the other for smaller municipalities (Ontario Ministry of Municipal Affairs and Housing Project Planning Branch, 1981, p. 84).

Because NIP was a fixed-termed, fixed-budget federal experiment in neighbourhood improvement, many questioned its long-term influence. NIP certainly improved social and recreational facilities in designated areas and RRAP had a positive effect on housing conditions, though it did not address all substandard dwellings. NIP alone, however, was not sufficient in scale and scope to reverse the deterioration of older neighbourhoods. The programme's focus was narrow, addressing community infrastructure and housing rather than incorporating a multidimensional approach encompassing employment, community economic development, social support programmes, and job training. Some evaluators argued that neighbourhood deterioration is a multidimensional problem that has to be addressed by a multidimensional programme (Lyon and Newman, 1986, pp. 24, 54).

However, NIP did result in a significant reorientation of municipal and provincial policy towards older neighbourhoods. Areas that in the past could not successfully attract public or private investment were the focus of renewal activity. The rationale of the programme was certainly not in question; the programme was needed and it was a welcome reorientation of government policy compared with renewal approaches of the 1950s and 1960s. There was also general support for its continuation, although with modifications that would make it a more multidimensional approach.

THE POST-NEIGHBOURHOOD IMPROVEMENT PROGRAM ERA

The evolving federal role

Despite considerable support for NIP, the programme was not renewed in 1978, though federal commitments did continue under NIP's replacement, the Community Services Contribution Program (CSCP). CSCP really combined NIP with two other programmes: the Municipal Infrastructure Program, which since 1960 had provided grants and loans of $2.2 billion for the planning and construction of sewage and water supply systems, and the Municipal Incentive Grant, which since 1975 had encouraged land development by providing a $1,000 per unit grant for modest-sized, moderately priced housing at medium densities.

CSCP was supposed to make federal assistance available to municipalities for a wide range of neighbourhood improvement activities ranging from sewage treatment and sewer and water systems to social, cultural, and recreational facilities; housing; and waste management. CSCP's focus was not on rehabilitating poorer areas or on arresting neighbourhood deterioration; neither did it encompass neighbourhood participation or multifunctional programming. However, CSCP was consistent with changing urban and housing policies in their movement towards encouraging increased private investment in housing and neighbourhood improvement, so as to allow a corresponding decrease in federal expenditures. Simultaneously attempts were made to transfer more responsibility to the provincial level by establishing more flexible federal/provincial relations. The following four principles defined the change in federal policy (Canada, Minister of Supply and Services, 1986, pp. 9–14):

- a desire to devolve federal responsibility to the private sector and the province;
- federal disengagement from programmes that were housing related but did not directly produce additional or improved units;
- an intent to retarget social housing assistance to ensure only the most needy are recipients; and
- an intent to limit any direct federal role to one concerned with weakness or failure in the housing market.

These principles ruled out any extensive federal involvement in the multi-dimensional programming required to address neighbourhood deterioration. In fact, the late 1970s and early 1980s were characterized by a very pronounced withdrawal of the federal government in most aspects of urban policy, as highlighted by the federal government's decision in 1979 to disband the office of Secretary of State for Urban Affairs.

Municipal initiatives

After the substantial withdrawal of the federal government, provinces and municipalities were left with the task of maintaining the momentum in neighbourhood improvement; many continued the initiative. In 1982 Ontario introduced the Ontario Neighbourhood Improvement Program patterned after the federal programme. In 1983 the province introduced the Ontario Downtown Revitalization Program, making available to municipalities loans with a one-time interest charge of 10% for the acquisition and clearing of land, reconstruction of public services, development of off-street parking, and projects to improve employment in inner city neighbourhoods. The municipalities were to repay the loans by returning one-third of the resulting increased tax revenue to 10% of the loan amount. In 1985 this was followed by the Ontario Commercial Improvement Program, a one-third grant/two-thirds loan arrangement and in 1986 by PRIDE (Program for Renewal Development Improvement and Economic Revitalization), with a similar grant/loan funding formula (Duffy, 1988, pp. 24–26).

The province of Alberta introduced AMPLE (Alberta Municipal Partnerships in Local Employment), a system of loans and grants to help municipalities replace old cast-iron sewers, water pipes, and combined sewers and storm drains, and upgrade roads (*City Trends*, 1986, pp. 8–9). The municipality of Regina has continued a Neighbourhood Improvement Area Program designed to upgrade decaying infrastructure in older neighbourhoods. Expenditures over the last ten years have exceeded $10 million.

Similar activity in other provinces and municipalities illustrates that provincial and municipal efforts continue the neighbourhood improvement initiative. These initiatives, however, all face the same difficulties. Funding has been too limited to address the full extent of the problem. The overwhelming cost is illustrated by the fact that in just three Edmonton neighbourhoods (Oliver, Westmount, and Englewood) the estimated cost of infrastructure improvement is $48 million, suggesting that costs in urban areas are beyond the combined funding capacities of the provincial and municipal governments (*City Trends*, 1986, pp. 8–9). In addition, municipalities are not interested in extensive loan programmes that increase their debt burden. Also, recent initiatives have not been multidimensional enough to address the complex set of circumstances associated with neighbourhood deterioration.

RRAP has continued to rehabilitate deteriorating housing but its impact has been weakened by the decision to open the programme to all households rather than restricting it to designated older neighbourhoods. Two successive national surveys (1982 and 1985) show very little reduction in the percentage of dwellings needing major repair and that substantially more dwellings in older residential areas of the inner city than in suburban areas need upgrading (Canada Mortgage and Housing Corporation, 1987, pp. 2, 7). Although expenditures for renovation and repair have been increasing more rapidly than expenditures on new construction—climbing 11.6% per year from 1976 to 1986 compared to 5.1% for new construction—the average private expenditure on repair and upgrading of the existing stock is substantially less than what is required to bring the housing stock up to acceptable standards. The shortfall in necessary expenditures exceeds $5 billion (Canada Mortgage and Housing Corporation, 1987, pp. 3–4).

Winnipeg's core area initiative: an intergovernmental comprehensive model

The multidimensional approach required to address neighbourhood deterioration is perhaps best illustrated by Winnipeg's Core Area Initiative. Winnipeg's core area includes the downtown and surrounding older neighbourhoods. Approximately ten square miles in area, the core includes one-fifth of the city's population and one-quarter of the dwelling units (Canada–Manitoba Subsidiary Agreement for the Development of the Core Area Initiative, 1986a, p. 2). Historically the area was the city's focal point for economic and social activity but over the last 35 years suburban development has dominated, resulting in the social, economic, and physical deterioration of the inner city.

The core is now significantly different than the rest of the city. Demographically it has been losing population since 1941. The proportion of young singles and older people has increased while the proportion of two-parent families with children has decreased. Much higher in the core area is the incidence of special needs groups such as single-parent families, aboriginal Canadians, and ethnic migrants who face barriers to full social and economic participation in the community because of limited education and employment skills. The aboriginal and ethnic groups also have difficulty establishing themselves in the urban environment because community and business values and conditions are different from those of their origin. The incidence of poverty is two and a half times greater than in other areas of the city and the unemployment rate is double (Canada–Manitoba Subsidiary Agreement for the Development of the Core Area Initiative, 1986a, pp. 3–5).

The physical environment is characterized by poor quality housing and deteriorating commercial buildings. Approximately 30% of the houses need major repairs, one of the highest incidences of poor housing among Canadian cities (Canada–Manitoba Subsidiary Agreement for the Development of the Core Area Initiative, 1986a, p. 4). Investment in suburban areas has also undermined commercial, light manufacturing, and service industry development in the core. Out-migration of investment has reduced core area employment and expenditures; much of the commercial floor space is under-utilized.

In recognition of the serious nature of the problem the Core Area Initiative (CAI), an ambitious trigovernmental (federal, provincial, and municipal) urban revitalization effort was undertaken in 1981. Funds totalling $96 million, shared equally by the three levels of government, were provided over the 5-year period, 1981 to 1986. Recently a second 5-year agreement was signed with a total funding of $100 million, shared similarly (Kiernan, 1987, p. 23).

The project's comprehensiveness and its trigovernmental delivery structure, without precedent in Canadian urban problem solving, has raised strong national and international interest. Overall management lies with a policy committee consisting of a principal federal minister, a principal provincial minister, and the mayor of Winnipeg. This committee issues policy guidelines and directives to a trilevel management board consisting of deputy minister-level representation, which provides operational directions. Below this the CAI office staff provide programme delivery; co-ordination; consultation with individuals, community groups, and investors; and evaluation. The multidimensional initiative addresses not just the bricks and mortar of the deteriorating urban core, but attacks simultaneously the physical, economic, and social problems in a comprehensive and integrated fashion.

At the end of the first 5-year agreement the impressive list of accomplishments included the investment of $21 million in 260 units of new market housing, the development of 330 units of social housing, repairs to over 5,000 older homes, the refurbishing of 30 heritage buildings, the establishment or expansion of 140 small businesses, the development of 15 inner-city industries, investment of over $40 million in community facilities, the construction of a $300 million mixed-use development, the creation of over 3,000 jobs and training opportunities, and the investment of $3 million in education programmes. Projects vary from programmes to combat adult illiteracy to the construction of a $300 million shopping complex. The $96 million public investment has leveraged $250 million in private sector capital plus another $170 million from complementary government programmes for a total investment of over $500 million (Kiernan, 1987, pp. 25–26).

Is this the model for arresting inner city decay in the future? Are there lessons to be learned from CAI? The integral involvement of the three levels of government in such a comprehensive long-term development is unprecedented in Canada and offers a number of advantages. The model expands not only the available funding resources but also the technical and management expertise for planning, delivery, and evaluation. It enhances the ability to attract funds from complementary programmes in various departments at all three levels of government (Brennan, 1989, p. 11). The co-operation and co-ordination inherent to the programme's framework prevents the scattered and disaggregated investment that typically occurs when the three levels of government work on their own individual initiatives. This co-ordinated approach gives the programme an identity and a sufficiently focused level of activity to gain the confidence of the private sector and encourage its investment.

CAI has succeeded in strengthening community involvement and promoting community-based decision making through community development corporations and advisory boards for each programme area. These organizations have wide-ranging control over priorities and programme initiatives. CAI suggests that intergovernmental urban partnerships are not only desirable and practical, they may also be indispensable vehicles for addressing contemporary urban problems (Kiernan, 1987, p. 1).

THE CANADIAN EXPERIENCE

International transferability

Are the lessons from the Canadian experiences transferable to the international arena? Because the problems facing older areas of Canadian cities are certainly present in other cities of the developed world, the Canadian initiatives should have some international applicability. The Canadian experience suggests that intergovernmental urban partnerships, although far from perfect, are the most effective vehicle for dealing with urban decay. The magnitude of the problem requires a co-ordinated and focused approach and a level of funding that can only be provided by an intergovernmental partnership. The Canadian experience also demonstrates that programmes to address decay have to be long term and comprehensive in their treatment of the issues as opposed to a brick-and-mortar, project-by-project approach. Social, educational, and economic programming is necessary to complement and reinforce projects that provide improved housing and community infrastructure. The Canadian experience also demonstrates the necessity and utility of community involvement in the decision-making process. Finally, and perhaps most important, the Canadian experience suggests that senior levels of government must be involved in both policy development and programme delivery if urban decay is to be adequately addressed. Funding capacity, expertise, and political will are often insufficient at the municipal level to deal with the magnitude of problems associated with urban decay. CAI, which incorporates most, if not all, of these aspects may well be an international model.

Evaluation of Canadian initiatives

One consistent weakness of the Canadian approach to urban decay is the lack of reliable and substantive evaluations of programme initiatives. Planning and associated programming is anything but an exact science. Almost inevitably, programming does not unfold as expected because the context is constantly changing. Periodic checking and adjustment are necessary, and therefore evaluation should be an ongoing exercise (Levy, 1988, pp. 95–96). In Canada, however, evaluation has generally been on a follow-up basis. Also missing from most evaluations are time-series analyses to determine whether programmes have been successful in arresting decay over a long period of time (Dctomasi, 1979, pp. 56–73). Also, the evaluations tend to focus on direct results, such as units built or heritage buildings saved, as opposed to the indirect and induced impacts on the neighbourhood.

Many of these problems can be attributed to four basic parameters missing from programme implementation and design. (1) Most legislation associated with renewal programming does not require evaluation and periodic review and updating. As a result, information systems are not put in place at the outset to collect the necessary data. (2) Evaluation priorities are weakened because of the divided jurisdictional nature of programme initiatives in Canada (Cullingworth, 1987, pp. 453–469). Often the senior levels of government – the major sources of funding – place greater emphasis on cost accounting than on neighbourhood impact. (3) Little money is set aside to undertake evaluation studies. This is not surprising given the first two reasons. Even the comprehensive long-term CAI initiative allocated only four-tenths of 1% of budgeted funds to evaluation (Canada–Manitoba Subsidiary Agreement for the Development of the Core Area Initiative, 1986b). (4) Many evaluations are undertaken internally or by self-interested parties rather than being contracted out to unbiased parties with the necessary skills and expertise. Often the evaluations tend to be based on weak methods and lack critical analysis.

What of the future?

Neighbourhood blight and deterioration are still extensive in inner city areas and are spreading out into aging suburban areas built since the Second World War. These areas constitute an expense that no municipality can afford to carry. As blight sets in, tax revenues decline and, on the other side of the accounting sheet, the costs of municipal services, maintenance of streets, utilities, playgrounds, fire and police protection, schools, and other facilities tend to rise out of proportion to general municipal rates. Operating within the confines of the private market, gentrification has and will continue to improve some areas, but it also tends to displace substantial numbers of lower income households, which gravitate to expanding areas of deterioration, unclaimed by gentrification.

Multidimensional programming is required. Winnipeg's CAI may well be the type of vehicle that should be adopted on a national basis to address the complexities of neighbourhood deterioration. What is most needed, however, is the return of the federal government as a more active participant in neighbourhood and infrastructure improvement, both in the policy and funding contexts. Regardless of whether it is through specific initiatives such as the CAI in Winnipeg or through a more nationally based programme, the federal government must turn its attention to the decaying social and physical infrastructure of city neighbourhoods and the deteriorating housing stock they contain. Only prompt and appropriate policy and substantial funding from the senior government can prevent more extensive problems and expenditures in the coming decades.

REFERENCES

AXWORTHY, L. (1971) The housing task force: a case study. In: G.B. Doerm and P. Aucoin (eds) *The Structure of Policy Making in Canada*. Toronto: Macmillan.

BRENNAN, M.L. (June 1989) *The Central Business District and the Core Area Initiative*. University of Winnipeg.

Canada–Manitoba Subsidiary Agreement for the Development of the Core Area Initiative (10, October 1986a) Appendix A, Section B.

Canada–Manitoba Subsidiary Agreement for the Development of the Core Area Initiative (10, October 1986b) Appendix E.

Canada, Minister of Supply and Services (1986) *Housing Programs in Search of Balance*. Ottawa.

Canada Mortgage and Housing Corporation (1979a) *Evaluation of the Neighbourhood Improvement Program*, Vol. 1.

Canada Mortgage and Housing Corporation (1979b) *Evaluation of the Neighbourhood Improvement Program, National Housing Act – Main Report*. Ottawa.

Canada Mortgage and Housing Corporation, Statistical Services Division (1979) *Canadian Housing Statistics*, Table 74.

Canada Mortgage and Housing Corporation (July 1987) *A Consultation Paper on Housing Renovation*. Ottawa.

Central Mortgage and Housing Corporation, Neighbourhood and Residential Improvement Division (1977) *Evaluation of the Neighbourhood Improvement Program: Provincial Position Papers*, Vol. 4. Ottawa.

Central Mortgage and Housing Corporation, Neighbourhood and Residential Improvement Division (August 1979) *Evaluation of the Neighbourhood Improvement Program, National Housing Act – Analysis of Program and Case Study Data*, Vol. 2. Ottawa.

Central Mortgage and Housing Corporation and Province of Ontario (1975) *Neighbourhood Improvement Program: Administrative Guide*.

Central Mortgage and Housing Corporation and United States Department of Housing and Urban Development (1979) *Revitalizing North American Neighbourhoods: A Comparison of Canadian and U.S. Programs for Neighbourhood Preservation and Housing Rehabilitation*. Washington, DC.

Canada Statutes (1945) 9–10, George VI, C. 15. An Act to Incorporate the Central Mortgage and Housing Corporation.

City Trends (September 1986) Increasing the Appeal of Old Neighbourhoods.

CULLINGWORTH, B.J. (1987) *Urban and Regional Planning in Canada*. New Brunswick, NJ: Transaction Books.

DETOMASI, D.O. (1979) The evaluation of public projects: the CMHC evaluation of NIP. *Plan Canada*, **19** (1).

DUFFY, G. (1988) Lawener Nabru. *Canadian Housing*, **5** (2) Summer.

FILHION, P. (1988) *The Neighbourhood Improvement Program in Montreal and Toronto: The Reformist and the Neoreformist Approach to Urban Policy Making*. Waterloo: School of Urban and Regional Planning.

Government of Canada (1985) *Consultation Paper on Housing*, Appendix 2.

GUERRETTE, D. (1980) Citizen representation in neighbourhood improvement programs. Unpublished M.A. thesis, Faculty of Graduate Studies, School of Community and Regional Planning, University of British Columbia, Vancouver.

KIERNAN, M.J. (1987) Intergovernmental innovation: Winnipeg's Core Area Initiative. *Plan Canada*, **27** (1) March.

LEVY, J.M. (1988) *Contemporary Urban Planning*. Englewood Cliffs, NJ: Prentice-Hall.

LYON, D. and L.H. NEWMAN (1986) *The Neighbourhood Improvement Program 1973–1983: A National Review of an Intergovernmental Initiative*, Research and Working Paper No. 15. Institute of Urban Studies.

Ontario Ministry of Municipal Affairs and Housing Project Planning Branch (July 1981) *Neighbourhood Improvement Programs: An Evaluation — Final Report*. Toronto.

ROSE, A. (1980) *Canadian Housing Policies (1935–1980)*. Toronto: Butterworths.

Saskatchewan Department of Urban Affairs, Urban Development Branch (August 1978) *Neighbourhood Improvement Program: An Evaluation 1974–1977*.

YOUNG, A.B. (1979) Federal perspectives in the development of the Neighbourhood Improvement Program and Rehabilitation Assistance Program: 1969 to 1973. MCP thesis, University of Manitoba.

3 AMERICAN NEIGHBOURHOOD POLICIES: MIXED RESULTS AND UNEVEN EVALUATIONS[1]

Marshall Kaplan

The United States of America has not been able to achieve a comprehensive or co-ordinated urban policy. Political facts of life deny the United States the ability to sustain priorities concerning cities. The federal government, in light of competing political groups and competing claims for a finite federal budget, cannot grant clear preference to city interests over non-city interests or to one class or type of city over another type of city (e.g. larger over smaller cities, distressed cities over healthier cities, central cities over non-central cities) for extended periods of time. Further, competition among and between federal agencies and often overlapping competitive roles and missions among federal agencies limits the federal government's ability to use strategically whatever policies and programmes exist at any one moment in time. Finally, the lack of knowledge concerning what does and does not work regarding city problems makes it difficult to define and/or gain support for overarching policies or programmes benefiting cities.

Urban policy advocates have tried their best to bring the country's attention to the needs of older and assumedly needier central cities. They have justified their desire to concentrate federal dollars on them on equity and efficiency grounds. Simply put, older central cities, they argue, have some of the worst physical and social problems, including a decaying housing stock, a deteriorating and under-utilized infrastructure, the absence of amenities, and outmoded downtowns. Their people illustrate higher levels of poverty, unemployment, and underemployment.

Since the early 1960s, the U.S.A.'s urban policy, or what purports to be its urban policy, has focused, in part, on neighbourhood revitalization. While the names of the initiatives changed over time, the conventional wisdom did not: the federal government had a responsibility to and, perhaps more relevant, could help improve the physical condition of older deteriorating or already deteriorated urban neighbourhoods. Most often, neighbourhood revitalization policies have been viewed as synonymous with efforts to reduce or ameliorate poverty – a linkage that seemed obvious to most federal policymakers in light of the concentration of low-income households in poorer quality neighbourhoods. This linkage was also sometimes a political requirement for securing resources. Only recently have we begun to seriously examine the role and impact of the federal government in neighbourhood revitalization. Similarly, only recently have we begun to question

28

the assumed relationship between neighbourhood improvement and poverty reduction.

AMERICAN NEIGHBOURHOOD REVITALIZATION: MYTHOLOGIES AND POLICIES

Americans have had a romance with their neighbourhoods almost since the country's birth. In the nation's mythology neighbourhoods have represented the American way of life, the safety of familiar space, a cluster of like-minded families and kids, and service provision by government at a human scale. Neighbourhoods have been the building blocks of our community planning and education programmes. Appeals to a sense of neighbourhood have been used to foster civic concern for amenities, the protection of property values, and the expansion of group and household life-style choices.

Our continued attraction to neighbourhoods has troubled some and mystified others. Some scholars have questioned whether, given our mobility, many of us really live in neighbourhoods. They claim that most middle- and upper-class households are no longer constrained by the spatial limits of neighbourhoods in choosing friends and in fulfilling household, community, and economic roles. The spatial map they would use to describe how we live is much larger and is constrained mainly by transportation and telecommunication variables.

To some analysts, the neighbourhood has become an obstacle to social progress. For example, they would argue that protection of the neighbourhood school has become a code for resistance to school desegregation. Similarly, the protection or maintenance of neighbourhood values and integrity is coincidental with resistance to the development of housing for low-income households in middle- and upper-income neighbourhoods.

By and large, the support for national neighbourhood policies has reflected the positive attributes most Americans associate with neighbourhoods. But the actual content of these policies has reflected many of the ambiguities raised by scholars and practitioners. In this context, neighbourhood policies have focused either on places or on people who live in places (Table 1). Put another way, and perhaps more relevantly, they have focused on neighbourhoods as physical environments or on the 'disadvantaged' people who live in neighbourhoods. But, even here, distinctions are not always clear.

The programmes described in brief

Table 1 presents a summary of American neighbourhood-related programmes through the years, divided into *place policies* and *people policies*. Each programme is briefly defined below.

Urban Renewal/Redevelopment. A federal programme that provided financial support to cities to acquire, clear, and write down the cost of blighted land and/or buildings for subsequent reuse according to a publicly approved plan.

Table 1. Place and people neighbourhood-related programme initiatives

Place
Urban Renewal and Redevelopment
Federal housing programmes (support for production)
Model Cities
War on Poverty
Neighborhood Housing Services
Urban Homesteading
Neighborhood Strategy Areas
UDAG
Community Development Block Grants
Tax incentives (e.g. historical preservation)

People
Welfare assistance
Provision of or access to services
Social Security/income enhancement programmes
Federal housing programmes (subsidies for rent/lease; vouchers)
Tax incentives (e.g. tax deductions and tax exemptions, rate structure)

Federal housing programmes (production).   A varied kind of federal financial aid to profit and non-profit groups to produce housing for low- and moderate-income household.

Model Cities.   A federal programme providing assistance to cities and community groups to revitalize and provide services in deteriorated areas of cities inhabited by low-income households.

War on Poverty.   A federal programme that provided federal dollars to support community action programmes prepared by community action agencies — local public agencies often controlled by residents from poverty areas. The community action programmes generally focused on community services, services to low-income households (job training, health, etc.), and community development initiatives.

Neighborhood Housing Services.   A federally initiated programme to provide technical assistance and financial support to neighbourhood groups and low-income households within neighbourhoods to revitalize their area and rehabilitate their homes.

Urban Homesteading.   A federal programme that provided foreclosed federally assisted housing to households providing they agree to live in and rehabilitate the housing.

Neighborhood Strategy Areas.   A federal initiative that encouraged cities to focus federal assistance in defined neighbourhood areas.

UDAG.   A federal programme (Urban Development Action Grants) that provided cities with funds if they leveraged such funds with private sector money and used both for economic development purposes.

Community Development Block Grants. A federal programme that provided cities with flexible funds, according to a formula based generally on population and poverty indices, for the redevelopment or revitalization of older areas and/or for the provision of services to low-income households.

Tax incentives. Federal support permitting developers and/or owners of buildings to reduce tax burdens if they responded to varied federal objectives (e.g. production and renting of units for low-income households, restoration of historical buildings, etc.).

Welfare. Federal aid to different kinds of low-income households to provide them with threshold or basic income support.

Provision of services. Federal aid to low-income households earmarked to or for basic services (e.g. health, food, stamps, etc.).

Social security. Federal aid generated from payments into a trust fund by employed individuals to individuals who have retired or who are disabled.

Federal housing programmes (non-production). Federal aid directly to low-income individuals for the renting or leasing of vacant units in local housing markets.

Tax incentives for people. Federal initiatives that limit the tax burdens on low-income households through enabling them to avoid the paying of taxes on certain expenditures or on a specified amount of earned income.

Place policies

Since 1949, Congress has indicated that every American is entitled to a decent home in a suitable living environment. Congressional intent, while laudable, has never really been backed up by sustained and predictable initiatives or resources. Generally, however, Congress has provided an envelope for a variety of sometimes consistent and sometimes inconsistent neighbourhood redevelopment, revitalization, and service provision programmes. Among the more important are those given below.

Redevelopment. The federal government has supported the wholesale clearance of relatively large blighted areas of cities and their redevelopment for public use and/or purposes. In many instances neighbourhoods – whole or part – were demolished and the space put to varied uses, including but not limited to housing.

Revitalization and/or rehabilitation. The federal government has supported local efforts to engage in strategic clearance and/or development of blighted neighbourhood areas. Through varied means, they also have aided the efforts of local communities, non-profit groups, profit-making companies, and households to rehabilitate deteriorated housing units.

31

Service provision and delivery. The federal government has aided local government, non-profit groups, and citizen organizations in providing or delivering increased or, assumedly, better services in deteriorated or deteriorating neighbourhoods.

People policies

The federal government, through a variety of initiatives, has provided money (welfare) and/or surrogates for money (entitlements to health-care services, housing, food stamps, etc.) to low-income households. Although expenditures by the poor are not limited to their neighbourhoods, the implicit, if not explicit, assumption of many of the programmes is that increased income (and/or access to the goods that income will buy) will lead to more stable neighbourhoods and .the improved quality of neighbourhoods.

Additionally, the federal government has helped fund 'empowerment' efforts; that is, efforts by the poor or representatives of the poor to establish neighbourhood organizations to advocate and/or deliver programmes, ostensibly favoured by low-income inhabitants of neighbourhoods. It is assumed that permitting the poor to influence, if not control, the flow of resources into and the planning of their own neighbourhoods will help them secure a better fit between expenditures and need. More importantly, allowing the poor to gain access to power will reduce one of the key variables identified by some as resulting in poverty and poor neighbourhoods – the lack of capacity of poorer residents to control their own fate.

AMERICAN NEIGHBOURHOOD REVITALIZING POLICIES: EFFECTIVENESS

A vigorous debate exists concerning the effectiveness of federal policies and programmes initiated to help neighbourhoods and their residents. Indeed, there are data to support all sides of the impact question.

It is fair to say that the broad purposes of many federal neighbourhood policies have not been achieved. Most of the neighbourhoods receiving 'place'-type assistance remain prone to the kinds of problem that initially qualified them to receive assistance. Many of the neighbourhoods that appear to be in better physical shape seem to have improved their lot, in part, because of changing economic, market, and social conditions. Clearly, it is difficult to establish causal linkages between federal aid and improved neighbourhood status.

Importantly, the relationship between neighbourhood physical improvement fostered by the federal government and changes in the income and/or job, education, and health choices of the residents of older neighbourhoods is still to be determined in a definitive manner. While national policies, initiated during the late 1960s and early 1970s, aimed at adding to or complementing household income were successful in ameliorating the conditions associated with poverty and in reducing poverty among certain Americans (the aged), significant questions remain as to how effective they were in stimulating qualitative changes in neighbourhood status. Similarly, while anecdotes and case studies point to some successes in resident upgrading of the physical condition of certain neighbourhoods, it is not clear what impact such successes had on the income of residents. Physical improvement in many neighbourhoods appears to have occurred almost simultaneously with or subsequent to demographic changes in household class or income. The net effect, in these instances, on poorer residents who were forced to leave or who left voluntarily can be found only in anecdotes and evaluations of limited numbers or cases.[2]

Regrettably, despite more than several decades of uneven but sometimes vigorous federal intervention, poverty in urban America remains at relatively high levels. National economic growth has not floated all ships or areas equally. The relationship between increased urban poverty and race reflected in expanding neighbourhood ghettos in many cities seems clear. Low-income and minority households continue to reflect relatively poor housing conditions. Substandard housing conditions, while statistically minor by historical and perhaps world standards, appear on the increase in many cities, particularly among rental units occupied by poorer households.

NEIGHBOURHOOD REVITALIZATION POLICIES: WHY MIXED RESULTS?

Analyses of American neighbourhood policies suggest several, sometimes competing reasons why they have failed to secure more than mixed results.

Neighbourhood policies often failed to reflect consistent neighbourhood definitions

Federal neighbourhood initiatives illustrated varied views of neighbourhoods and their characteristics. Most federal efforts relied at least in part on local governments to describe the boundaries of their neighbourhoods assumed eligible for federal assistance. Many local governments, however, set relatively arbitrary, and often different, limits concerning population and/or area size. Similarly, many required relatively arbitrary, and often different, income, job, and housing characteristics. Finally, more than a few cities seemed to predicate the identification of a neighbourhood on the presence of political representation or the availability of an active group to speak for residents in the area.

The diverse federal initiatives implicitly, if not always explicitly, reflected varying views of what characterizes a neighbourhood. Lack of consistency and certainty concerning criteria to define neighbourhoods helped foster uncertainty and inconsistencies concerning revitalization approaches. As one former assistant secretary responsible for a number of neighbourhood programmes said:

> If we do not have a clear idea of what a neighborhood is . . . if we do not know whether to define a neighborhood in economic, social, or physical terms or any combination thereof . . . if we are not certain that neighbourhoods make sense as a viable way to describe a discrete

urban place, with distinguishable characteristics . . . then how can we develop effective policy approaches?

Use of neighbourhoods as a focus of federal aid often seemed related more to the need for a convenient political ledger or fiscal accounting sheet than to any clear set of ideas concerning their residents' future.

Neighbourhood revitalization policies have failed to be guided by an overall consistent theory

Consistent theories have rarely driven neighbourhood policies. Some understanding of the assumed theoretical underpinnings can be gained by journeying back in time to legislative testimony and/or the speeches of programme or policy advocates. For example, urban renewal seemed directed at aborting and redirecting market trends by dramatically changing the physical conditions of an area and its historical land use and related social patterns. Model Cities appeared focused on helping people in neighbourhoods adjust to or accommodate local market and social trends. Implicit in its approach was the stabilization of neighbourhoods for the people who lived in them through improved and expanded service delivery and through neighbourhood involvement in the planning and allocation of public funds. War on Poverty, through funding services and through granting residents power to plan, aimed at helping people find the means to break out of dependence and, conceivably, their neighbourhoods. Welfare programmes provided cash to help poor people secure threshold levels of service (Table 2).

Only recently have American academics paid much attention to defining hypotheses that lend understanding to the dynamics of neighbourhood change and to the relationship among public intervention, neighbourhood revitalization, and household income. Put another way, our policies until recently have been guided by a varied, often disparate, set of ideologies. Theories offering possible explanations of observed neighbourhood trends and their relationship to neighbourhood residents generally have been tested only by anecdote and by limited evaluations of specific cases over short periods.

We have been told that neighbourhood change is natural; that it relates to broader metropolitan area population and income trends; that these broader trends lead to neighbourhood segmentation along class and caste lines; that such segmentation in certain kinds of markets may either open up or limit housing choices. For example, according to Katharine Bradbury, Anthony Downs, and Kenneth Small (1982):

> United States urban development is dominated by the 'trickle down' or filtering process. No one person or group consciously designed that process: It evolved from separate decisions and actions taken by millions of households, developers, local governments, federal agencies, homebuilders, lenders, and politicians.

Speaking of new housing once built for middle- or upper-income households, the same authors indicate:

34

Table 2. Neighbourhood revitalization strategy – key federal initiatives*

Ameliorate effects of decline
Welfare
In-kind services
War on Poverty

Change physical character
Urban renewal

Stabilization
Model Cities
Urban Homesteading
Select housing assistance programmes
Community development block grants

Upgrading
Select housing assistance programmes – assisted and non-assisted
Neighborhood Housing Services
Neighbourhood strategy areas
Community development block grants

Gentrification
Economic development assistance
UDAG
Non-assisted housing programmes
Tax incentives

* The above attempt to classify federal initiatives around key neighbourhood strategies or initiatives is relatively subjective. Federal programme initiatives often reflected multiple and sometimes inconsistent strategies and were used by and in communities to secure multiple and sometimes inconsistent objectives. The typology, at a minimum, helps focus attention on the relationship between diverse federal efforts and neighbourhood strategies. Stabilization refers to activities aimed at halting or impeding neighbourhood change, physical or demographic; upgrading refers to activities aimed at improving the physical character and delivery of services in a neighbourhood by existing residents; gentrification refers to the in-migration of and a simultaneous or subsequent effort to improve the physical character and delivery of services in a neighbourhood by the in-migrants or newcomers.

But as they [the housing] got older, and new growth moved out beyond them, they gradually trickled down through the income distribution. They were successively occupied by groups with relatively lower incomes. During most of their history, these housing units provided good quality dwellings for their occupants. But in many cases, they eventually became occupied by households too poor to maintain them or to pay rents sufficient to induce landlords to maintain them. In U.S. metropolitan areas, most of the lowest ranking neighborhoods are close to the older cores of the area; most – but usually not all – of the highest ranking neighborhoods are close to the outer periphery; and most middle-ranked neighborhoods are somewhere in between. . . . The socioeconomic and ethnic segregation deeply embedded in U.S. urban development strongly contribute to physical decay and population losses in many older big city neighborhoods. (Bradbury *et al.*, 1982, pp. 165–166)

Another theory holds that neighbourhood differentiation both in terms of condition and occupancy is related primarily to transportation costs or to the linkages between job commutation costs and particular housing desires. In other words, high-density neighbourhoods are found in central cities because land costs are high and the lower income people who live in

35

them sacrifice housing for minimal journey-to-work costs. Apparently, higher income people are willing to bear the costs of commuting to gain larger, more amply endowed housing units on the fringes of urban areas where land costs are cheaper. The highest income households, ostensibly, can secure the benefits of inner-city living including good housing and low transportation costs. As portrayed by Michael Schill and Richard P. Nathan:

> Employment is concentrated in the urban core . . . the journey to work constitutes the major transportation cost for most households. In the core of the city, commercial, industrial, and residential users compete for scarce space, so land values are highest closest to the center and decrease with distance from the center. A particular household decides how it wants to make the trade-off between relatively cheap land in the suburbs and easy access to downtown in the center city . . . higher income households will locate at the periphery, thereby consuming more space than they could near the core while spending additional time and money commuting to their jobs in the center. The poor will locate in the center at high densities so as to minimize the costs of land and transportation.

In explaining why wealthy families or households sometimes move into older neighbourhoods, Schill and Nathan indicate:

> Well-to-do people who move into revitalizing neighborhoods value both land and accessibility, and can afford to pay for them both. They thus outbid all other groups for land close to the urban cores. (1983, pp. 14–15)

Analyses and related theories linking income and race to neighbourhood change are of relatively recent vintage. David Varady, in his book *Revitalizing America's Cities*, says:

> Although there is a relatively large body of research on neighborhood racial change and on ghetto expansion patterns, there has been minimal linkage between those subjects and theoretical works on neighborhood physical and social decline. (1986, p. 9)

Generally, all other things being equal, households with higher incomes will out-compete households with lower incomes. Over time this is likely to lead to neighbourhood homogeneity in terms of class. Racism in the form of publicly sanctioned and/or induced discrimination limits minority choices in urban and metropolitan housing markets. Indeed, racism combined with poverty appear to be key variables leading to ghettos or the compaction of poor minority households in single or contiguous, impoverished neighbourhoods — neighbourhoods that illustrate relatively high degrees of social pathology. Taken together, they also seem to be obstacles to the upgrading of the nearby neighbourhoods by their residents and the gentrification or revitalization of a neighbourhood area by the in-migration of higher income people.

Neighbourhood revitalization policies are premised on insufficient knowledge and analysis of cause-and-effect relationships

Our knowledge of the causes of neighbourhood change and the relationship of changes to the health and wellbeing of different kinds of households, while improving, remains uneven. For example, we still do not know the exact nature of the link between metropolitan growth patterns and neighbourhood transition. Similarly, we have formulated only preliminary hypotheses to explain why some neighbourhoods with similar physical and/or demographic characteristics reflect vastly different development trends. The role of historical variables in neighbourhood evolution, the role of different cultural and ethnic characteristics in neighbourhood renewal or decline, the role of public and private sector investment in hastening or inhibiting change, and the effect of different household decisions on neighbourhood dynamics and change are all yet to be definitively determined.

The relationship between household wellbeing and place-specific revitalization efforts has never been clear. Policies aimed at building better neighbourhoods and improved social services, if linked to subsidies that permit low-income families to remain in such neighbourhoods, could slow down mobility and possibly sustain long-term household income improvements. By comparison, policies aimed at providing people with supportive services to gain access to the job market, if not related to housing and neighbourhood initiatives, could, at least in the short term, leave them facing difficult living conditions. Finally, policies aimed at the physical revitalization of low-income neighbourhoods, if not matched with income-enhancement programmes, could encourage the in-migration of higher-income households and either force existing residents out or require them to pay a higher percentage of their already meagre income for housing.

Independent neighbourhood policies often fail to reflect explicit achievable objectives and/or objectives that are consistent with other neighbourhood policies

Measurable objectives have rarely been a strong feature of American neighbourhood revitalization efforts. More often than not the objectives are generalized to avoid offending different constituencies or, more positively, to build support among different constituencies. Frequently, they read like a menu of all that is good under the sun to gain public and congressional acquiescence. Model Cities provides a good example of the norm. Its mandate was to cure slum conditions in selected neighbourhoods and to provide extended jobs, education, and health services to the residents of such neighbourhoods. It also aimed to encourage neighbourhood involvement in the development of revitalization plans. All objectives were to occur within a relatively short period—less than a decade. Similarly, the War on Poverty initiatives contained multiple, often non-quantifiable, objectives. Its programmes were to ameliorate poverty, permit the poor to control their own lives and the future of the areas in which they lived, reform the delivery and affect the content of public services, make the poor self-sufficient, co-ordinate public delivery systems, and reform those delivery systems.

Neighbourhood initiatives sometimes either joined place and people objectives in a confusing and potentially inconsistent manner or granted priority to one initiative without acknowledging its likely effect on the other. For example, Model Cities, in mixing objectives concerning physical revitalization and amelioration of poverty, sometimes made it tough to achieve either objective. Successful revitalization often required deep subsidies that frustrated the start-up of service-related programs. Successful revitalization in some areas generated household migration and encouraged new household in-migration; both resulted in unplanned benefits to some and costs to others. Minimal funding only exacerbated difficulties in achieving the programme's multiple goals.

The goal of War on Poverty to empower neighbourhood residents helped frustrate another proposed goal – the co-ordination of federal, state, and city programmes. It proved difficult for neighbourhood groups to secure co-operation from public entities concerning programme delivery and reform while they were attacking or criticizing them for incompetence or worse. 'Power to the people' had a ringing sound and it made for nice speeches. But, if and when converted into adversarial relationships between the newly empowered and the historically powerful, it rarely generated resources for the former and help from the latter.

The Urban Homestead and Neighborhood Housing Services programmes were premised on the hope that public initiatives would generate multiple neighbourhood spill-over effects. Both programmes often let their supporters down and leave their evaluators short of positive stories to tell. Public investments and actions were not able to achieve the desired private investment objectives or related private household actions. Both programmes failed to meet their objectives.

Neighbourhood policies rarely have consistent or precise strategies

Without guiding theories and clear-cut objectives, neighbourhood policies in the United States have rarely reflected definitive strategies. As indicated above, some programmes attempted to provide people with opportunities to secure threshold or improved services and make their lives better; some attempted to allow people to break out of poverty and gain income and neighbourhood mobility. Only recently have we focused on the kinds of discrete spatial strategies that could be related to different kinds of neighbourhood characteristics. Only recently has the literature on neighbourhoods attempted to distinguish efforts to stabilize areas from efforts to upgrade areas. Only recently have analysts focused on linking the objectives of various federally assisted neighbourhood redevelopment strategies to the impacts resulting from the possible range of initiators of such strategies, for example, investors, developers, community groups, newcomers, and residents. Only recently have we begun to place a time and resource dimension on diverse neighbourhood improvement efforts. Finally, only recently have policymakers begun to raise questions concerning the effect of regional and local housing markets on neighbourhood revitalization efforts. Without appropriate federal housing initiatives, filtering and trickle-down processes – processes that lead to a *decline in housing prices* – may be the most effective way to *improve the housing conditions* of relatively large numbers of poor households. In a nutshell, in weak housing markets or markets that generate a surplus stock of housing, housing prices weaken generating a demand by middle- and upper-income households to improve their housing situation. In theory, at least, their willingness and desire to move up to better housing opens up vacant units to lower-income households. Often abandonment of the worst units occurs when lower-income households leave their unit for better housing. While, sometimes, the process works to expand housing choices and improve housing conditions, it is slow and does not generally encompass the majority of low-income families and individuals living in bad housing.[3]

In tight housing markets, federal intervention to abort the decline of neighbourhoods or to stabilize neighbourhoods, without compensating strategies, may negatively affect the quality of life and housing conditions of those least able to fend for themselves. Federal policies, in this context, at times have added to the upward price or rent spiral. In helping revitalize the physical condition of neighbourhoods, they, in many situations, have created demand, forced up housing costs, and forced lower-income families either to pay a higher share of their income for housing or leave the area.

Neighbourhood policies and programmes have rarely been subject to sustained, useful, and policy-relevant evaluation concerning their impact

It has been and remains difficult to subject American neighbourhood policies and programmes to evaluation. While the literature is growing, the techniques of evaluation often remain quite subjective, the choice of neighbourhoods for study relatively few, the factors or variables used in distinguishing neighbourhood development patterns narrow, the time spans of the analyses restricted, and the use of surrogate measures for signs of neighbourhood improvements relatively conventional (e.g. housing, household satisfaction).

Measurements of performance often focus more on input (dollars spent, units rehabilitated) than on output (effects on people's lives and long-term effects on neighbourhoods). Perhaps as relevant as the lack of measurement criteria in inhibiting effective evaluation efforts has been the short and often chaotic life of neighbourhood policies and programmes. They have been governed more by the policy (or political fad) of the moment than by a long-term commitment to defined objectives. In a similar vein, and directly related to their episodic character, they often have been significantly underfunded and/or — a variation on a theme — limited in scale.

The small size of many programmes, their uneven support, and their short life spans have made it difficult to distinguish between nonproject-related and programme-related variables and impacts. Put another way, factors affecting the national or even local economy and factors associated with other federal or local policies often blur recognition of the sought-after effect of specific neighbourhood initiatives. Sometimes it is next to impossible to define and evaluate cause-and-effect relationships with any degree of confidence.

Sustained evaluation of neighbourhood programmes has faced other obstacles. We have yet to establish an 'evaluation culture', one that supports the possibility of critical data and conclusions resulting from federally funded studies. Federal and local administrators rarely like to be told they are wrong or that they are administering a flawed or failed programme. Evaluation as a function is often assigned or has a strong relation to political officers who have strong stakes in 'success' stories. Further, longitudinal studies generally require the certainty of appropriations and the commitment of agencies for many years, both difficult to achieve when election cycles are relatively brief and the probability of leadership changes is frequent. Finally, federal initiatives to secure neighbourhood improvements were reduced to the barest minimum by the Reagan administration. The President and his colleagues viewed most federal neighbourhood initiatives as a variation of Gresham's law: allocating federal dollars to distressed cities or areas was throwing good and limited resources into bad situations. It was inefficient or worse. In this environment, federally funded evaluation efforts were at best marginal and episodic.

Neighbourhood policies have infrequently been linked to other urban and non-urban policies in America

Ideally, neighbourhood policies would be part of a comprehensive set of urban policies and would be related to non-urban policies, where and when relevant. But, as noted at the outset of this paper, our nation has not been able to develop a comprehensive urban policy or a set of reasonably refined and co-ordinated objectives from which resources flow and programmes are designed.

As a result of the failure to link urban policies together and to relate neighbourhood policies to other kinds of urban and, indeed, non-urban policies, we often face the situation of the right hand not knowing or caring what the left hand is doing. More perversely, perhaps, programmes initiated by good and decent people have negatively affected programmes initiated by other good and decent people. Without relating non-neighbourhood urban policy to the neighbourhood, anticipated and hoped-for revitalization impacts are muted and/or positive objectives are turned into negative happenings (Table 3). For example, urban renewal, particularly in its early days, cleared a lot of land and resulted in the relocation of many disadvantaged people. It did this often during periods of and in areas with housing shortages. The effect in some parts of the nation was to force people or households to seek shelter in already deteriorating or deteriorated areas — areas frequently subject to federal initiatives to either expand the housing choices of their residents and/or to improve the physical and social conditions of the area. The net result was overcrowding and the further compaction of poverty problems and related neighbourhood difficulties. Similarly, America's love affair with federally supported highways and freeways began in the mid-1950s. Many analysts view the interstate highway system and the advent of beltways around cities as heightening decentralization trends and weakening the social and economic health of downtowns and older neighbourhoods; yet, this occurred simultaneously with other federal initiatives

Table 3. Inadvertent negative neighbourhood effects of select federal initiatives

Initiative	Effect
Fostering housing production in suburbs	Weakening of older neighbourhoods
Urban renewal	Displacement of low-income households, their concentration in declining neighbourhoods
Highway and beltway construction	Facilitate decentralization of population, weakening of older neighbourhoods

Tax reform:
    Lowering of marginal rates
    Changes in depreciation
	Minimize investor interest in municipal bond market, rental units

Restricted or tight monetary policy	Higher costs for mortgages
Development of subsidized housing	Concentration of low-income households in select neighbourhoods
Welfare assistance	Rules sometimes impede household mobility

aimed at encouraging the return to downtown and to older neigbourhoods of the middle class.

Inside the Department of Housing and Urban Development, the federal agency most responsible for urban policy initiatives and formation, tension has existed between the 'housers' and the neighbourhood revitalization folks. Both have laudable objectives, but sometimes they compete. Federally insured housing production, by and large, takes place in the suburbs where it is cheaper to build. Building large numbers of units in the suburbs, particularly in markets with high vacancy rates, weakens the housing market in older neighbourhoods. Federally assisted or subsidized housing units, if located in neighbourhood areas struggling to remain viable, sometimes negatively affect federal initiatives aimed at securing neighbourhood stabilization and improvement. The concentration of public housing in certain urban neighbourhoods has limited the ability of such neighbourhoods to retain an integrated population and income mix and has often limited household as well as commercial investment incentives.

LEARNING FROM ABROAD

Many Western European nations and Israel have attempted to develop neighbourhood revitalization programmes. While differences exist among them, many pervasive themes seem common. For example, most European and Israeli initiatives, contrary to the United States' experience, appear able to outlast changes in political administrations. Similarly, most European and Israeli initiatives, unlike United States programmes, provide a clear link between or merger of precise people and place strategies. Finally, most European and Israeli initiatives, unlike the United States' efforts, appear to emanate out of a cohesive national policy and to be driven by national definition. Regrettably, as in the United States, in-depth evaluations of European and Israeli neighbourhood policies and programmes have been limited. Those evaluations that exist have been oriented more towards 'process' or how-we-did-it studies than to product or what occurred and how it

41

benefited the area and residents. Joint or comparative inter-nation evaluations of results or outputs would provide insights and wisdom to all involved
nations, including the United States.

STARTING OVER: DEMONSTRATION AND EVALUATION

A new administration has taken over in Washington. Budget deficits combined with an uncertain national economy make it difficult to mount
any new large-scale neighbourhood revitalization policies in the near
future. It is a good time, therefore, to take stock of where we have come
from and to initiate careful analyses of what has worked and what has not.
It is also a good time to attempt to reconcile social welfare and neighbourhood revitalization strategies. It is to be hoped that the federal government, along with state and local governments, will initiate demonstrations
that test and reflect the degree of coincidence between both strategies. Both
the demonstrations and their evaluations should be structured to help
generate efficient and equitable neighbourhood revitalization efforts by all
levels of government in the United States and by the public and private
sectors as well as by community groups. Paraphrasing that old but wise
policymaker, Socrates: 'An unexamined neighbourhood policy is not worth
having.'

NOTES

1. This article is based on a presentation in Stockholm and has been published in *The
Future of National Urban Policy*, which this writer has co-authored with Franklin
James (Duke University Press, 1990).

2. According to HUD's recent Annual Housing Surveys, most Americans appear satisfied
with their neighbourhoods, but considerable variation exists. It appears to relate, in
part, to the distress level of the cities in which neighbourhoods are located and to the
income and race of neighbourhood residents. Several housing analysts, among them
William Apgar, Jr, have indicated that low-income renter households have been
squeezed of late by a declining availability of units in cities, by the absence of purchase
options, and by competition from younger buyers priced out of the ownership market.
Their continued inability to pay increased housing costs likely will result in a visible
increase in housing problems in central cities and their neighbourhoods. Many inner-
city poor neighbourhoods remain subject to high concentrations of very low-income
minority households. As William Wilson notes: 'It is the growth of the high and
extreme poverty areas that epitomizes the social transformation of the inner city, a
transformation that represents a change in the class structure in many inner-city
neighborhoods as the nonpoor black middle class and working classes tend to no
longer reside in these neighborhoods, thereby increasing the proportion of truly disadvantaged individuals and families' (1987, p. 86).

3. Several impediments limit the usefulness of the filtering process in expanding housing opportunities for poor people. The process relies on the availability of a surplus
of housing to work. When a surplus exists and markets soften, production of new
units slows down simultaneously with the abandonment of units and the increase in
the number of households in the market. Competition for limited units heats up and
lower income households find themselves unable to out-compete higher income
households. Other factors that limit the positive impact of filtering include: the
limited ability of many low income households to move because of jobs and/or the
absence of available financing for lower income households, etc. Finally, if prices

soften because of vacancies, owners of rental units lack incentive to maintain such units. Conditions decline and abandonment occurs.

REFERENCES

BRADBURY, K., A. DOWNS and K. SMALL (1982) *Urban Decline and the Future of American Cities*. Washington, DC: Brookings Institution.

SCHILL, M. H. and R. P. NATHAN (1983) *Revitalizing America's Cities: Neighborhood Reinvestment and Displacement*. Albany: State University of New York Press.

VARADY, D. P. (1986) *Revitalizing America's Cities: Neighborhood Reinvestment and Displacement*. Albany: State University of New York Press.

WILSON, J. (1987) *The Truly Disadvantaged: The Inner City, the Under Class, and Public Policy*. Chicago: University of Chicago Press.

4 URBAN RENEWAL: THE BRITISH EXPERIENCE

Colin Wood

This chapter traces the progress of urban renewal policy in Britain, or, more specifically, England and Wales, during the latter part of the twentieth century. It concentrates on housing renewal, by which is meant clearance and replacement of older, poorer housing, or the improvement of older housing to a higher standard.

After the Second World War, housing renewal followed a number of distinct courses. Immediately after the cessation of hostilities, efforts were directed towards tackling the housing shortage brought about by the destruction of or damage to properties as a result of war-time bombing. As the major new housebuilding programmes began to reduce the problems of actual shortage, more emphasis was given towards improving the quality of the housing stock, and by the late 1950s many of the larger urban authorities were beginning to resume slum clearance programmes that had begun in many areas during the 1930s before the outbreak of hostilities.

By the late 1950s and into the 1960s the slum clearance programmes were in full swing, but by the mid-1960s increasing doubts began to be cast on the wisdom of demolishing large tracts of older housing and replacing them with, for the most part, housing estates provided and managed by the local municipalities. Towards the end of the 1960s the emphasis had begun to swing towards improving areas of older dwellings where they were basically sound and provided the opportunity for continued good-quality accommodation if suitably upgraded. Many thousands of dwellings were improved with the assistance of government grants channelled through the local authorities. But this approach, too, came under criticism for, among other things, failing to deal with the poorest properties and for neglecting the plight of households in the greatest housing need. In a further policy shift, therefore, efforts and resources were concentrated ostensibly on tackling areas of physical and social deprivation using higher grant thresholds to encourage the improvement of older houses in private ownership. At the same time housing associations (funded at the time largely by central government and local authorities and run by voluntary committees to provide and manage housing) were being promoted to play a bigger role in the renewal of older areas.

Throughout the remainder of the 1970s and 1980s the main thrust of housing renewal policy was directed towards the improvement of older housing rather than its demolition and replacement. The major slum clearance programmes in the larger conurbations had for the most part come to an end by the early 1970s.

The last decade or so has seen a dramatic reduction in the amount of funding available to local housing authorities for dealing with housing problems in their areas, a greater reliance on the sale of capital assets, especially dwellings and land, to supplement the income of local authorities, and a much greater emphasis on the contribution of the private sector in providing and maintaining housing accommodation. During this period there has also developed a growing awareness of the problems of disrepair in the public housing sector, and a variety of initiatives have been introduced in an attempt to address these. Housing policy directed to older and predominantly privately owned areas of poorer housing has undergone a further recent review, and the intention now is to focus attention on larger renewal areas where a combination of selective clearance and improvement activity would seek to upgrade housing conditions, where private investment and private developers would be encouraged to play a major role, and where financial resources would be targeted more on the basis of need. This represents a shift in emphasis from an approach that concentrates on improving the housing stock irrespective of occupants' incomes towards one that purports to pay more regard to the individual needs and resources of people living in older housing.

This chapter charts the progress of these various phases in the development of renewal policy in England and Wales, sets the wider context within which each phase has been played out, considers how far the stated intentions of each phase have been realized in practice, and highlights any lessons that might help to inform a successful approach to housing renewal. The final part of the chapter addresses wider issues that have a bearing on the extent to which the problems of poorer housing can be tackled through renewal policies alone. Before going into further details on housing renewal activity, however, it seems appropriate to provide a broader context to housing in Britain that helps to explain the renewal issues that have arisen and the various approaches adopted in trying to tackle them.

THE CONTEXT OF BRITISH HOUSING AND URBAN RENEWAL

In 1986 there were an estimated 18.8 million dwellings in England and Wales. Of these 11.8 million (63%) were owner-occupied, 4.5 million (24%) were owned and let by local authorities or the New Town Corporations (responsible for running the new post-Second World War planned settlements designed to ease congestion in the major conurbations), and the remaining 2.5 million (13%) were rented furnished or unfurnished by tenants of private landlords or housing associations or were vacant. Out of the total stock, nearly 5 million dwellings (26%) were built before the First World War, nearly 4 million (21%) were built between the wars, and the remaining 9.8 million (53%) were constructed since 1945. In 1986, 909,000 dwellings were classified as unfit, 463,000 lacked one or more of the basic amenities, and 2.4 million were in a state of disrepair (Department of the Environment, 1988).

The tenure pattern of housing in the 1980s is markedly different from that at the beginning of the twentieth century, when 90% of all properties were rented from a private landlord. The decline in the private rental sector and the growth of owner-occupation and municipal housing represent perhaps the strongest sustained features of housing trends in Britain in this century. The reduction of the numbers of privately rented houses has had many contributory causes, with purchase for owner-occupation, the effects of slum clearance policies, and the relative unattractiveness of investing in accommodation for private rental being seen as among the most significant (Balchin, 1989, pp. 107–109).

It is in the residual rump of the privately rented housing stock and in the older owner-occupied dwellings, many of which have been acquired from the private rental sector, that most of the problems of unfitness and disrepair are to be found in the non-public sector. Surveys show that these properties are often occupied by low-income households, many of whom are elderly, many of whom, also, have lived at the same address for a very long time (Department of the Environment, 1988).

During the First World War rent controls had helped limit the exploitation of housing shortages by unscrupulous landlords, but they also reduced the attractiveness of providing this type of accommodation. After the war, the reduction in the number and proportion of privately rented homes greatly accelerated. Sitting tenants began to purchase the houses they occupied, and the local authorities, with the encouragement of central government, launched a major drive to provide municipal rental housing – 'Homes Fit for Heroes'. A series of legislative measures in the 1920s and 1930s saw the development of housing estates by local authorities on the expanding periphery of many cities and towns throughout the country, comprising dwellings built to generous space standards at low densities (Merrett, 1979).

The 1920s and 1930s, too, saw a major expansion in the provision of new homes for owner-occupation, with the building societies playing an increasingly influential role in determining the scale and location of housing investment. The urban expansion that took place around this time was seen as representing a threat to open countryside and agricultural land, and legislation was introduced to check 'ribbon development', the construction of dwellings along the frontage of roads linking separate towns. This period, too, perhaps represented the first major shift in funding and investment from the heart of the older cities and towns towards the newer suburbs.

In the 1930s, also, there was growing concern about the future of the older industrial areas following the Great Depression, and about the rapid growth and increasing congestion in the Southeast, and the London area, in particular. Several commissions were set up to investigate and advise on the distribution of population and industry, rural issues, and land taxation, and these provided the basis for much of the early post-war legislation aimed at providing a better living and working environment (Hall, 1987). The establishment of the New Town Corporations and the development of new settlements to ease pressures in the older congested conurbations saw major housing provision in the early post-Second World War years spearheaded by the public sector. Legislation also facilitated the planned expansion of

46

existing towns, with parallel measures introduced to protect and enhance the countryside. The mid-1950s to mid-1960s witnessed continued high levels of dwelling production, but with an increasing emphasis on building for owner-occupation under the Conservative administration.

Housing for owner-occupation, initially championed primarily by the Conservative Party, was receiving support from all the established political parties. Significant financial incentives, including mortgage tax relief, lack of capital gains tax on the sale of the principal home, and—from 1963—abolition of taxation on the imputed rental income of owner-occupied accommodation, made owning one's own home an increasingly attractive proposition. House price rises in the early 1970s, much in excess of the general retail price index, and interest on savings increased the incentive to buy rather than rent. For a long time, too, owner-occupiers and landlords had access to grants and loans for improvement and repairs that were denied to tenants. The promotion of owner-occupation went so far as to lead some critics to question whether this was always the most appropriate tenure, especially for people on fluctuating incomes and for the elderly (Karn, 1979). Growing concern was expressed about the number of older owner-occupied properties in unfit condition or poor state of repair.

Under the Thatcher government the emphasis on home ownership became even more pronounced. It has been paralleled and promoted by a series of measures aimed at reducing the stock of local authority housing and the role of the local authorities in the name of increasing freedom and choice for tenants. The 1980 Housing Act introduced the 'Right to Buy', enabling those tenants who so wished to purchase the house they occupied with discounts on notional market value, which increased with length of residence. Despite the resistance of some local authorities to this sales policy, over one million local authority or New Town houses had been sold by 1986, 200,000 in 1982 alone (Balchin, 1989, pp. 217–218). Further legislation was passed designed to enable tenants to transfer the management of local authority housing estates to alternative agents, while Housing Action Trusts (HATs) could be designated in areas of local authority housing suffering from severe physical and social problems with boards appointed by the Secretary of State and imposed, if necessary, against the will of the local authority. Recent changes to the system of housing finance curtail local authorities' ability to cross-subsidize their housing revenue account with funds raised through local taxes, which will lead to increased rents for local authority tenants and, it is anticipated, persuade those who can afford it to forsake local authority tenancies for owner-occupied accommodation. At the same time, the amount of money available to local authorities for spending on housing and environmental services has been reduced substantially since 1978 (Treasury, 1985). Very few authorities now have a building programme, while slum clearance that relies on the availability of relets or new accommodation has virtually ceased.

The discussion of housing renewal in the next sections, therefore, should be seen against overall housing trends that can be characterized by a swing away from major slum clearance and public sector new construction towards the improvement of older houses; an increasing reliance on the private sector and market forces in tackling housing issues; a reduced role for local authorities in the direct provision, improvement, and management of dwellings with greater emphasis on the 'enabling' role; local authority housing increasingly seen as last-resort housing for the most needy rather than for general housing needs; and an increasing social polarization between owner-occupation and local authority housing, between the inner cities and the suburbs, and between the Southeast and the North. Simultaneously in many areas problems of disrepair in the older privately owned sector and much of the local authority stock show evidence of increasing rather than decreasing.

HOUSING RENEWAL

Slum clearance and comprehensive redevelopment

Many of the older cities and towns had commenced slum clearance programmes in the 1930s, but these were interrupted by the Second World War and postponed after the war as the major drive was concentrated on producing new dwellings to replace those destroyed or irreparably damaged.

The programmes were revived in the mid-1950s and were directed for the most part at areas of older, terraced housing built at high densities in the inner rings surrounding the town and city centres and close to the factories and workshops that afforded employment to many of the residents. Most of these dwellings were constructed in the mid- and late nineteenth century and were predominantly rented from private landlords. They were occupied for the most part by indigenous working-class families and were located in areas, often described by urban sociologists as 'residual areas', which were socially relatively stable (Gittus, 1969).

These areas of older housing were surveyed by officers from the Department of Public Health (called 'Environmental Health' after 1974), who classified the poorest dwellings as unfit according to criteria set out in the 1957 Housing Act. Clearance areas were declared, indicating properties for which demolition was deemed appropriate, either because they were unfit or because they needed to be acquired by the local authority for demolition so that the whole area could be satisfactorily redeveloped (English *et al.*, 1976). The twin policies of slum clearance and comprehensive redevelopment came to be seen as part of the same process. Many of the clearance areas were redeveloped by the local authorities themselves with rental housing, often in the form of flats or maisonettes in deck-access or tower blocks, using generous government subsidies that were made available to facilitate system-building techniques. It is many of these types of dwellings that now constitute a significant element of the major problems of disrepair that face many urban authorities.

Although slum clearance policies were clearly designed to provide better housing for people who were deemed to be experiencing inadequate conditions, there were other motives as well. Slum clearance and comprehensive redevelopment offered the opportunity for urban restructuring and the replacement of outworn roads and infrastructure that were no longer considered appropriate to meet the requirements of the late twentieth century.

Many of the large municipalities, too, were becoming increasingly 'image conscious', and the removal of what were seen to be unattractive areas of older cramped housing and their replacement by new structures of contemporary design was all part of a demonstration of civic progressiveness and ambition. The larger authorities vied with each other to see which could demolish the most old houses and which could build the most new ones. Some commentators saw in slum clearance the opportunity for town and city councils to reap some of the benefits, such as increased rates, which might accrue from the redevelopment of expensive inner city sites by more lucrative forms of investment. There was also the belief in some quarters that the removal of slums would also remove some of the social and economic problems with which they were often associated, and that slum clearance would reduce the threat of the spread of disease and poverty into more middle-class areas. It was also thought that a workforce housed in more congenial surroundings might be more productive. Furthermore, there was also the suspicion that slum clearance programmes were pursued in some areas for largely ideological or political reasons, as part of an attempt to eliminate private rentals and to alter constituency voting patterns.

In spite of the progress that many local authorities made in removing unfit housing and providing more modern living standards, the twin policies of slum clearance and comprehensive redevelopment came under increasing challenge. Concern was expressed about the effect that the programmes were having on working-class communities. Strong sentiments were expressed that the demolition of older dwellings and the rehousing of families in houses sometimes many miles away was destroying the social fabric of the older parts of towns and cities and breaking links between work and home (Jennings, 1962; Vereker *et al.*, 1961; Young and Wilmott, 1957). However, other critics argued that attempts to retain 'communities' were based on notions that ignored the real social dynamics of these areas and would deny their residents the opportunities of geographical and social mobility available in the wider society (Rosser and Harris, 1965).

There was increasing opposition from former tenants of condemned unfurnished properties who often had to pay considerably more for their council accommodation than they had been used to paying in tenancies protected by rent controls. Owner-occupiers, too, voiced protests about having to accept what many of them saw as a decline in housing status, as compensation provisions were rarely sufficient to enable households to purchase their own alternative accommodation prior to clearance. Indeed, the opposition to slum clearance and comprehensive redevelopment intensified as the programmes started to encroach on areas with a higher proportion of owner-occupiers. Residents' groups were formed in many cities and towns in areas affected by clearance programmes, with organized protests coinciding with a greater general public concern about involvement in decisions affecting the environment, and the exposure of the planning profession to the ideals of public participation (Ministry of Housing and Local Government, 1969a).

There was a greater questioning about what many saw as the imposition of bureaucratic values that were at odds with the views and interests of individuals directly affected by the clearance policy. The designation of properties as unfit began to be challenged more often as people recognized that this was more a matter of judgement than fact (Davies, 1972; Dennis, 1972).

Moreover, residents of clearance areas were often dissatisfied with what they saw as a lack of choice in their rehousing by the local authority. Some municipalities imposed a limit on the number of offers they were prepared to make to residents in clearance areas, their argument being that to allow unrestricted choice would mean slowing down the clearance programme and condemning other families to live in unsatisfactory and deteriorating properties for longer than was desirable or necessary. In many areas people who moved into clearance areas after the date of representation were not entitled to be rehoused by the local authority, and other groups of residents, such as lodgers, were also often excluded.

There was growing dissatisfaction, too, with the type and location of alternative housing available to clearance area residents. Many were unhappy with the high-rise and deck-access schemes that were being constructed in many cities to rehouse people displaced from clearance areas, and with the 'overspill' schemes built in adjoining authorities to house those who could not be accommodated locally (Stones, 1972). Criticisms were levelled at authorities for failing to co-ordinate the various strands of the clearance and comprehensive redevelopment programmes. Areas of land remained cleared and undeveloped for long periods in some areas, for example, as new construction failed to keep pace with demolition (Muchnick, 1970).

There was also increasing concern about the costs of the programme at a time in the late 1960s when the national economy was relatively weak and the government faced major economic problems. Moreover, a National Condition Survey in 1967 revealed that excepting 1.8 million unfit dwellings, there were 2.3 million that lacked one or more of the basic amenities (such as sinks, wash-basins, and inside WCs), and 3.7 million that were in a state of disrepair (Ministry of Housing and Local Government, 1969b). There was a growing realization that clearance and rebuilding alone were not going to be sufficient to tackle the full extent of the problem of inadequate housing on a reasonable time scale.

The Housing Act 1969 and General Improvement Areas

A number of influential reports produced in the mid-1960s, including that of the Denington Committee (Denington Report, 1966), paved the way for the publication of Old Houses into New Homes (Ministry of Housing and Local Government, 1968), which advocated a change in emphasis in housing renewal policy, with far greater attention than hitherto being placed on the retention and improvement of the older housing stock. The paper led to the 1969 Housing Act. While improvement grants had been available for over 20 years to owners wishing to modernize properties falling below a certain standard, the 1969 Act increased the grant amounts and relaxed some of the conditions attached to them. Funds were made available to local housing authorities from central government to enable owners and landlords to apply for mandatory standard grants for the provision of basic amenities and

50

discretionary grants for improvements, repairs, and conversions. Dwellings had to be upgraded to a 12-point standard after improvement for owners or landlords to be entitled to the discretionary improvement grants. This was intended to equip the improved dwelling for a 30-year life. Grants were designed to match pound-for-pound the applicants' authorized expenditure up to the maximum grant level.

The Housing Act 1969 also introduced General Improvement Areas (GIAs). These were intended to be areas of between 300 and 800 basically sound, older housing that could benefit from modernization. Compulsory purchase powers were made available for local authorities to acquire the properties of owners or landlords whose unwillingness to meet their share of the improvement costs threatened to jeopardize the success of the improvement area strategy. In addition to providing grant incentives for the improvement of dwellings, limited finance was also made available for environmental improvements such as the treatment of alleys separating blocks of properties, tree planting and landscaping schemes, and provision of car parking spaces.

General Improvement Areas and the emphasis given to the rehabilitation of older properties received all-party support. The Labour administration, responsible for introducing the measures, saw improvement as a cost-effective way of dealing with housing problems at a time when the national economy was rather weak, while the Conservative Party viewed the 1969 Act and home improvement policy as a means of boosting the private sector and owner-occupation. Rehabilitation of older houses was seen as a way of improving housing conditions that avoided many of the criticisms levelled against slum clearance and comprehensive development. In particular it was felt that this type of renewal activity would enable residents of improved areas to remain in their properties, and that communities would not be disrupted as they were by clearance and rebuilding. It was also felt that improved older housing would provide the sound, low-cost housing that was needed in many of the urban areas of England and Wales, and that rents would continue to be lower than for new council accommodation.

Following the Housing Act 1969, the number of grant-aided improvements increased from 109,000 in 1969 to 398,000 in 1973 (though this was partially due to the preferential grant rates available under regional policies through the Industry Act 1971). Expenditure in discretionary grants increased from £40 million to over £300 million over the same period. In 1973 there were more grants issued for the improvement of older houses than there were new properties built. By 1971 the 1.8 million unfit properties recorded in 1967 had been reduced to 1.24 million as a result of combined clearance and improvement action. By the end of 1973, 733 GIAs had been declared in England and Wales, comprising 223,000 dwellings.

By the early 1970s, however, this new policy was also being attacked. It was argued that improvement grants were operating regressively in that it was the better-off owner-occupiers and developers who were the main beneficiaries. Not only were they receiving cash hand-outs that were seen by many critics to be unwarranted, but they also gained from the untaxed appreciation in the capital value of the improved property in areas of high demand. Small landlords, on the other hand, could often not afford their contribution towards the cost of improvements, even with grant assistance. Instead many chose to wait for vacant possession so they could sell their property for owner-occupation, or alternatively, they sold to larger landlords. Larger landlords could often make substantial financial gains if they improved or converted properties and then let them on new tenancy agreements, or sold them for owner-occupation. Stories of cash hand-outs as inducements to sitting tenants to vacate their accommodation ('winkling') and physical threats and intimidation were commonplace, especially in London (Babbage, 1973). The result was a reduction in the amount of unfurnished accommodation for private rental and greater pressure on an increasingly overcrowded private furnished rental sector from displaced low-income households. In parts of London the character of certain areas changed as previously privately rented accommodation for low-income families was improved with grant aid to be sold off for owner-occupation or converted into luxury apartments for upper-income households, a process known as 'gentrification' (Ferris, 1972). In these areas the policy of improvement was resulting in the break-up of communities almost as effectively as slum clearance.

A House of Commons Subcommittee on House Improvement Grants was established in 1972 to investigate how the legislation was working in practice, and to see who was benefiting from the grant system and what effects it was having on the housing stock. Their deliberations and the evidence of many professional bodies and interest groups led to the publication of *Better Homes: The Next Priorities* (Department of the Environment, 1973). To overcome the exploitation of the grant system that was seen to be operating, particularly in parts of inner London, the paper proposed that where improvement grants were to be made to private landlords, the properties should remain available for letting for a period of 7 years; that if they were sold within this period the grant should be repaid with compound interest; and that local authorities should have the discretionary powers to require unwilling landlords to carry out improvements or undertake the work themselves and recharge the costs. The paper also envisaged the use of compulsory purchase powers to enable local authorities to buy and improve empty properties. The paper also recommended the establishment of a new type of renewal area – the Housing Action Area (HAA).

The Housing Act 1974 and Housing Action Areas

The Housing Act 1974 was heavily influenced by three main considerations. First, whereas the 1969 legislation had been introduced to complement slum clearance, opposition to the bulldozer was by now so strong that improvement action was envisaged as an alterative method of renewal. Second, the aim of the 1974 legislation and HAAs was to target improvement action to those households and properties most in need, something that the 1969 Act has failed to achieve satisfactorily. Third, the intention was to devise a more discriminating form of grant structure avoiding much of the abuse that had characterized the 1969 system.

52

The 1974 Act introduced HAAs and Priority Neighbourhoods to add to the existing, and continuing, GIAs. Priority Neighbourhoods were designed to prevent housing conditions from deteriorating in those areas immediately adjoining HAAs and GIAs. HAAs were intended to be areas of some 400 to 500 dwellings that combined poor physical conditions with evidence of social stress. Social stress indicators included multiple occupation; overcrowding; a high proportion of rental accommodation; and concentrations of households likely to have special housing needs such as the elderly, large families, single-person households, and those on low incomes.

The aim was to achieve a rapid improvement in the physical and social conditions of HAAs within 5 years (extendable, with Department of the Environment approval, for a further 2 years). Important considerations were the effective use and management of the housing stock and the wellbeing of existing residents. A revised system of grants saw a general increase in grant limits for eligible improvement expenses, higher grant rates (the proportion paid by the government) in HAAs, and the introduction of new grants for repairs. Grants for the provision of basic amenities were renamed 'intermediate' grants. Conditions were imposed on the future occupancy of properties that received improvement grants to avoid the speculative purchase, grant-aided improvement, and sell-off and gentrification that had undermined rehabilitation policy particularly in the London area under the 1969 Act. Local authorities were also given powers to require that improvements be carried out and to acquire properties for improvement in HAAs. The central government stressed in 1975 the need for local authorities to devise comprehensive local housing strategies to deal with housing issues in their areas, and emphasized the role that HAAs and GIAs could make as part of those strategies (Department of the Environment, 1975). A major role was envisaged for housing associations in acquiring and improving older properties and retaining them as part of the stock of socially rented accommodation.

To chart the progress of HAAs, local authorities were invited to make a series of quarterly statistical returns. A series of in-depth studies was commissioned in several HAAs, and annual progress reports were prepared. In the first year of operation, 73 HAAs were declared, covering some 22,200 dwellings. Some authorities, such as Birmingham and Liverpool, were quick to embrace the new initiative while others were more cautious. In the early days, HAAs were seen by some as appropriate only for the larger conurbations, given the emphasis on social stress, even though the areas of older housing in most authorities showed some signs of stress.

The 1981 English House Condition Survey revealed that 19% of dwellings in HAAs had received some form of improvement, though there were marked regional variations (Department of the Environment, 1983). Generally, improvement activity seemed to be more prominent and successful in HAAs where the local authority had registered a strong presence by pursuing compulsory improvement and the acquisition of properties. Progress was also related to the length of life of the HAA, with activity tending to peak in the third and fourth years. The detailed case studies showed that 70% of the occupied dwellings in HAAs that had been in existence for at least 5 years had some kind of improvement work and just over one-half of this had been undertaken by the local authorities themselves or by housing associations (Niner and Forrest, 1982).

Although, overall, nearly one-half of all improvement activity in HAAs was undertaken by private owners, a number of factors limited private investment in many areas. Not least was the attitude of the local authority, as the suspicion often persisted, in the early years at any rate, that HAA declaration and the 5-year intensive action was merely a way of forestalling immediate clearance (Paris and Blackaby, 1979). Building societies in the 1970s often regarded areas of older housing as poor risks for their investors and prospective liabilities for would-be purchasers, and were reluctant to provide mortgage finance for house purchase in areas that included existing or potential HAAs—a process known as 'red-lining' (Duncan, 1976; Weir, 1976; Williams, 1977). As improvement activity often followed the acquisition of older properties, in many cases by newly formed younger households, restrictions on the purchase of houses in certain parts of older towns and cities did little to stimulate their upgrading.

Even with HAAs' more generous grant rates many low-income households found it difficult to pay their part of the improvement costs, especially during the period of high inflation that followed the 1974 legislation. The original grant limits were determined at £3,000 for improvement grants, and were kept at that level until August 1977. During this period building prices increased markedly, with rehabilitation costs in Birmingham ranging from £4,500 to £6,000 by the end of 1976 (Department of the Environment, 1979). This meant that owners receiving 75% grants had to finance up to £3,600. Improvement activity was not assisted either in those areas where the local authority required rehabilitation to be carried out to the full 12-point standard, even though the occupants did not always want, and could not afford, all those measures.

Economic factors that constrained the rate of improvement included what are called the 'Prisoner's Dilemma' and the 'Valuation Gap'. In the case of the former, it seemed to be against the interest of individual owners to invest in improving their own properties unless their neighbours did so at the same time. Unless a terrace of properties were improved, an individual improved dwelling would not produce as attractive a return as other forms of investment. Meanwhile, the owners of the improved properties could be benefiting from these other forms of investment and, to some extent, from the improvements carried out by their neighbour (Davis and Whinston, 1961). The Valuation Gap was the difference between the cost of improvement of an older property and the increase in its market value. In areas of low demand this was often a negative sum, a further disincentive to expenditure on rehabilitation (National Home Improvement Council, 1980).

Certain restrictions on grant provision designed to overcome the speculative use of state financial incentives also had unforeseen consequences that affected the improvement of some older, poorer properties and certain lower income households. No improvement grants were available, for example, for owner-occupied properties with a rateable value of over £175 (£300 in Greater London), in the year immediately following the 1974 Act. This was introduced as a means of better targeting grants. In the absence of an income test, it was seen as a measure of the condition of the property and of an owner's ability to pay for the work. The rateable value, however, was not necessarily a good indicator of dwelling condition as there was wide local and regional variation in the rateable value of similar types of property. Neither was there a reliable relationship between the rateable value and household income. While there was a broad correspondence between average incomes and average rateable values, there was likely to be wide variation in the incomes of individual households living in similar houses even in the same area (Department of the Environment, 1976).

The difficulties of encouraging improvement action in the private rental sector, where most of the worst problems were to be found, remained. Research for the Department of the Environment published in 1979 showed that 30% of all completed grants in HAAs had gone to rental accommodation, although these comprised 43% of all properties. With one or two exceptions, few local authorities made such use of their compulsory improvement powers, which were generally found to be unwieldy and time consuming.

By the end of the 1980s housing associations were playing the more dominant role demanded of them in the 1974 legislation and subsequent government advice. They owned 10% of all houses in HAAs by 1981, but were responsible for almost 30% of improvement activity. However, they faced their own problems, which prevented faster progress. First, their acquisition and improvement proposals had to undergo a series of detailed checks by the Housing Corporation, which had been set up by central government to oversee their affairs. While a necessary vetting of the use of public funds by housing associations was clearly necessary, these lengthy procedures slowed action in areas of poorer housing, which sometimes thwarted acquisition and improvement as owners chose to sell to other interests, or where inflation produced cost revisions that made the scheme inviable. Second, housing associations had to operate within cost yardsticks that did not always adequately reflect current acquisition and improvement costs. Sometimes this meant reduced standards of improvement creating longer term maintenance problems. Third, the price that housing associations could pay for dwellings they acquired was determined by the district valuer whose valuation did not always reflect prevailing market values during a period of house price inflation. This meant that housing associations could be outbid for older properties and lose out on the opportunity of acquisition and improvement. This did not necessarily mean that the property would not be improved by its new owner, but the chances of rehabilitation were usually greater if it were purchased by a housing association. Fourth, the system of annual budgeting required by the Treasury of housing associations meant that any unspent funds could not be carried forward into the next financial year, which made long-term planning difficult and tended to ignore the practical realities and timetabling difficulties associated with the purchase and improvement of older dwellings (Thomas, 1986, pp. 85–86).

The mid-1970s saw reductions in public expenditure on housing that were to persist for the next 15 years. The public expenditure White Paper published in 1975 reduced expenditure on home improvements from £423 million in 1974–75 to £297 million in 1975–76 (Treasury, 1975). Although there was an increase in the number of acquisitions by local authorities, there were fewer resources to deal with them. Improvement grants declined from 242,000 in 1974 to 71,000 in 1977 with other contributory factors being a recession in the property market, high rates of interest and financial difficulties affecting the construction industry, and the more stringent conditions attached to improvement grant approvals. Limitations on the recruitment of staff imposed by tighter financial restrictions on local government also meant that progress in HAAs – with their staff-intensive demands – was slower than it might have been.

Despite the best intentions of HAA policy, statistical returns in the early 1980s indicated that they were only addressing a small part of the problem of inadequate older housing. Thirty per cent of houses in HAAs had been improved by 1980, representing around 56,000 dwellings in total. Birmingham City Council, however, estimated that there were 93,000 dwellings in that city alone that needed major repair and improvement (Birmingham City Council, 1981). By mid-1982 just over 500 HAAs had been declared in England covering approximately 173,000 dwellings. This represented about 3% of the entire pre-1919 stock of dwellings throughout the country. Analysis of the 1981 House Condition Survey suggested that 408,000 mainly pre-1919 dwellings fell within potential HAAs (Department of the Environment, 1982), and that over 75% of properties suitable for potential HAA action were not within a current programme (Department of the Environment, 1983). The 1981 House Condition Survey findings were not easy to compare with the results of previous surveys, particularly on the state of repairs, but all the evidence pointed to increasing deterioration throughout the older housing stock over the previous 5 years. Perhaps the best that could be said for HAA initiatives was that conditions had deteriorated rather less rapidly in these areas (Thomas, 1986, p. 94).

Enveloping

To overcome the problems posed by the 'Prisoner's Dilemma' and the patchy pattern of improvement activity in renewal areas, the Birmingham City Council pioneered a new form of renewal initiative in the latter part of the 1970s. This involved the complete repair and renovation of all roofs and external structures of whole blocks of older, terraced housing, a process that came to be known as 'enveloping'.

Initially developed as a pilot scheme funded through the Urban Programme, the idea was that if the exterior of dwellings were improved at no cost to the owners, this would provide the incentive for occupiers to use grant aid to modernize the interiors. There were some reservations on the part of the Labour government at the time about providing substantial resources for this type of initiative, regardless of the occupiers' ability to pay, but the incoming Conservative government in 1979 approved the scheme on an experimental basis and set aside a sum of £6 million over 3 years, sufficient to fund a programme of 500 dwellings per year.

Other experiments along similar lines were conducted in Leeds, Leicester, and Hull and in October 1982 a national programme was announced with a 75% level of contribution from exchequer funds. The decision to adopt enveloping on a nationwide basis was prompted to some degree by the findings of the 1981 National House Condition Survey, which revealed growing problems of disrepair in the older housing stock. The new initiative, however, was slow to take off, partly because many authorities felt that the measure was more appropriate to the scale of obsolescence and type of properties to be found in Birmingham and partly because of government delays in funding (Perry, 1983).

A number of perceived advantages were put forward in support of enveloping prior to its adoption as a national scheme. Because, initially, no cost fell on the owners of properties, it was argued that this would speed the process of renewal by obviating the need for individual grant processing. It would also be more appropriate to the scale of the problem. It was estimated that enveloping would cost only one-half the amount needed for municipalizing the older housing stock, and would retain properties in private ownership, a policy that appealed to central government and those concerned about controlling the influence of larger municipalities over housing in the inner areas. Economies of scale were also anticipated for administration and construction work where contracts could encompass whole blocks at a time rather than individual properties on a piecemeal basis. Higher standards of work and a greater sense of visual and structural uniformity and coherence were also put forward as potential advantages. Moreover, enveloping was seen as an important mechanism for promoting confidence in an area, encouraging further investment by owners, landlords, housing associations, and building societies (Thomas, 1986).

Some problems were encountered, however, particularly the disruption caused to areas undergoing enveloping as a result of the nature of the works being carried out. The anticipated economies of scale sometimes did not materialize to quite the extent expected owing to the high overheads experienced by the large contractors attracted to the work. In the early part of the programme, too, there were marked variations in the quality of work, reflecting differing standards of performance between contractors. The programme was also expensive, despite costing less than municipalization, and there remained concern about the use of public funds for this type of renewal regardless of the occupants' ability to pay.

Nevertheless, enveloping appeared to be a popular initiative. In a survey of residents, over 90% thought the scheme was a good idea, and nearly three-quarters of owner-occupiers believed it had increased house prices significantly (McCarthy and Buckley, 1982). Evidence also suggested that fewer people moved out of enveloped areas than out of HAAs generally, and that there was perhaps greater social and community stability in these areas as a result. The longer-term questions, though, as to whether enveloping would have an impact on general levels of investment and maintenance remained to be answered.

Other initiatives

A number of other initiatives have been introduced to tackle the problems of older, poorer houses. The Housing Act 1980 included provisions to enable central government to make a contribution to local authorities and housing associations so that they could acquire and improve older dwellings for sale. By the end of 1985, 1,265 dwellings had been sold by local authorities and a further 8,085 by housing associations under this improvement for sale initiative.

Homesteading is another method of encouraging the renewal of older homes, pioneered by the former Greater London Council (GLC). This involved the sale of unimproved homes by the GLC for improvement by the purchasers. Many of these properties had been acquired by the council as a result of road proposals that had subsequently been abandoned. By September 1984 over 7,000 dwellings had been sold by local authorities and new towns under the homesteading scheme.

Housing Improvement Zones (HIZs) are another type of renewal area initiative, in this case pioneered by the London Borough of Hammersmith and Fulham. HIZs are aimed at areas of generally better-quality older housing that are not suitable for GIA or HAA treatment, and where co-operation between the local authority and private agencies, including Building Societies, is intended to attract considerable private funding to assist in tackling problems of disrepair. They are fairly staff intensive, and involve the establishment of multidisciplinary project teams working in area offices within (or easily accessible from) the HIZ. The first HIZ was designated in north Fulham in January 1982. Reduced staffing levels brought about by local government expenditure cuts have made proper evaluation of this type of scheme rather difficult, but there is no convincing evidence that private sector finance on the scale required can be generated (Chambers and Gray, 1985).

Yet another series of projects aimed at areas of older private housing has been set up by the Neighbourhood Revitalisation Services (NRS) agency, an initiative developed by the National Home Improvement Council. NRS projects are intended to be comprehensive improvement programmes geared to the needs of local communities, and based on partnership arrangements between a variety of interested organizations. Initial projects were set up in Sheffield, Bedford, Oldham, and Gloucester. The programme was extended in 1987, with a £2 million grant from the Department of the Environment being matched by a similar contribution from private sources. Targeted areas are quite large, covering up to 3,000 dwellings, where the majority of accommodation is owner-occupied. Comprehensive agency services are designed to assist residents to upgrade their homes by providing information and advice on improvements, repairs, and maintenance. The involvement of local communities is actively promoted through local area committees (National Home Improvement Council and NHIC Educational Trust, undated).

RECENT TRENDS AND CURRENT POLICY DIRECTIONS

The support for private sector renovation meant that public expenditure on housing renovation increased from £573 million in 1982–83 to £1,064 million in 1983–84, and the number of improvement grants reached an all-time high of 320,000 in 1984. Despite the attempts to target grants more carefully there was still evidence of abuse of the grant system in parts of west London (Balchin, 1989, p. 101). The Treasury was increasingly concerned about the cost effectiveness of improvement grant expenditure in the light of the large sums being allocated for private renovations and the need, as it saw it, to hold down public spending. In 1984 Value Added Tax (VAT) was extended to home improvements and alterations at the rate of 15%, and the repairs grant rates were reduced from 90 to 75% except in cases of hardship. Concern and confusion about the amount and timing of funds for improvement led several authorities to impose a moratorium on improvement grant applications.

Housing Improvement: A New Approach (Department of the Environment, 1985a) heralded a further move by central government to target subsidies more carefully via the introduction of means-tested grants and discretionary loans. A subsequent paper, *Housing: The Government's Proposals* (Department of the Environment, 1987), was intended to provide the basis for legislation geared towards targeting grants to the worst housing and households in greatest need. It proposed a single mandatory grant for households living in accommodation that fell below a newly revised standard of fitness, with discretionary payments for improvements above this standard related to the cost of the work and the household's ability to pay. These discretionary grants were repayable on a sliding scale if the properties benefiting were sold within 3 years, above a specified price. Urban Renewal Areas were to replace GIAs and HAAs, and would combine rehabilitation clearance and new building activity. The March 1988 Budget, however, introduced a further disincentive to improvement by disqualifying homeowners from mortgage tax relief on rehabilitation works.

The Local Government and Housing Bill 1989 contains most of the provisions in the 1987 paper, establishing that Renewal Areas are to comprise areas of 500 dwellings and upwards, and are intended to provide a more comprehensive approach to renewal, involving initiatives to upgrade the local economy as well as housing and environmental improvements. Mandatory grants are available to enable applicants to upgrade properties to a new standard of fitness, revised for the first time since 1957. This new standard implies that more properties will fall below acceptable levels. Without increased resources, however, many authorities with large numbers of unfit dwellings (defined according to the new criteria) will find it difficult to fulfil their duties, under the new legislation, of ensuring that these dwellings are improved to the new standard.

The 1986 English House Condition Survey

The legislation affecting older private housing was being prepared at the same time that the results of the most recent National House Condition Survey, carried out in 1986, were becoming available (Department of the Environment, 1988). It is estimated that 909,000 dwellings were unfit in 1986 (4.8% of the total stock), 463,000 lacked one or more of the basic amenities (2.5%), and 2.4 million were in poor repair (12.9%). Just over 200,000 (1.1%) failed on all three criteria and 730,000 (3.9%) failed on two or more. In total, nearly 2.9 million dwellings (15% of the stock) failed on one or more criteria.

About three-quarters of the unfit properties (classified on the 'old' standard) were built before 1919, and one-quarter of them were vacant. One-half of the households in properties lacking basic amenities and one-third of those living in unfit accommodation had net annual incomes of less than £3,000. A high proportion of dwellings in poor condition were occupied by persons aged 75 years or over. The survey showed that since the previous exercise in 1981 there had been a substantial fall in the number of dwellings lacking basic amenities, a small reduction in the number of unfits, but no significant change in dwellings in serious disrepair. Analysis indicated that 1.6 million private homes had been subject to some form of improvement or repair action between 1981 and 1986. Forty per cent were in southeast England, although the 1981 House Condition Survey suggested that the area contained less than one-quarter of all the nation's unsatisfactory dwellings. Evidence indicated that housing conditions may have worsened rather than improved in regions other than the Southeast and the North.

The survey also indicated that two-thirds of all improvement grants issued between 1981 and 1986 went to properties identified as unsatisfactory in the 1981 survey, and about the same proportion went to owner-occupiers with a net household income of below £9,000 a year. Those aged 75 years or over, however, received only 3% of all improvement grants.

Public sector conditions and action

Poor housing conditions are not confined to the older privately owned and rented stock. The housing survey of 1986 revealed that some 475,000 dwellings in local authority or new town ownership were in poor condition, some 10.6% of the total publicly rented stock. While the mean costs of repairs for both owner-occupied and local authority-owned inter-war accommodation were broadly the same, the repair costs per dwelling for post-war local authority properties were almost twice those of the owner-occupied stock of the same period (Department of the Environment, 1988, para. 4.19). The same survey showed that about one-half of all local authority flats were affected by problems in common areas, such as vandalism, graffiti, litter, and rubbish (para. 5.20).

In response to the growing awareness of problems in the public sector a detailed survey on the repair and improvement of local authority dwellings was undertaken in 1985 (Department of the Environment, 1985b). This revealed that, out of a total stock of 4,654,000 dwellings, repair or improvement work was required on 3,836,000 (82%) at an estimated cost of £4,900 per dwelling. The survey concluded that the total cost of renovation would be over £18.8 million. The main categories of work and costs were repairs to structure and fabric (£7.3 million), and modernization of internal arrangements, kitchens, and bathrooms (£3.6 million).

Government-sponsored initiatives to tackle the problem of run-down local authority housing include the Priority Estates Project (PEP), Estate Action, and provisions allowing for the establishment of Housing Action Trusts (HATs). The PEP was set up in 1979 with three pilot projects established in Bolton, Hackney, and Lambeth. These were designed to provide intensive, locally based area management on housing estates suffering from poor living conditions and an unpopular image. PEP stressed the need for close liaison between the various local government departments responsible for service delivery to tenants in these areas, and for more information and advice to tenants on such matters as welfare rights and housing benefit entitlements (Power, 1987). Alice Coleman (1985), who worked with the Design Disadvantagement Team, produced a book exploring the relationship between local authority dwelling types and estates' lay-out and antisocial behaviour, which recommended that no more flats should be built, that existing flats should be modified to remove their worst design features, and that the design faults of the previous decade in local authority housing should be removed.

In June 1985 the Urban Housing Renewal Unit (renamed Estate Action) was launched by the government in an effort to tackle the problems of run-down local authority housing estates. The aims of Estate Action are to diversify housing tenure by encouraging privatization, the right to buy, and the involvement of housing associations and co-operatives; improving management and maintenance by building on the experience of PEP and promoting resident participation and involvement in decisions affecting their home and environment; and attracting private resources and finance. In its first full year of operation (1986/87), Estate Action had a budget of £50 million, which increased the next year to £140 million. By 1987/88 there were nearly 200 schemes in operation. About one-fifth of Estate Action's resources goes towards the refurbishment and improvement of local authority housing, with other funds being used for affordable heating, security works, management facilities, and tackling homelessness by bringing empty properties back into use.

A third weapon in central government's armoury to deal with the problem of run-down local authority housing estates is contained within the provisions of the Housing Act 1988. This allows for the designation by the Secretary of State of HATs, where he considers it expedient to do so, considering the condition of the housing, the way it is managed, and the general social and environmental conditions of the area. HATs aim to secure the repair and improvement of housing, its proper and effective management, greater diversification of tenure, and the improvement of social and living conditions of the area generally. They are run by boards comprising the chairman (appointed by the Secretary of State), a deputy chairman, and between five and eleven other members. In constituting the board, emphasis is expected to be given to persons who live in, or have special knowledge of, the locality. The Secretary of State also has powers to approve the appointment of the chief officer and the number of other officers who will service and advise the board. HATs may acquire, hold, manage, reclaim, and dispose of land and other property; carry out building and other operations; ensure the provision of gas, water, and other services; and carry out any related business or undertaking. Many of the powers and functions of local housing authorities are conferred upon them, including the provision of accommodation and the power to serve repair and enforcement notices, and they may also exercise certain planning and public health powers. An amendment to that part of the bill dealing with publicity and consultation now provides for a ballot of tenants, and a proposed HAT may not be confirmed now if a majority of voting tenants are opposed to it. In July 1988 proposed HATs were announced for Lambeth, Southwark, Tower Hamlets, Leeds, Sandwell, and Sunderland, subject to the approval of both Houses of Parliament and confirmation of the necessary designation orders. An annual sum of £190 million has been allocated for the first 3 years of the programme. HATs are expected to make a significant impact over a limited period in upgrading the housing and general environment of run-down estates, and to transfer the property on completion of their work to new public and private landlords. Tenants wishing to revert to a council tenancy after refurbishment will be able to do so subject to local authority agreement.

HATs have been strongly criticized by local authority organizations, who argue that their imposition against the wishes of the affected local authority is an infringement of local democracy; that the boards themselves are not locally accountable; that tenants will face significant rent increases after refurbishment unless they are compensated by an increase in housing benefit; and that HATs will do little to meet the needs of the homeless for whom they have no specific responsibilities. The local authorities also argue that they could tackle the job of improving run-down areas themselves given the level of resources to be devoted to HATs and many see this instrument as yet another means of transferring power from local authorities and weakening their control.

Much of the thrust of current central government policy appears to be based on the belief that many of the problems of run-down council estates can be traced back to poor management and maintenance by the local authorities, and by the 'low-rent philosophy', which many of them practice. There is concern at the national level that repairs, improvements, and maintenance have been funded in many cases too much through capital spending, grants, and contributions from the rate fund rather than through rental income. Current legislative proposals will control borrowing and effectively 'ring fence' housing revenue accounts so that councils will be unable to subsidize rents from the new community charge or vice versa and require authorities to operate their housing revenue accounts like a trading body. The effect is likely to be a further increase in rents, which have risen as a proportion of average male manual earnings from 7.2% in 1978 to 9.4% in 1988 (Smith, 1989, p. 712). With so many local authority tenants unable to pay current rents without assistance, however, unless housing benefits are pegged, increased rents may mean merely that the burden of subsidy is transferred to another arm of central government.

DISCUSSION AND CONCLUSION

The description and analysis of the changing scale and nature of neighbour-hood decline and housing obsolescence and the policy responses for dealing with it can now be summarized, and an assessment made of the progress so far. The numbers of properties considered to be unfit for human habitation have been reduced as a result of both slum clearance and improvement pro-grammes, especially the former, though there is evidence that the rate of pro-gress in dealing with the poorest properties is slowing. Dwellings lacking basic amenities have been steadily reduced in numbers, though the number of dwellings in a state of disrepair has not changed much over recent years. Dwelling conditions generally may have deteriorated in many parts of the country outside the Southeast and the North. Problems in the public sector in many parts of the country now match those in the older private sector.

Renewal emphasis has changed over the past forty years. In the mid-1950s, 1960s, and early 1970s the emphasis was on demolishing the oldest and poorest properties inherited from the last century in slum clearance pro-grammes that were started in the larger cities and towns in the 1930s. Towards the end of the 1960s it was realized that slum clearance alone was unlikely to prove adequate to deal with the scale of the problem, and increas-ing emphasis was given not only to clearance but also to the rehabilitation of sounder areas of older housing. By the early 1970s, opposition to slum clearance and comprehensive redevelopment was at its height. There was also concern that public grants for house improvements were being exploited and that the people in the worst circumstances were not benefiting. The focus switched to concentrating resources on the worst areas and compre-hensive redevelopment was effectively replaced by a philosophy of gradual renewal with the emphasis on rehabilitation.

Over the last decade or more there has been a steady reduction in the amount of public resources available for dealing with housing renewal, with a higher proportion of those shrinking funds being devoted to the improve-ment and repair of older private housing. Slum clearance and new construc-tion in the public sector are at rates lower than at any time since the war. The emphasis has shifted to targeting grants to the worst properties and tying funds for general improvements more closely to households' ability to pay. Problems in the public sector have been tackled by a variety of methods involving disposal of estates to the private sector and other measures to diversify tenure, improved management techniques, and estate refurbish-ment schemes. Current initiatives in both private and public sectors stress the need for housing and environmental initiatives to be closely linked to other measures designed to improve local economic and social conditions, and stress the importance of promoting private investment.

Throughout the post-war history of housing renewal, however, the atten-tion given to geographical areas has remained constant, with slum clearance areas, GIAs, HAAs, and Renewal Areas succeeding each other in older areas of private housing, and PEPs, Estate Action, and HATs focusing on partic-ular local authority housing estates. While clearance and improvement of individual properties or small groups of properties has taken place outside area schemes, the arguments for focusing action within defined boundaries has been persuasive. Such action concentrates financial and manpower resources, is a more effective use of money and skills, provides a more visible return on capital outlay, and creates confidence among residents and would-be investors. It can be argued on the grounds of equity, too, in that many of the poorest people and the worst conditions are to be found in these areas, and improvement of housing conditions can help to break the cumulative cycle of decay and deprivation that affect them.

However, a policy that pays too much attention to relatively small geographic areas can also be criticized. It could be argued that they only constitute a proportion, perhaps a relatively small proportion, of the total scale of the problem; that some of the households and dwellings that benefit from area treatment might not require the use of public funds; and that it is unjust for people in immediately adjoining areas who may experience very similar conditions.

The overall extent to which area-based action contributed to improving housing conditions between 1981 and 1986 was, indeed, relatively small, as these programmes took in only 12% of the private sector stock that was unsatisfactory in 1981 (Department of the Environment, 1988, para. 8.17). Moreover, many properties in the renewal areas do not require improvement. Even in HAAs, where generally the worst conditions are to be found, one in three dwellings were deemed satisfactory (Department of the Environment, 1988, Table 8.19). Neighbourhood Priority Areas, introduced by the Housing Act 1974, and intended to ameliorate housing and environmental conditions in areas immediately adjacent to HAAs, have not appeared to play a prominent role in renewal activity, and little research has been undertaken to establish how many were declared and how successful they have been in meeting their objectives.

Measured in terms of proportion of dwellings undergoing improvement works, level of satisfaction of residents, and relative social stability following improvement, enveloping could lay claim to being the most successful renewal initiative. But little research has been undertaken on the extent to which external works provided at no cost to the occupant have stimulated internal improvements or been followed up by regular maintenance. The issue of continuing maintenance is an important one, as the 1986 English House Condition Survey reveals that over 25% of private dwellings that had work done or had been included in area schemes since 1981 were in poor condition again by 1986 (Department of the Environment, 1988, Table A8.28). This suggests that the reasons for neighbourhood decline and housing decay need to be better understood if policy is to address itself effectively to these problems.

Housing may decay either because it was constructed to low standards in the first place, because it has been inadequately maintained, or as a result of a combination of these factors. Much of the older, poorer, privately owned housing, built to poor standards during the growth of Britain's industrial cities and towns in the last century, was demolished during the slum clearance programmes in the 1930s and the post-war era. Decay arising from social misuse and inadequate repair and maintenance is a more complex process and may have a variety of causes. Property owners may be unwilling to invest in the maintenance and improvement of this accommodation. This may apply to those larger slum landlords who spend the bare minimum (or less!) on repairs and maintenance to maximize profits from rental income. It may also apply to those owners and landlords in areas affected by the 'Valuation Gap', where expenditure on repairs and improvements is not reflected in a commensurate change in the capital value of their property. Moreover, some residents of older properties may express satisfaction with accommodation that policymakers regard as inadequate. Conflicts between the views of residents affected by slum clearance programmes and the professional judgements of local authority officials has been well documented.

Dwellings may also deteriorate and neighbourhoods decay as a result of policy decisions taken by a range of public and private organizations. Neighbourhood decline may be the unintended consequence of decisions affecting other areas or wider policy fields. The red-lining policies of building societies in the 1970s contributed to a loss of confidence among existing and potential residents of affected areas, and a reluctance to repair and maintain properties. The displacement of people who did not qualify for local authority rehousing during the major slum clearance programmes put pressure on accommodation in adjoining areas, leading to the subdivision of properties, overcrowding, and consequent deterioration. It could be argued that in some cases slum clearance actually contributed to the formation of new slums. The expansion of older cities and towns (despite planning policies of containment), facilitated by the growth in car ownership and road construction, the political influence of the housebuilders' lobby, and the growth in new house construction in the private sector as part of a policy of encouraging home ownership, have all contributed to a transfer of investment from the older central parts of cities and towns towards the outer suburbs. This has left a legacy in many older neighbourhoods of vacant or underutilized dwellings, and reduced expenditure on repairs and improvements.

Less tangible factors may also have had a significant bearing on investment in property in both private and public sectors, not only in terms of economic criteria but also in terms of social value and psychological commitment. A prevailing political and economic climate that treats newness as an indicator of social status helps to explain why most people, given the choice and the resources, would probably opt for a new owner-occupied house in the leafy suburbs and why older terraced housing tends to be occupied by people whose choices are more constrained and whose ability to influence decision makers to bend resources in favour of their neighbourhoods is more limited. A system that stresses the importance of owner-occupation as the preferred tenure, that rewards owner-occupiers in terms of financial incentives and higher social status, and that emphasizes the weaknesses and shortcomings of local authorities as housing managers may help to explain why conditions on many council estates are so poor and why some schemes were 'slums' almost from the day they were completed.

Apart from poor construction, an unwillingness to maintain properties (for whatever reason), unforeseen consequences of various policy measures and the cumulative economic and social process that together shape people's perception of the housing stock, there is another factor that has a significant, perhaps the most significant, effect on housing conditions. This is the ability, as distinct from the willingness, of households to maintain their accommodation to a reasonable standard, and the effects of low income on repair and maintenance. The 1986 English House Condition Survey draws a clear relationship between poverty and poor housing conditions: 'Half of all households lacking amenities, one-third of those in unfit housing, and 27 per cent of those whose homes were in poor repair had net incomes of less than £3,000' (Department of the Environment, 1988, p. 44).

One-fifth of the unemployed lived in housing in poor condition in 1986 and they were 50% more likely to live in such housing compared with all households at the national level. Households headed by someone aged 75 years or over were three times more likely than other households to live in dwellings lacking basic amenities and one-and-one-half times more likely to live in unfit dwellings. The combined effects of low income and a reluctance to undergo the disruption associated with improvement action means that many elderly households are likely to experience poor housing conditions. Any effective renewal strategy, therefore, will need to address these economic and social realities.

An effective renewal strategy, too, would need to recognize that poor housing conditions are unlikely to be eradicated by private initiatives and the workings of the free market alone, or by policies that focus solely on small geographical areas. Such refurbishment as has already been undertaken by the private sector, most notably of difficult-to-let and run-down council estates, has generally been on the back of significant public subsidies that have underwritten any risk involved while enabling the firms to retain most or all of the profits. The dangers of focusing too much on small areas is highlighted by the 1986 English House Condition Survey which showed that the majority of dwellings in poor condition were found in areas where the rest of the housing was in generally good condition. Only 11% of the stock in poor condition fell in areas where the majority of the housing was run-down (Department of the Environment, 1988, p. 39).

An effective renewal strategy is likely to recognize the need for appropriate alternative accommodation for elderly people currently living in poor conditions so that if they are so prepared they can make their homes available for purchase and improvement by a younger household, a housing association, or the local authority itself. Better incentives may be required to encourage households to repair and improve their dwellings instead of the present distribution of subsidies that tends to favour housing consumption, under occupancy, and 'trading up', especially in the owner-occupied sector. The reintroduction of tax relief mechanisms tied to expenditures on repairs and improvement for owner-occupiers and landlords of poorer housing and the abolition of VAT on repairs and improvements would be modest steps in the right direction, especially if coupled with speedier processes available to the local authority to enforce repair and improvement in the case of unwilling landlords. The imposition of capital gains tax on the sale of houses might reduce personal mobility but might also encourage people to adapt and improve their existing homes rather than trade up to something more expensive.

More radical measures might address the wider issues of planning, land taxation, and housing. A tax on the increases in land values combined with a less discretionary statutory planning regime would limit the amount and location of new development to those areas where it was genuinely required in the wider community interest and at the same time raise very substantial revenues that could be used by the government to regenerate the older urban areas (Reade, 1987, pp. 200–205). A fairer distribution of subsidies between tenures would help to reduce the stigma associated with local authority renting and enable smaller landlords of poorer properties to spend more on repairs and improvement.

Effective housing renewal is likely to be associated in the poorer, run-down areas with a variety of other measures to improve the general environment, regenerate the local economy and raise income levels. Current area-based initiatives being promoted by central government recognize the importance of these links between housing conditions and other economic and social factors. But unless the resources needed to make these initiatives work are forthcoming and without more general and adequate income support measures for people living elsewhere in poor housing conditions, they may be largely symbolic gestures, part of the rhetoric of renewal rather than the real thing.

ACKNOWLEDGEMENT

I would like to thank Henryk Adamczuk of the Department of Planning and Landscape, Birmingham Polytechnic, for his thoughtful help and advice.

REFERENCES

BABBAGE, A.G. (1973) House improvement in stress areas. *Environmental Health*, Vol. 81.

BALCHIN, P.N. (1989) *Housing Policy: An Introduction*. London: Routledge & Kegan Paul.

Birmingham City Council (1981) Housing Investment Programme Submission, 1981/82 (unpublished).

CHAMBERS, D. and F. GRAY (1985) Housing Improvement Zones: a right move for area improvement? *Housing Review*, **34** (3), May/June.

COLEMAN, A. (1985) *Utopia on Trial: Vision and Reality in Planned Housing*. London: Hilary Shipman.

DAVIES, J.G. (1972) *The Evangelistic Bureaucrat: A Study of a Planning Exercise in Newcastle upon Tyne*. London: Tavistock.

DAVIS, O.A. and A.B. WHINSTON (1961) The economics of renewal. In: J.Q. Wilson (ed.) *Urban Renewal: The Record and the Controversy*. Cambridge, MA: Harvard University Press.

Denington Report (1966) *Our Older Homes: A Call for Action*. Central Housing Advisory Committee. London: HMSO.

DENNIS, N. (1972) *Public Participation and Planners' Blight*. London: Faber and Faber.

Department of the Environment (1973) *Better Homes: The Next Priorities*. Cmnd. 5339. London: HMSO.

Department of the Environment (1975) *Renewal Strategies*. Circular 13/75. London: HMSO.

Department of the Environment (1976) *Local Government Finance: Report of the Committee of Enquiry (the Layfield Report)*. Cmnd. 6453. London: HMSO.

Department of the Environment (1979) *Housing Action Areas: An Analysis of Annual Progress Reports for 1977*. Improvement Research Note 5/78. London: HMSO.

Department of the Environment (1982) *English House Condition Survey 1981*. Part 1: *Report of the Physical Condition Survey*. London: HMSO.

Department of the Environment (1983) *English House Condition Survey 1981*. Part 2: *Report of the Interview and Local Authority Survey*. London: HMSO.

Department of the Environment (1985a) *Housing Improvement: A New Approach*. Cmnd. 9513 (Green Paper). London: HMSO.

Department of the Environment (1985b) *An Inquiry into the Condition of the Local Authority Housing Stock in England*. London: HMSO.

Department of the Environment (1987) *Housing: The Government's Proposals*. Cmnd. 214 (White Paper). London: HMSO.

Department of the Environment (1988) *English House Condition Survey 1986*. London: HMSO.

DUNCAN, S.S. (1976) *The Housing Crisis and the Structure of the Housing Market*. Working paper 2. Urban and Regional Studies, University of Sussex.

ENGLISH, J., R. MADIGAN and P. NORMAN (1976) *Slum Clearance: The Social and Administrative Context in England and Wales*. London: Croom Helm.

FERRIS, J. (1972) *Participation in Urban Planning: The Barnsbury Case. A Study of Environmental Improvement in London*. Occasional Papers on Social Administration, No. 48. London: G. Bell and Sons.

GITTUS, E. (1969) Sociological aspects of urban decay. In: D.F. Medhurst and J. Parry Lewis (eds). *Urban Decay: An Analysis and a Policy*, pp. 27–35. London: Macmillan.

HALL, P. (1987) *Urban and Regional Planning*. London: Allen & Unwin.

JENNINGS, H. (1962) *Societies in the Making: A Study of Development and Redevelopment within a County Borough, Bristol*. London: Routledge & Kegan Paul.

KARN, V. (1979) Low-income owner occupation in the inner city. In: C. Jones (ed.) *Urban Deprivation and the Inner City*. London: Croom Helm.

MCCARTHY, J. and M. BUCKLEY (1982) *Birmingham Enveloping Schemes Survey*. London: Research Bureau Ltd. (for Department of the Environment).

MERRETT, S. (1979) *State Housing in Britain*. London: Routledge & Kegan Paul.

Ministry of Housing and Local Government (1968) *Old Houses into New Homes*. Cmnd. 3602. London: HMSO.

Ministry of Housing and Local Government (1969a) *People and Planning*. Report of the Committee on Public Participation in Planning. London: HMSO.

Ministry of Housing and Local Government (1969b) *House Condition Survey, England and Wales, 1967*. London: HMSO.

MUCHNICK, D.M. (1970) *Urban Renewal in Liverpool*. Occasional Papers on Social Administration No. 33. London: G. Bell & Sons (for London School of Economics).

National Home Improvement Council (1980) *The Market Value of Housing Improvement*. London: NHIC.

National Home Improvement Council and NHIC Educational Trust (undated) *Neighbourhood Revitalisation: Why You Should Help Stop the Rot*. London: NHIC.

NINER, P. and R. FORREST (1982) *Housing Action Areas Policy and Progress: The Residents' Perspective*. Research Memorandum No. 91. Birmingham: Centre for Urban and Regional Studies, University of Birmingham.

PARIS, C. and B. BLACKABY (1979) *Not Much Improvement: Urban Renewal Policy in Birmingham*. London: Heinemann.

PERRY, J. (1983) What boom? *Roof* **8** (6) November/December.

POWER, A. (1987) *The PEP Guide to Local Housing Management*. Three volumes for the Department of the Environment.

READE, E. (1987) *British Town and Country Planning*. Milton Keynes: Open University Press.

ROSSER, C. and C. HARRIS (1965) *The Family and Social Change: A Study of Family and Kinship in a South Wales Town*. London: Routledge & Kegan Paul.

SMITH, M.E.H. (1989) *Guide to Housing*. London: Housing Centre Trust.

STONES, A. (1972) Stop slum clearance—now! *Official Architecture and Planning* **35** (2), February.

THOMAS, A.D. (1986) Housing and urban renewal: residential decay and revitalisation in the private sector. *Urban and Regional Studies*, No. 12. London: Allen & Unwin.

Treasury (1975) *Public Expenditure to 1978/79*. Cmnd. 5879. London: HMSO.

Treasury (1985) *The Government's Expenditure Plans*. Cmnd. 9428. London: HMSO.

VEREKER, C., J.B. MAYS, E. GITTUS and M. BROADY (1961) *Urban Redevelopment and Social Change: A Study of Social Conditions in Central Liverpool 1955–56*. Liverpool: Liverpool University Press.

WEIR, S. (1976) Red line districts. *Roof* **1** (4), July.

WILLIAMS, P.R. (1977) *Building Societies and the Inner City*. Working paper 54. Birmingham: Centre for Urban and Regional Studies, University of Birmingham.

YOUNG, M. and P. WILMOTT (1957) *Family and Kinship in East London*. London: Routledge & Kegan Paul.

5 COMMUNITY INVOLVEMENT IN NEIGHBOURHOOD REGENERATION: A BRITISH PERSPECTIVE

Rose Gilroy and Richard Williams

This chapter concentrates on the problems facing low-income neighbourhoods and housing estates and on the variety of policy initiatives and approaches being adopted to overcome these problems and achieve regeneration. Both central government policies and locally generated initiatives are explored, primarily in England, drawing upon both national sources and on the authors' knowledge of and research in northeast England. A social and community renewal perspective is taken, and the attempt is made to offer a comprehensive review of policy and procedure.

This chapter first discusses the major issues facing residential neighbourhoods, their recent policy history, and the broader policy context in which the issue of regeneration must be seen. The second section is devoted to the analysis and illustration of current regeneration policies and broadly classifies them as either top-down initiatives — those coming from central government — or bottom-up initiatives — those taken by local government or directly from communities. The themes and examples reflect the authors' view that the most innovative and potentially significant current initiatives are those that mobilize human resources within the community to achieve renewal and a new self-image for residents of run-down neighbourhoods. The chapter ends with an evaluation of some important recent initiatives, the processes of change, and the current regeneration effort, and arrives at a general conclusion about regeneration efforts in the United Kingdom.

CONTEXT FOR RENEWAL

The policymaker seeking to address the issue of neighbourhood regeneration in the United Kingdom must seriously consider its urban history. Urban industrialization began two hundred years ago with the mass construction of housing for migrants from the countryside who formed the new industrial working class. This legacy is important to remember, not because large numbers of examples of low-income housing survive from the early nineteenth century, but because of the long history of urban culture and the sense of community and identity built up in the major cities of the United Kingdom and because of the political ideas, public health reforms, and new planning concepts provoked by nineteenth-century urban conditions.

The early form of low-income housing in England and Wales was typically the terrace house (two-storey walk-up), built to minimum space, lighting, and public health standards. Some urban neighbourhoods built after the landmark Public Health Act of 1875, particularly after the turn of the century, still exist and were subject to regeneration policies during the 1970s and 1980s. Housing built to minimum standards prior to 1875, plus much of that built up to the 1890s, was demolished for redevelopment during the twentieth century. For the most part, nineteenth-century housing was rented from private landlords, whereas the bulk of the replacement housing (especially after the 1919 Housing Act) was built by local authorities (municipalities) as council housing.

Council housing became, in the post-war period, the dominant mode of housing provision for lower-income households as Table 1 shows.

Table 1. Housing tenure in Great Britain 1914–87

	Owner occupied (%)	Public rented (%)	Private rented (%)
1914	10	0	90
1945	26	12	62
1951	29	18	53
1961	43	27	31
1971	50	31	19
1981	56	31	13
1986	63	27	10

Sources: Boddy (1980). Figure 2.5 (Department of the Environment, 1977). Census of population, 1981, and Building Society Association estimates. Taken from *The Changing Social Structure* (Hamnett, 1989).

At its peak, council housing accounted for approximately one-third of all dwellings nationally, and up to 50% of all dwellings in several larger industrial cities. Prior to the 1980s, both Conservative and Labour governments promoted council housing, but in the 1980s the policy of offering the 'right to buy' to sitting council tenants has had the effect of reducing municipally owned stock and increasing owner-occupation in all but the lowest income ranges.

Council housing is distinct from the social housing programmes developed in other European countries, in giving municipal authorities a dominant role as landlords. This distinct United Kingdom policy dates back to the 1919 Housing Act.

Another important aspect of the housing regeneration legacy is that replacement housing reflects the prevailing architectural and planning orthodoxy at the time of construction. Generally, council housing of the 1920s and 1930s is outdated but often capable of improvement, although some problem estates remain from this period. Dwellings built in the 1950s are generally satisfactory and many have been purchased by tenants under the 'right to buy' provision in the 1980 Housing Act. Redevelopment, which reached a peak in the 1960s and 1970s, unfortunately left a legacy of appallingly unsatisfactory council housing, often beyond improvement and for which the only solution is the very costly one of demolition.

Thus, in the United Kingdom, neighbourhood regeneration is concerned partly with the regeneration of improvable older neighbourhoods and with the much bigger task of rehabilitation or replacement of failed

71

redevelopment projects. Some neighbourhood deterioration resides in the age of the dwellings or in misconceived architectural concepts. Problems here are exacerbated by the limited investment in the maintenance and physical renewal of these properties. A further problem in many of the more run-down council estates, where not only has the physical fabric deteriorated but incomes are low, unemployment high, and the majority of households dependent on welfare benefits, is that of stigmatization and the negative consequences of social polarization. Traditional British council housing is readily identifiable because of the estates' distinctive architecture and layout (Eversley, 1975; Hallett, 1976) and residents are often discriminated against (by their address) in the job market and in their attempts to obtain credit, reinforcing unemployment and low living standards. The residents are stigmatized in a way that rarely occurs in Germany, where the social housing is much more physically and socially integrated into the mainstream. Social polarization in the council sector has increased in the 1980s (Hamnett, 1989).

Nevertheless, a secure community and continuity of identity survive in many working-class neighbourhoods. Unfortunately, respect for this identity and the wishes of local communities has not always been a feature of regeneration policies. But where these features are present, a successful outcome is more likely to occur.

During the 1960s the scale of redevelopment and new construction was without precedent. Many town centres and residential areas had been comprehensively redeveloped, with more buildings being demolished than destroyed by bombings during the Second World War. The national government promoted a massive building programme with the target (never quite achieved) of 500,000 new dwellings per year. To build on this scale, industrialized system building methods were necessary. These, combined with the architectural fashion for tall buildings and deck-access streets, led to the creation of housing projects that were physically unsound and vulnerable to the wind and weather. Great social stress ensued as residents were relocated to the new dwellings from familiar neighbourhoods and they discovered their isolation from playgrounds, employment opportunities, and shops and facilities. The new estates brought worries about vandalism and personal safety (Newman, 1973) and for many, a sense of alienation (Power, 1987). Many of the new housing projects were not only badly designed and built, but also contrasted totally with any form of housing ever experienced or aspired to by the population.

By 1969 policymakers realized that all was not well with the massive housing redevelopments of the 1960s. The 1967 gas explosion and collapse of Ronan Point, a tower block in east London, triggered a loss of confidence in housing professionals. Growing awareness of the social and economic cost of wholesale redevelopment led to the 1969 Housing Act, which introduced the concept of large-scale neighbourhood improvement through the policy measure of General Improvement Areas (GIAs). The argument in support of GIAs was that the cost of extending the life of better-quality old housing by 30 years would be less per year than that of redevelopment and new construction for an 80-year design life. Furthermore, neighbourhood improvement would preserve community identity, minimize relocation, and avoid the social costs of redevelopment.

GIA programmes involved improving the environment around dwellings by traffic control measures, provision of play spaces, and landscaping and providing grants for the improvement of individual dwellings. This physical approach to neighbourhood improvement led to 'gentrification', whereby neighbourhoods became more desirable and fashionable. Gradually funds were released for the purchase of dwellings and the neighbourhood populations became more affluent and middle class, displacing the original residents and intended beneficiaries.

Legislation was enacted in 1974 which introduced the concept of Housing Action Areas. These placed less emphasis on the physical improvements of dwellings to certain defined standards, and more emphasis on improvement appropriate to the socio-economic status of the residents. Therefore improvements were avoided which would impose unsufferable rent increases or which would restructure multi-occupancy dwellings into orthodox family dwellings contrary to the lifestyle of the occupants. This legislation was intended to achieve regeneration consistent with the needs and circumstances of the existing residents and thus overcome the problems of gentrification. The latter had become a widespread phenomenon, sometimes associated with harassment of residents to persuade them to move. Gentrification still persists in several cities, with the worst example being found in the neighbourhoods around Docklands in London. In Whitechapel, immigrant communities are under threat because of escalating house prices and commercial rents.

The major urban policy innovation of the 1970s was the identification of inner cities as a focus for policy and the development of a more holistic approach to the problems of the inner cities, in the sense that programmes addressed social, environmental, and economic problems concurrently. Social aspects include the improvement of housing and community facilities, race relations, and benefit take-up campaigns. Environmental aspects include derelict land reclamation, improvement of the environmental quality of inner city housing and industrial areas, and image improvement. Economic aspects include urban economic development and promotion of employment near housing estates in industry, commerce, and retailing. Although the regeneration of older housing areas has been very much a part of inner city policy, the main impact of inner city funds on housing policies was more evident on landscaping, environmental improvements, and especially on the demolition of some notorious 1960s blocks of flats and maisonettes (Williams and Butler, 1981).

RENEWAL POLICIES

Two different strands can be identified in the full spectrum of neighbourhood regeneration policies: those intended to improve quality of life for the indigenous population and those with political and social engineering objectives that are directed to land and property development. Through the 1980s there has been a definite drift away from the people-oriented policies.

Top-down initiatives

A people-oriented policy, tenants' 'right to buy', which was initiated by the 1980 Housing Act, gave local authority tenants the right to purchase their homes at substantially discounted cost. Critics of the policy state that the reduction in the supply of rental housing has led not to neighbourhood regeneration but to polarization as good estates become better through personal investment, while poorer estates have been neglected because of shrinking capital allocations to local authorities. (Their work in recovering poorer estates is discussed below.)

Other top-down initiatives offer central government funding for which local authorities must make very detailed bids. Two examples include Estate Action and Urban Development Grants.

Estate Action (originally termed Urban Housing Renewal Unit) was set up by central government in 1985 with the aim of revitalizing run-down local authority estates through benefits to tenants and through property development. Through the first strand, many local authorities have used Estate Action funding to improve housing services to tenants by opening neighbourhood offices or by establishing estate management boards in which the landlord and the tenants in partnership manage the properties and the environment.

To gain additional funds, local authorities are encouraged through resource blackmail to make part of the estate vacant and sell the property to private developers or housing associations who will improve the property for owner-occupation. Often it is only by pursuing such a policy that sufficient resources can be made available to carry out improvements for existing tenants.

We may call this neighbourhood regeneration because improvements are made to the stock. The presence of owner-occupiers and the combined investment of the private sector, individuals, and building societies may promote greater confidence in an estate, reduce tenant turnover, and make the property easier to let. An important question, however, is: What of the tenants who moved out to allow redevelopment to take place? Were their housing circumstances improved? The housing allocation system allows tenants in clearance property to jump to the top of waiting lists and have a good choice of property. Estate Action, however, is used on difficult-to-let estates, often those with poorly designed block dwellings, which are often let to young singles by default since they are unsuited to families with children or to the elderly. Unfortunately, this owner-occupation initiative is making inroads on the availability of local authority housing for young singles.

Through Urban Development Grants, an inner city policy with antecedents in the United States' Urban Development Action Grant, central and local government funds have been used to lever in private sector funding with the aim of building homes for owner-occupation on poor-quality sites or for renovating local authority dwellings for owner-occupation. Again, this may be termed neighbourhood regeneration but perhaps at the expense of the immediate population (Cameron, 1987).

The Urban Development Grants policy was reincarnated in 1988 in the form of City Grants, with the significant omission of local government as part funder. This may represent a cost saving to local authorities, but it is another link in the chain by which central government has reduced local control and decision-making power and imposed greater central control.

This ideological aim of central government is seen most clearly in its proposals for Housing Action Trusts (HATs), introduced by the 1988 Housing Act. Through HATs, the central government appoints agents to take on the ownership and management of designated council estates. The controversy that surrounded the initial selection of estates in July 1988 without consultation with local people became more heated when the Secretary of State vehemently denied the right of tenants to have a say in the HAT proposal—a position that government was forced to reverse. The future of HATs now seems doubtful as central government has called off three of the five proposed schemes: Leeds, Lambeth (London), and Sunderland. Ironically, HATs' only claim to regeneration may be through tenant mobilization. Nationwide, tenants whose homes were to be affected joined CASE (the Campaign Against Selling Estates)—organizing media activities and promoting awareness of the issues.

It is interesting to consider the financial rationale behind the proposal. Central government declared that its intention was 'to focus on the use of scarce public money more effectively so that tenants are given a better deal' (Department of the Environment, 1987). Yet, if local authorities were given adequate capital spending power, could not more and better regeneration of communities be undertaken? Instead, in the poorest municipal housing neighbourhoods, where the right to buy is irrelevant because of low income or the condition of the housing stock, central government has starved the local authorities of adequate resources and then sought to impose unilaterally its own flagship regeneration projects on certain problem estates.

The view from below

Through the Thatcher era, central government has introduced an ethos of choice. This concept of choice has discredited representative democracy and promotes participatory democracy involving consumers shaping the services they receive. However, the ability to make choices in the marketplace is dependent on the ability to pay. Such a strategy can only widen the gap between those who can acquire 'good quality services in the private sector or in the market place of the public sector [and those] forced to rely on a basic no-frills state system' (Stoker, 1989, p. 164).

In the spheres of council housing and education of school children, central government has encouraged citizens to evaluate services from the local authority and compare them with the performance of other providers. The 1988 Housing Act has introduced the mechanism of 'tenant choice' by which council tenants are able to examine a range of management possibilities, including self-government, through tenant co-operatives and neighbourhood housing associations to takeover by a large housing association. Another mechanism, 'voluntary transfer', gives local authorities the opportunity to divest themselves of the landlord function and set up a housing association or simply transfer their stock to an existing association.

This is complicated by changes to the role of housing associations in the United Kingdom. Prior to 1988, housing associations were seen as a part of the public sector in that they were non-profit making bodies, run by voluntary committees, providing houses, hostels and associated amenities funded largely by housing corporations (central government) money. Housing associations are now asked to raise part of their development funds from the private money markets and to charge assured market level rents which are higher than the 'fair rent' system under which they used to operate. Tenants moving to the housing association sector find their housing costs rise: they also find that they have lost their right to protest and be heard. The major weakness of housing associations is their lack of public accountability — surprising in view of their past reliance on public money. This concern is not just a British problem: in the Federal Republic of Germany, where housing association stock holdings are on a par with British municipal landlords, there is a growing demand for a more tenant-responsive style of management (Novy and Norton, 1990).

For any consumer choice to be effective it must be based on clear information. However, no one can determine the exact impact of various policies on rental costs. Tenants affected by the tenants' choice or voluntary transfer programmes face higher rents but the level of rent increase is uncertain. Should consumer subsidies (housing benefits) not keep pace with escalating rents, and central government's past performance indicates that they will not, housing associations will have to cater to a more prosperous and therefore less needy client group than they previously targeted.

Tenants considering HAT proposals also have limited choices. They are comforted that:

> if your home needs improvement work, or your block needs major alterations, the Trust will give you a rent freeze until the work has been carried out. Your rent would then move to catch up with rents in similar Council properties in the area. (Department of the Environment, 1988)

Hardly a reassurance, since the question of affordability is also echoing in town halls. The Local Government and Housing Act 1989 will cause council house rents to escalate and if producer or consumer subsidies fail to take the strain then rents will have to be made affordable by reduced spending on repairs and management resulting in poorer service. Recalling Stoker's comment on the 'no-frills state system', it seems that 'threadbare' rather than 'no frills' will be more precise.

Housing associations are unrestricted in their selection of tenants. Through moving up-market they can gain funding and political favour at the cost of abandoning their original governing principles. For local authorities this has never been an option. Their duty remains to provide housing for the homeless and the needy. With decreasing capital resources and tenants increasingly dependent on the local authority for all services, how can local authorities continue to play a part in the regeneration of poorer neighbourhoods? Indeed, is there any scope for regeneration in these areas?

In the early 1980s regeneration was characterized by the Oliver Twist approach of 'Give us more money and we will improve our housing, our schools, our services.' By the late 1980s policymakers recognized that more money was not forthcoming and that the focus should shift to the other major resource of local government—the people. Many writers, both academics (Stewart, 1988; Stoker, 1989) and politicians (Blunkett, 1982; Hodge, 1987), spoke of the need for local government to respond to the challenges set by central government by opening up local government to greater citizen involvement.

This repoliticizing of local government comes at the close of a decade when many commentators were pointing out the issues of political alienation (Scarman, 1981; Archbishop of Canterbury's Commission on Urban Priority Areas, 1985; Lawless, 1989) and the irrelevance of the political system to residents of council estates in both the outer edge and inner city.

This problem is one of residualization. In the Northeast particularly, low property prices have meant that 'owner occupation is now the majority tenure for the economically active sectors of the working class (on virtually any definition of that class)' (Ball, 1982, p. 63). For the excluded, left behind on council-owned estates, life is often bleak. A former senior policymaker at the Middlesbrough District Council (the area of the case study below) said the situation was one of large estates on which thousands of unemployed people sat around all day.

Middlesbrough's strategy was to recognize the reserves of untapped talent in their community, as eloquently stated by a politician from Walsall, a Midlands authority also committed to greater involvement:

> Repairing the damage the system does to people, that's only half the story. The other part is giving the community confidence in itself. All the pride and decency of working people, and the talents that are there, waiting to be used. We have to build on what we have, use what's there. (Powell, 1984)

The strategy involves survival issues:

> The country cannot take for granted the continued support of the local population if it eventually faces emasculation and dismemberment. The government, after all, justifies its present policy by claiming that local government cannot deliver what people want. The onus is on us to prove that assertion wrong. The more people feel involved in what the Council does for and with them, the more likely are they to notice and object when its existence is threatened. (Cleveland County Council, 1989, p. 132)

In a housing context, a local authority landlord that is responsive to its tenants may present an unassailable target. It is strongly felt in the North that Sunderland was chosen for HAT primarily because it is perceived as a remote landlord.

The first steps toward greater democratization in Middlesbrough came in 1980 with the establishment of innovative housing projects on two estates built in the 1920s and 1930s known as Brambles Farm and St Hilda's Estates, both areas of difficult-to-let dwellings. These new projects were intended not only to improve housing but also to help and support community initiatives through community development workers. Part of their brief was to increase the involvement of tenants in decisions that affected their lives and to arrest the process of professionals running the show.

One example from the period shows the clash between professionals and consumers. A new shopping centre was planned for St Hilda's that was to include new dwellings for rent. The architect proposed two-storey dwellings (maisonettes) above the shops, but the people of St Hilda's knew they did not want this kind of dwelling. The architect argued for the aesthetics of a continuous building line. The community argued that these were not the properties they aspired to. The community won. Gradually it became established at St Hilda's that officers would submit all proposals to the Management Project and its committee. While the management committees of the projects had only advisory powers their views were passed on to decision-making committees. Furthermore, each committee had £5,000 for assisting self-help community groups.

Middlesbrough turned to this model when seeking ways of fulfilling the promise set out in the Labour election manifesto of more open government. Community councils were established in 1986 in ten of the most deprived wards in the borough, while an eleventh was set up in a more prosperous area encompassing the desirable Coulby Newham council estate built in the 1970s. The latter was chosen as a control to be used in evaluating this move to greater democratization.

The pledge of the community councils was to create openness, public accountability, and a real democracy.

> Democracy isn't about going and putting a cross on a piece of paper once every five years, or even once a year if you remember to go and vote in the local election. It's about being involved in decisions that affect all your life all the time. (Powell, 1984, p. 80)

Every six weeks front-line officers, residents, and councillors meet to discuss local issues, which might include street repairs, use of a recreation ground, or a proposed development by the borough council. The community council addresses issues beyond the departmental concerns of the district council for housing, engineering, and planning. The Hemlington Community Council, for example, was concerned with crime and vandalism. Officers and residents met with the local police commander and formed a residents' neighbourhood watch group with a telephone hot line to the police from a resident's flat.

The councils have only advisory powers but it is now customary for any matter pertaining to those eleven wards to be brought to the committee for consideration. Each council has a budget of £3,000 to prime local projects and self-help schemes and to ease matters of local stress, such as poor street lighting, that might otherwise not find their way into mainline budgets. Residents have secured funds for such projects as equipping a boys' football team and producing leaflets warning of the dangers of glue sniffing following the death of a resident's child from solvent abuse.

In Middlesbrough, housing management has also been decentralized with the setting up of neighbourhood offices on estates of greatest deprivation. In this way, more consumers are involved in the decision making. The recent move in these projects to committees with a majority of elected tenants speaks of a development of confidence in local government's ability to resolve the various interests and values within the community. The neighbourhood council's views can be overturned by the area committee, which is dominated by councillors, but this is unlikely to happen often. To begin the process of sharing or transferring power to the community is to begin an unstoppable process. As residents become involved they gain confidence and seek greater involvement.

The Middlesbrough venture is not without its critics; largely from officers who feel that residents are still not well equipped to cope with the transfer of power and need training if they are to contribute meaningfully to the decision-making process. Some neighbourhood councils may allocate some of their budgets to tenant training.

The ability of tenants may be judged from the work undertaken by the first tenant management co-operative in Langridge Crescent, an area of difficult-to-let dwellings that professionals had determined were fit only for demolition. Built in the 1950s, the Crescent's three-storey walk-up blocks were largely empty and vandalized units in a concrete and tarmac environment. The first priority was, therefore, improving the dwellings and their environment, a task in which the new co-operators were able to play a full part in determining priorities and choices.

Capital works completed, the tenant co-operative, with advice from a secondary co-operative and the borough council, now deals with neighbour disputes, repairs, allocation of dwellings, and spending the co-operative's budget. The co-operative is not just a landlord nor is it a utopian community. What has developed is a community of tenants who want to exercise greater control over their neighbourhood. Through their commitment the area has been revitalized, both in physical terms and in morale and self-confidence.

It is community action that Middlesbrough relies upon for neighbourhood regeneration. Through involvement in deciding spending priorities and by taking advantage of pump-priming funding, communities may experience a greater sense of self-worth. Middlesbrough hopes to prove that confidence is not promoted only by owner-occupation and share ownership (the Thatcherite measures) but through government by the people.

EVALUATION AND CONCLUSIONS

This chapter has argued that it is vital that local people have some role in directing the investment in neighbourhood regeneration. Unfortunately, many of the initiatives undertaken in the 1980s have shifted away from this concern. Fred Robinson comments:

> The flavour of the decade, evident in so many cities is the theme of property and physical development – centred on land, building, and places, rather than people and communities. (1989, p. 40)

Some may feel that such an approach cannot be termed 'neighbourhood regeneration' since neighbourhood encompasses more than just physical space. It is tightly bound up in the inhabitants and the community. Neil Kinnock (1988) has commented:

> Regeneration may come about through changing the nature of the population living in that area rather than through improving the economic circumstances and life chances of those already there.

This leads us to a consideration of two questions: Who benefits from neighbourhood regeneration? and What is the problem? Boyle, commenting on Glasgow, focuses on the first question :

> Frequently, the road to urban revival was seen as beginning with a reconstruction of an image of a city and its business community. Exactly the same message lies at the heart of development partnership being pursued in cities such as Glasgow, Manchester, and Liverpool. The combination of image reconstruction, physical modernisation, and the possible product of economic regeneration is indeed seductive for many older cities faced with economic transition. (1989, p. 25)

Boyle and other commentators discuss the impact of these ventures and find that:

> Profit becomes the goal; the original, much wider objectives covering the economic and social condition of the city begin to fade. (Boyle, 1989, p. 24)

Any visitor to Glasgow cannot help but be impressed by the Merchant City Quarter and the newly cleaned and floodlit nineteenth-century buildings. The parks, museums, and the Pompidou Centre-like shopping complexes dispel any thoughts of 'No Mean City'. However, those who venture out to the vast outlying estates find that while the 'Glasgow's Miles Better' has worn thin, there *are* projects, albeit more low key, which are revitalizing neighbourhoods though community-based housing associations, housing management co-operatives, homesteading projects, and community ownership of former council-owned blocks. All of these initiatives give local residents control over public services and are dependent on public money — local authority capital and revenue and Housing Corporation funding — for their inception and for their continuation.

By contrast, central government's current inner city policies, which are dependent on private sector involvement and interests, fail to invest in those people who daily experience the worst of urban problems. Cash grants from central government are needed to 'cajole the private sector to place the inner city problem on its agenda' (Usher, 1989, p. 38). As Usher states, 'the response has been lukewarm'.

The business community might assert that its proper concern is not and cannot be the promotion of social well-being; this is the responsibility of central and local governments. To the private sector, then, the answer to the question 'What is the problem?' is a physical one — derelict land, decaying buildings, and the intangible problem of image. But are these the only problems? An easy, short-term solution to the problem of run-down areas of public sector housing is physical improvement and better public estate management, but Malpass and Murie come nearer to the real problem:

> Housing policy is in itself inadequate to the task of tackling the current housing crisis. The point here is that although it is obviously important to devise and implement good housing policies, it is also necessary to locate housing in the wider economic context and to recognise that a return to economic prosperity in the country as a whole, including a big reduction in unemployment, would have a considerable impact on the housing problem. (1987, p. 317)

An initiative currently under way in Newcastle is attempting this more holistic approach. The inner west of the city is known for its high-rise blocks and deck-access flats. It is an area of petty crime and high unemployment. Newcastle is making improvements to the local authority housing using its own mainstream allocation and funding available through Estate Action. A group of tower blocks now have a receptionist backed up by electronic door locking and video camera surveillance. The deck-access blocks now have private gardens and access points that serve only a few dwellings. The estate's concrete environment has been replaced with a softer approach dominated by stained timber in bright primary colours.

These physical solutions were decided on through intensive consultation with tenants. A community-based initiatives centre has also been set up that has helped more than 30 local people find employment. Plans have been made to start up a trust that will promote community-based businesses to meet local needs for a launderette and a good child-care facility that will enable women, particularly single parents, to seek work.

The local authority alone could not have achieved these objectives. It has used funding from the Department of Employment and also from local businesses that have been persuaded by The Newcastle Initiative to make a commitment. TNI is a group of local business people, councillors, and professionals, brought together by the Confederation of British Industry, whose aim is to regenerate the inner city by persuading the business world to invest in Newcastle. The difficult challenge in the inner west is securing job pledges from local employers to train and employ the long-term unemployed.

In Middlesbrough, as in Newcastle, we see the same holistic vision. Improving housing without improving the lives of the people who live in the dwellings is not dealing with the real problems and is a waste of the opportunities provided by local government.

Formal evaluation in Middlesbrough has not been extensive, but includes a 1987 tenant-satisfaction survey and a series of seminars that enabled public and private sector residents to discuss pressing issues with officers. The survey indicated that most households were satisfied with services although there was criticism of the response time to tenants requests for repairs and concern with petty crime and vandalism. These issues were put on the agenda of the housing department and the community councils.

Of major importance in the survey was testing levels of awareness on issues of tenant participation. When asked if they knew of any residents' organizations in their area, 60% of the respondents could name one or more, and of these 17% (10% of all respondents) had attended meetings and taken part in activities. Respondents were asked specifically about the community council and only 15% knew that there was one operating on their estate. This might be a disappointing response but it should be noted that not all of the estates have councils (Cleveland County Research and Intelligence Unit, 1987). The feedback in the seminars was used to set the agenda for future action by the community councils.

The monitoring of resident participation is a continuing process. Resident response to new initiatives and the level of ongoing commitment to community action is a way to test the success of the approach. Policies centred on people must recognize the different needs of individuals. Many tenants and neighbourhoods may not wish greater involvement while others may be seeking full empowerment and looking for self-help initiatives. The Middlesbrough approach recognizes that there is no blueprint for success. The only rule is that the local authority should consider the needs of the community whatever those needs might be.

It is not the purpose of this chapter to argue that community-oriented renewal is the only way to achieve regeneration. Physical planning, environmental improvement, and landscape design all have vital roles to play at a local level, as have improvements in economic conditions and employment opportunities.

Much has been written elsewhere, however, about physical renewal strategies, and it is our firm conviction that community-based, bottom-up initiatives can make a bigger contribution to regeneration than has often been recognized, that the human resources present in housing estates can be harnessed as part of a regeneration strategy, and that to do so increases the commitment to and identity with a neighbourhood. The case of Middlesbrough is a valuable and innovative example, whose approach could be more widely developed and adapted to other contexts elsewhere.

REFERENCES

Archbishop of Canterbury's Commission on Urban Priority Areas (1985) *Faith in the City*. London: Church House Publishing.

BALL, M. (1982) Housing provision and the economic crisis. *Capital and Class*, No. 17, p. 63.

BLUNKETT, D. (1981) Struggle for Democracy. In *New Socialist*. September/October.

BODDY, M. (1980) *The Building Societies*. London: Macmillan.

BOYLE, R. (1989) Partnership in practice. *Local Government Studies*, March/April.

CAMERON, S. (1987) *Recent Approaches to Problem Council Housing in Tyneside*. Working Paper Series, No. 3. Department of Town and Country Planning, Newcastle University.

Cleveland County Council (1989) Economic, demographic, and social review. In: *Learning from the Public*. London: LGTB.

Cleveland County Research and Intelligence Unit (1987) *Tenant Satisfaction*. Survey of Middlesbrough District Council.

Department of the Environment (1987) *Housing: The Government's Proposal*. London: HMSO, Circular 214.

Department of the Environment (1988) *A Housing Action Trust for Sunderland?* London: HMSO.

EVERSLEY, D. (1975) Local government in perspective. In: R. Rose (ed.) *The Management of Urban Change in Britian and West Germany*. London: Sage Publications.

HALLETT, G. (1976) *Housing and Land Policies in West Germany and Britain: A Record of Success and Failure*. London: Macmillan.

HAMNETT, C. (1989) Consumption and class in contemporary Britain. In: C. Hamnett, L. McDowell and P. Sarre (eds) *The Changing Social Structure (Restructuring Britain)*. Open University in association with Sage Publications.

HODGE, M. (1987) *Post Election Strategy for ALA*. Paper presented to the Association of London Authorities Labour Group, 26 June 1987.

HMSO (1988) *The Housing Act 1988*. London.

KINNOCK, N. (1988) Keynote address at the Institute of Housing, National Conference, 15 June 1988.

LAWLESS, P. (1989) *Britain's Inner Cities*, 2nd edn. London: Paul Chapman Publishing.

MALPASS, P. and A. MURIE (1987) *Housing Policy and Practice*, 2nd edn. London: Macmillan.

NEWMAN, O. (1973) *Defensible Space: People and Design in the Violent City*. London: Architectural Press.

NOVY, A. and K. NORTON, eds (1990) *Sociale Wohnpolitik der 90er Jahre*. Basle: Birkhäuser.

POWELL, B. (1984) In J. Seabrook (ed.) *The Idea of Neighbourhood*. London: Pluto Press.

POWER, A. (1987) *Property before People*. London: Allen & Unwin.

ROBINSON, F. (1989) *Urban Regeneration Policies in Britain in the Late 1980s: Who Benefits?* Discussion Paper No. 94, Centre for Urban and Regional Development Studies, University of Newcastle.

SCARMAN, L. (1981) *The Brixton Disorders, 10–12 April 1981, Report of an Inquiry*. London: HMSO.

STEWART, J. (1988) *A New Management for Housing Departments*. London: INLOGOV.

STOKER, G. (1989) Creating a local government for a post-Fordist society: the Thatcherite project. In: J. Stewart and G. Stoker (eds) *The Future of Local Government*. London: Macmillan.

USHER, D. (1989) Building solutions with public money: the exercise of city grant. *Northern Economic Review*, Autumn.

WILLIAMS, R. and P. BUTLER (1981) Inner city partnerships and established policies. *Policy and Politics*, **9** (2), 125–136.

6 NEIGHBOURHOOD SOCIAL DEVELOPMENT POLICY IN FRANCE[1]

Jean-Paul Tricart

The Neighbourhood Social Development (NSD, or Développement Social des Quartiers) policy was launched by the new left government, established in 1981, as one of many national initiatives dealing with the grave problems of poverty, exclusion, and other symptoms of the economic and social crises in the large estates built in the 1960s.

NSD's ambitious objectives include the establishment of broad-based partnerships, active resident participation, and integrated improvement strategies. NSD mainly comprises extensive volunteer interventions in urban neighbourhoods considered to be particularly neglected or disadvantaged. The aim is to promote a dynamic of change in these neighbourhoods, through concrete actions simultaneously addressing all the problems affecting the daily life of residents: housing, education, social integration, job creation, vocational training, culture, health, and recreation. The programme depends on national support, the mobilization of state services, and local management of specific measures.

The NSD policy was gradually expanded from 16 to 22 experimental sites. (These are called 'national sites' because NSD was initially implemented under the responsibility of the national government.) In 1984 the policy was extended to 120 and then 150 neighbourhoods all over the country. (These are called 'regional sites' because the decentralization acts of 1982–83 gave the regional authorities new responsibilities and competencies in the field of urban policies.) Between 1983 and 1987 NSD had a strong influence on 1.5 million residents living in 350,000 housing units (half were rehabilitated).

During this same period, the state devoted two billion francs (FF 6 is approximately equivalent to US $1) to housing transformation and one billion francs to social improvement action. The regional councils contributed up to 700 million francs for housing and up to 600 million francs for social actions. The local authorities, as well as various public authorities, made their own contribution to these national and regional efforts. It has been said that when the state places one franc on the table, more than three francs fall into the district's kitty on account of the intergovernmental partnership. This means that NSD is a significant part of the current social policies in France.

THE ORIGIN OF NSD: A NATIONAL IMPULSE

The NSD constitutive act was signed in October 1981 by the Prime Minister during the national meeting on social housing districts. The act created the National Commission for Neighbourhood Social Development (CNDSQ, Commission nationale pour le développement social des quartiers). This national meeting was initiated by the General Commissariat for Planning (Commissariat général du plan), the Ministry for National Solidarity (Ministère de la solidarité nationale — the former Ministry for Social Affairs), and the Federation of Social Housing Organizations (Union nationale des fédérations d'organismes Habitations à Loyer Modéré). The primary reason for this national meeting was the growing concern among these housing organizations regarding the dilapidation of the hastily planned and constructed large estates of the 1960s. An additional impetus to the establishment of NSD was the preoccupation of the new government with the problems of delinquency, failure at school, and the integration of young people into the labour market and society.

There was also a circumstantial interest in these issues. In the 'hot' summer of 1981 incidents in the suburbs of several large towns had brought to light an undercurrent of social violence, intercultural tension, and the rebelliousness of young people faced with no future.

From the outset NSD acknowledged the visible crises of the housing estates: their physical degradation as well as the deterioration of relationships among residents, and the concentration in these estates of a population facing various handicaps to its ability to withstand the economic crisis occurring in France. Many of these families are immigrants and have not been given the chance to become socially integrated. The majority of the youth are unemployed and are labelled as foreigners even though they were born and brought up in the estates. These residents live in an environment of sad-looking and abandoned gardens far removed from the life of the city. The estates symbolize their exclusion from and rejection by mainstream society (Tricart, 1981).

The major challenge of this assessment was combating the growing dualization of society and marginalization of large segments of the population and of the neighbourhoods where they reside. The social deterioration in housing estates observed by NSD officials agreed with observations made in analyses, studies, and reports during the late 1970s. New forms of poverty were emerging in France resulting from increased unemployment, changes in the family structure, and failures in the social protection systems.

Perceiving the limitations of previous urban policies like Housing and Social Life ('Habitat et vie sociale') launched in the 1970s, which were no longer able to cope with the grave problems in these estates, France's social affairs organizations wished to replace these policies with ones more responsive to the social effects of the ongoing economic crisis. If exclusion or social problems affect not only isolated individuals, but also large groups or neighbourhoods, then new social programmes must be implemented with a more ambitious and coherent focus, oriented towards community and local development and not towards individual assistance. In this context, NSD was launched, as one example of the attempt to redefine social policy in France.

THE KEY PRINCIPLE: PARTNERSHIP FOR A COHERENT LOCAL STRATEGY

The first role of the NSD National Commission was to define methods and procedures for intervention in the deteriorating neighbourhoods. The main problems were unemployment, poverty, and insecurity, therefore NSD could not be simply limited to a programme of urban renewal plus social work. Rather, NSD, in formulating its goals, borrowed extensively from the model of community development in rural areas (i.e. in rural areas in developed countries). In the Third World, NSD expanded the focus of local social programmes by integrating and co-ordinating urban, economic, and social concerns.

In 1982 the NSD National Commission presented a report to the Prime Minister, which described the key principles of its actions at the national sites. Entitled *'Ensemble, refaire la ville'* (Together, Restoring our Towns), it shows the main orientations of the proposed policy: working together, mobilizing various actors and institutions, launching a new start for urban areas, and making the local intervention part of a more general urban policy.

'Partnership' is a key word in understanding the framework of NSD. No fewer than 11 ministries were involved in the NSD National Commission. Partnerships were formed between the national and local levels. Partners emerged from all sectors: councillors (i.e. elected members at local and/or regional levels) and state officials, volunteer associations, trade unions, social housing authorities, social workers, various experts, and, of course, residents, who are the most concerned about the transformation of their districts.

At the national level, partnership means that the NSD National Commission, which is in charge of defining the main guidelines of the programme, brings together the relevant ministries, the Federation of Social Housing Authorities, trade unions, residents' associations, and other organizations. Comparable partnerships exist in the NSD Regional Commissions which are set up at regional level. At the local level, where the actions are implemented, the mayor conducts the operation through a project director. Actions are decided on and implemented through a local committee composed of neighbourhood actors; representatives of public services, social institutions, and local associations (volunteer and residents' organizations); and economic partners.

The partnership is necessary both for broad-based mobilization and for achieving a global approach to social problems and an integrated strategy. The multidimensional approach of NSD requires various actors to co-operate in finding new strategies, forging new links, and developing new synergies between concrete activities and the actors' diverse areas of expertise. For example, one possible strategy is to use building rehabilitation as an opportunity for vocational training or job experience for neighbourhood youth.

This measure can also improve the inhabitants' sense of belonging to the local community.

Partnership is, thus, a major factor in the determination of a coherent strategy of local development. Through these partnerships all the problems can be addressed in an integrated manner and this, in turn, contributes to the definition of new urban policies.

In this approach, efficiency and legitimacy rest with the local authority. As the local programmes involve many partners, co-ordination and motivation are necessary, and they can be ensured only by the mayor, as the public officer responsible to the local community. In the early 1980s, this approach was new in France (Ion and Tricart, 1987), not only because of the traditional centralization of the administration but also because many local councillors had a limited interest in social problems and social work, especially in poor and disadvantaged neighbourhoods. Experience shows that NSD succeeds only where the mayor and the local councillors are active in the management of the programme.

The main characteristics of NSD are as follows:

- NSD evolved from a national impulse, but it relies on the acknowledgement and support of local initiatives. Local programmes come under the responsibility of the mayor who must mobilize all the partners who can intervene in a given area.
- This policy is multidimensional and encompasses various sectors. It tries to achieve integrated development through the establishment of durable partnerships and measures that cross various professional groups and administrative levels.
- This policy is a contractual one, based on national solidarity, but implemented through decentralized procedures and specific contracts agreed on by the state, the regional councils, and the local authorities.
- This policy is pragmatic: without a specific doctrine as to what social development must be exactly, the policy acknowledges that local actors must define their priority objectives according to the needs and characteristics of the local areas. The policy also acknowledges that the local programmes include an experimental aspect.

THE LOCAL PROGRAMMES

Local NSD programmes show great disparities. In one place, the programme may deal with a very small neighbourhood; in another with a large estate housing tens of thousands of inhabitants. The city council may actively develop specific actions in one neighbourhood but assume only distant responsibility for another. At one site, emphasis may be placed on job training, employment, and economic development, where policemen, judges, teachers, and health workers may be active partners; at another site, on urban planning and housing renovation, the programme may involve only social workers and social housing administrators. These disparities are not surprising. They are the result of differences in the intensity of the social problems to be tackled and in the degree to which forming partnerships is successful in the particular local context. They result also from the unequal abilities of the actors at the various sites to forge co-operative partnerships and to achieve effective compromises or consensus about local priorities.

To these disparities among the sites is added the heterogeneity of the local programmes. Many consist of separate measures; others of an integrated and structured whole. This heterogeneity is implicit to NSD since it is structured so that interventions are started in multiple fields and with multiple actors. However, the heterogeneity is also a product of the uncertainty about the exact content of the social development ideal that is to be realized. This uncertainty results in the co-existence of distinct, and sometimes contradictory, theories and objectives. In addition, NSD is considered by some actors to be mainly or only an interesting procedure to obtain credit (or funds) for realizing traditional local objectives, rather than an incentive for the development of new ways of acting.

These disparities and heterogeneity do not appear only in the content of the programmes. They can also be found in the structure and implementation of the programme. For example, some municipalities have seen the policy as providing an opportunity to develop new management methods that involve more resident participation. In these places the councillors and municipal services personnel have used the treatment of districts in crisis as an experiment of 'territorialized' management. In France, many policies at the national level are organized on the basis of target groups or of administrative sectors. NSD is an attempt to integrate these policies in a multidimensional and coherent approach on the basis of local and community development. By contrast, other programmes are managed by the local authorities in a traditional manner. In these places, the programmes seem to be only marginal experiments.

CONCLUSION

Even if NSD has not been able to cope with all the social problems of poor neighbourhoods, it is agreed that it is an appropriate response to the problems and a useful opportunity for redefining the practical interventions and methods of social and urban management. It is significant that the change to a more conservative government between 1986 and 1988 has not undermined NSD, although both conservative and liberal political forces have exerted some pressures on it.

A national administrative group was constituted in 1987, under the aegis of the General Commissariat for Planning, to determine the main lessons of the NSD programmes and to make recommendations for needed changes (Lévy, 1989). This administrative group viewed positively NSD's cost-effectiveness and the viability of the successful partnerships. It also identified some of NSD's weaknesses: the lack of monitoring and local evaluation, the complicated financial procedures, the weak involvement of the local authorities or of economic partners in a number of sites, and the insufficient skills of some of the professional participants. Finally, the group observed that the success of a local programme such as NSD also depends on changes in other national policies (housing, employment, and economic development). The groups unanimously concluded, however, that NSD should be continued as an outstanding procedure for establishing solidarity in poor neighbourhoods. Poverty is a national concern and as NSD is a social policy involving national solidarity (and national funding), it is legitimate and well founded to continue it for sites where there is a concentration of problems. NSD should be part of a new urban policy that would integrate the various initiatives launched in the 1980s to combat exclusion, poverty, and insecurity. The creation of an Interministry Delegation for the Cities and for Urban Social Development (Délégation interministérielle à la ville et au développement social urbain) in 1988 indicated this general agreement on the success of NSD.[2] The delegation is in charge of the coherence of urban policies, including NSD. Its creation is partly a response to the recommendation for a new urban policy that would integrate various initiatives. In 1989 the decision was also made to expand NSD to a large number of sites—about 300. This decision threatens to convert NSD's initial experimental approach into an ordinary procedure.

The national group, which included administrative representatives and researchers, based its work on enquiries at various local sites and on reports submitted by various national, regional, and local actors involved in NSD. Although the group's conclusions do not constitute a scientific evaluation, they do take into account the observations of the few researchers involved in studies or monitoring of NSD programmes. Credibility can therefore be assigned to the group's positive but moderate conclusions, especially concerning NSD's partnership dynamic and contribution to new forms and methods of social policy. Nevertheless, NSD faces three important challenges.

First, local NSD programmes have not been equally successful. Only a few qualify as convincing successes and they are mainly in cities, generally small or medium sized, where the mayor (usually of the left or centre) was directly and actively managing the local programme and/or where there was a skilled project leader. (These sites include Cahors, Chanteloup-les-Vignes, Grande-Synthe, Mantes-la-Jolie, Poitiers, Quievrechain, Reims, Romans, Valence, and some housing estates in Lyon and Marseille.) This suggests that NSD sites should be selected according to these criteria.

The second challenge requires a thorough study of the transferability of the experimental approaches developed in the local programmes. At each of the sites listed above, the local programmes emerged and developed differently. One was organized around cultural activities, another around resident participation, and others around modernization of local services or activities in the fields of health or employment. Successful local development, therefore, seems to result from specific multidimensional schemes structured according to the priorities and the skills of the key actors in the local area. It means that the success of a NSD programme does not result from the implementation of 'recipes' found elsewhere but from the ability of local actors to work together to launch a dynamic and indigenous programme of social change—a much more difficult challenge.

Finally, NSD programmes will have to be linked, from now on, with various initiatives aimed at promoting social integration. These initiatives are launched within the framework of the implementation of the minimum income scheme created in 1988. The creation of this scheme (Revenu Minimum d'Insertion) demonstrates the need for new tools to combat poverty, especially by providing financial resources to the poorest households and by offering them specific support for social integration. This improvement in social protection provisions may facilitate the success of local programmes such as NSD. The challenge is therefore to link these measures concretely in a coherent strategy to combat poverty.

The recent expansion of NSD, if not implemented with these challenges in mind, may well undermine the future success of the programme.

NOTES

1. The views expressed in this article are the author's and do not necessarily reflect the opinion of the Commission of the European Communities or the Community Member States.

2. In addition to NSD, this delegation administers policies called 'Banlieues [Suburbs] 1989' and 'Prévention de la délinquance', but not the policies for education ('Zones d'éducation prioritaires') or for youth ('Insertion sociale et professionnelle des jeunes').

REFERENCES

ION, J. and J.P. TRICART (1987) *Les travailleurs sociaux,* 2nd edn. Paris: La Découverte.

LÉVY, F. (1989) *Bilan − perspectives des contrats de plan de développement social des quartiers*. Paris: Rapport du groupe de travail présidé par La Documentation Française.

TRICART, J.P. (1981) Pauvreté et précarité, l'évolution des grands ensembles dans un contexte de crise durable (Preparatory report for the national meeting on social housing districts). In: *Vivre ensemble dans la cité*. Paris: Unfohlm.

7 POST-WAR OUTER HOUSING ESTATES IN THE FEDERAL REPUBLIC OF GERMANY: PROBLEMS, STRATEGIES, PROSPECTS

Fritz Schmoll

Post-war housing estates are generally seen as very large developments of multi-storey buildings that were planned in the 1960s (many were still under construction in the 1970s and some even into the 1980s) and built on the outskirts of large cities to house tens of thousands of people. We tend to regard these residential areas as the least desirable, loaded with physical, infrastructural, and social problems. However, there was a time not long ago when these estates were one of the achievements that filled the designers of the West German welfare state with pride.

In the Federal Republic of Germany (F.R.G.) there are seven estates containing 10,000 to 20,000 flats each — three of them in West Berlin, and one each in Munich, Nuremberg, Brunswick, and Bremen. Altogether there are approximately 120 estates with a thousand or more dwellings each. The very large estates, however, are not always the most problematic: whether an estate is 'doing well' depends on a wide range of factors, including the social and physical structure of the estate and the economic, political, and demographic developments in the respective regions. In addition, it is important to consider who is diagnosing an estate or the people living there as a 'problem', and whose interests are involved in these value judgments.

In Germany the discussion about 'problems' in outer estates peaked in the mid-1980s. Now public interest and political action is directed to other housing and urban issues. In this chapter it is indicated that the central problems discussed some five years ago have not been solved, but have been masked by a housing shortage. Thus, it is difficult to evaluate the success or failure of programmes and projects that were started when conditions in the housing market were considerably different from today's.

HISTORY

The construction of peripheral estates of several thousand flats each was the outcome of historic housing and planning trends that originated in the nineteenth century. Even before the November 1919 revolution that brought the Social Democrats to power in Germany, housing had already been one of the key issues in domestic politics. During the First World War the Kaiserreich had developed legislation for housing subsidies and rent control, aware that the sharp decrease in construction before and its standstill during the war would cause a severe housing shortage when the army was demobilized

91

(Niethammer, 1979). Thus the Social Democrats inherited a legal foundation upon which they could build their programme of 'light, air, and sun' for the homes of the working class. What they still needed was money for financing it. By introducing a special tax on rental income (*Hauszinssteuer*) after the end of inflation in 1924, the state acquired the means to offer interest-free housing loans to encourage new construction. The famous projects of Ernst May in Breslau and Frankfurt am Main, of Martin Wagner and Bruno Taut in Berlin, and of Fritz Schumacher in Hamburg were financed in this way.

Compared with contemporary construction, the large *Siedlungen* (settlements or outer estates) of the 1920s seem modest in size, with a maximum of 2,000 units in a single scheme (von Saldern, 1987). However, after the Second World War, planners, architects, and housing companies would look back to the *Siedlung* of the 1920s as the paradigm and would develop it to the extreme. The early *Siedlungen* seemed to ideally combine the ideas of social reform through housing reform and urban planning through zoning, two concepts that had been discussed for more than a half century in professional and academic circles.

The planners of the 1960s were also personally and philosophically influenced by elements of Hitler's fascism (Durth, 1988). Nazi propaganda had stressed the idea of the neighbourbood (originally developed in the Chicago School of Social Sciences) as a planning unit. The Nazis had also initiated the idea of private cars as a mass commodity. Fascism had accelerated the concentration of capital in the building and housing sector, above all through the *Gleichschaltung* (subordination under Nazi leadership) of the limited-profit housing companies. Last but not least, fascism had undermined class consciousness and class-based social structures in the German working class and instead had promoted values of job efficiency, individual consumption, and privatism. Thus important preconditions for both efficient large-scale production and socially unquestioned use of outer estates as a form of mass housing were created in the 1930s.

In a certain sense the modernization and Americanization of the F.R.G. after 1945 did not bring an end to certain developments that had begun in 1933 but rather safeguarded the continuity of societal modernization. In the F.R.G. the developments of mass housing through state subsidies for the construction of large-scale suburban estates relied on both well-established traditions and a widespread endorsement of modernism.

OUTER ESTATES IN PUBLIC OPINION

The bombing of Germany during the Second World War and the influx of refugees after the war caused an extreme housing shortage that was exacerbated in the 1960s by the rising standard of living, which in turn increased expectations of what constituted decent housing. This apparently infinite demand led the housing and construction industries to develop increasingly large housing schemes. Not until 1974 did the housing sector experience a glut, its first since 1910: large numbers of flats, built mostly for sale to owner-occupiers, turned out to be unmarketable. Although this glut did not really touch the social housing sector, no new schemes for large outer estates were developed after the mid-1970s, and the few still in planning were cut back and altered.

Simultaneously changing life-styles and local politics began undermining the appeal of the outer estates. In the mid-1970s the professional middle class began to appreciate the merits of living in flats in inner city areas. Moreover, because of changes in the taxation system in 1972, which allowed municipalities to raise revenue via income tax, it was in the interest of local authorities to keep upper-income residents within the municipal borders. The tendency of owner-occupiers to build new homes in the outskirts of big cities had become a fiscal problem for the core cities. Cultural and fiscal reasons thus led to a shift away from the large outer estates to the development of housing projects at more central sites through urban rehabilitation and the construction of smaller housing schemes, restricted by the size of inner city plots.

In general, the outer estates were not regarded as a problem until the mid-1980s, in spite of isolated, though nevertheless spectacular, actions by residents' groups in some estates as early as 1968 (Bodenschatz, 1987; Pfotenhauer, 1977). It was the economic recession of the early 1980s, causing rising unemployment and a slump in housing consumption, that led to difficulties in letting flats in the outer estates. The reorientation towards the inner city created an atmosphere in which it seemed less attractive than ever to live on a large suburban estate. Those who could afford to tried to move back into the city or to build their own home on the rural outskirts.

Letting difficulties and long-term vacancies of flats were a new experience for the limited-profit companies, which owned the bulk of the affected blocks. They called for additional government subsidies to bring down rents and improve the buildings to make them more competitive in the rental market. The federal government reacted by launching an inquiry in 1984 among the local authorities on the situation in large outer estates, which was carried out by the governmental BFLR (Bundesforschungsanstalt für Landeskunde und Raumordnung, Bonn) (Schmidt-Bartel and Meuter, 1986).

The federation, as well as most of the *Länder* and larger municipalities, started programmes for the improvement of outer estates. In 1988 the federal Minister for Housing and Planning submitted a report to the Bundestag (federal Parliament) on the situation in post-war estates (Bericht, 1988). Parallel to this official reaction, public discussion and academic research focused on the outer estates; articles appeared and the media reported on the item. The arguments brought forward in these discussions were not totally new, but soon it became clear that there were in fact new developments that were aggravating the well-known problems of these estates. A consensus emerged that the problem was a complex one.

ECONOMIC STRUCTURE

To understand the particular nature of the problems in West Germany's outer estates and of the strategies adopted here for improvement, it is necessary to explain the economic structure of the country's social housing sector.

The limited-profit housing companies, the main owners of large estates, were also their main developers in the 1960s and 1970s. The 1940 law on limited-profit housing agencies, which was recently abolished, codified the conditions under which these companies work. As autonomously organized firms — either joint stock, joint companies, co-operatives, or foundations — they were restricted to owning and managing houses. (They could not run building firms or engage in other economic activities.) The profits distributed to the shareholders could not exceed 4% of the par value capital, and they were obliged to reinvest any surplus. In exchange for these restrictions they were exempted from the taxes private firms have to pay. The largest single group of shareholders of these companies was the local authorities (holding 100% or a majority of shares in more than 30% of the companies), followed by the unions (the DGB, the unions' federation, held all of the stock of the formerly largest housing corporation Neue Heimat, which was disposed of by the unions in 1986 and is in liquidation now), the state (Länder and the federation), and large industrial firms. Each category held the majority of shares of approximately 15% of the companies (Fuhrich, 1984).

The 1988 tax reform law abolished the tax exemption of the limited-profit housing companies (excluding co-operatives) as of 1990 and, in consequence, their business restrictions. These firms now operate under the same conditions as any private investor. Both the possible rent increases and the possibility of privatization of whole buildings and individual flats have now become strong economic incentives to the owners of social housing. This could soon lead to widespread structural changes in the whole social housing sector.

The main purpose of the limited-profit housing sector has been building and managing subsidized housing (comprising 73% of their stock), but they also develop, own, and manage other forms of housing, and act as developers on behalf of private investors. Social housing has been subsidized by the Länder through loans with no or reduced interest and increasingly since 1970 through regressive rent subsidies paid quarterly directly to the owner. (These are direct subsidies as compared to indirect tax reductions given to the private sector.)

Tenants' qualification for social housing is based on family income, but the maximum is rather high. It is estimated that more than 60% of all households would qualify, and in certain metropolitan areas the percentage might even be higher. Tenants in the social sector pay a 'cost rent', the calculation based on the owners' outlays (interest on loans, running costs, etc.) and on a limited interest rate on the investor's capital, minus subsidies. The rent subsidies are reduced yearly or every three or four years by a certain proportion and so cause an automatic increase of the affected social rents. Rents are not pooled but individually calculated for each building, so that different financing conditions produce different rent levels even for housing of equal quality.

Because any investor can qualify for direct subsidies, provided the guidelines are followed for rent calculation and letting conditions, private owners and companies (who can accumulate both indirect and direct subsidies), limited-profit companies, and co-operatives all compete for these subsidies.

Similar grants and additional tax benefits, which are available to owner-occupiers, have been increased continuously since 1970. They now comprise more than 60% of all direct subsidies (Grüber, 1981). In this way the tendency towards owner-occupation has been enforced continuously by the state policy.

The definition of a building as 'social housing' is not permanent: when public money is repaid and/or rent subsidies have ended, the owner's possession of ground and building is unrestricted. Before the new tax legislation, the limited-proof companies still had to meet certain rent calculation guidelines, but these have now ended.

This economic structure, however, has led to a sharp decrease in the social housing stock since the mid-1980s. The amortization of loans from the 1950s and 1960s — the peak years of social housing programmes — has taken about 30 years, and has led to the dismissal of a good deal of social housing into the free market. The problem was aggravated in 1981 by the introduction of rebates for early repayment of state loans. Thus the social housing stock is shrinking dramatically and will continue to do so. It is estimated that by 1995 it will be half its peak size. Increasingly the remaining stock is tending to house marginalized social groups, which is one major cause of the problems in outer estates.

During the reconstruction era of the 1950s and early 1960s, the financing conditions and subsidies allowed the limited-profit housing companies to play a growing role as developers and owners of outer estates. They built up tight-knit networks of communication and co-operation with the municipal planning departments, the *Länder* departments for housing subsidies, the building industry, and the finance sector. The initiative for planning, acquiring land, and developing outer estates in many cases did not come from the local authority, but from a housing company. Today 16% of the housing stock of the limited-profit sector is in the form of estates built in the 1960s and 1970s with more than 500 housing units each (Schmidt-Bartel and Meuter, 1986).

Developments in housing policy and in the housing market after 1980, however, had a negative impact on the subsidized rental housing sector, particularly on the estates built in the late 1960s and 1970s. On the one hand, the increasing subsidies for owner-occupied flats and houses and the decreased demand for housing caused prices to stagnate in the private sector. Meanwhile, the regressive rent subsidies, increased interest rates for public loans, and a high interest rate for loans from the capital market caused an increase in social rents. In some cases the rents in the social sector exceeded the limits of qualification for rent allowances (subsidies given to individual households with low incomes to cover a part of their rent outlays), so that the affected tenants not only had to pay the increased rent but also lost their allowances or had them reduced. Those households that qualified for social housing on the basis of income when they moved in, but no longer do so because of increases of their income, are subject to an additional compensation fee introduced by some of the *Länder* in 1981. For these tenants social housing has become even more expensive and less attractive than a house of their own in financial terms.

On the demand side, the recession of the early 1980s in the F.R.G. had highly selective consequences. Those who kept their jobs had to face income stagnation for only a short period. Consumer prices and housing costs in the private sector, however, stagnated for nearly five years. These developments gave those who were economically secure a range of housing choices. But West Germans with a reduced or insecure income found it increasingly difficult to keep their flats. The alternative for these groups was to look for an older flat, particularly among those available in the social stock of the 1950s and early 1960s or in the unrehabilitated pre-1919 private rental stock. Both options offered more affordable rents.

SOCIAL PROBLEMS

Social scientists in the F.R.G. have probably studied no subject more than the outer estates. Since the late 1960s a countless number of empirical studies have been published on social structures, planning processes, infrastructure, and living conditions in these areas, but few of these studies have offered conclusions that can be accepted uncritically.[1] In spite of the methodological problems, the studies agree that the larger outer estates generally shared certain problems from the beginning: a lack of public transport, of facilities for children, the elderly, and for general community activities; and of private services like shops and medical care; and a rather homogeneous population of lower middle-income families with children. (The proportion of children in outer estates was significantly higher than that of the respective municipal area.) Most of the studies criticized the monotonous design of sites and buildings and the absence of a stimulating environment.

In addition, in spite of the heavy subsidies, rents per square metre in the outer estates in the 1960s were generally much higher that those in the rent-controlled pre-war stock. The rent differential between the old and new flats was exacerbated by the fact that households moving into a new estate often did so to acquire a larger flat. The financial strain was further aggravated when new furniture and a car had to be bought, often on credit. Part-time employment opportunities near home for housewives were rare in outer estates. Thus, the change from an old inner city flat or rural home to a new estate could cause severe problems for the family budget.[2]

Nevertheless for those first families moving into a new estate must have seemed attractive. The quality of the flats' technical equipment and the layout and amount of floor space were comparatively high and still improving throughout the 1960s and 1970s. The construction and finish of the buildings in most cases were also good, especially as compared to social housing in other European countries. Only Scandinavian construction achieved an equal or even higher technical standard. Even before the oil crisis of the mid-1970s, when heat insulation standards were increased in the F.R.G., dampness and condensation problems were an exception in newly built flats. Many of the young families who moved into the outer estates had been living with their parents or relatives, often in the inner city, which offered stimulation but also danger to young children. Their new homes

96

lacked the familiar infrastructure—shops and transportation—but offered open space and social facilities.

As far as can be determined, people moved into the outer estates partly because of the general housing shortage and the poor living conditions in inner cities, and partly because they were attracted to the new, modern, and progressive possibilities and image of the outer estates. Only in the 1970s, with the advent of urban renewal demolition programmes and the necessary relocation of displaced residents who had not chosen to move, did people feel forced into the new estates or at least duped by the offer of a modern flat that turned out to be hardly affordable.

In some cases attempts have been made to tackle the social problems through the creation of additional institutions and facilities. Moreover, problems with children and teenagers in the outer estates stimulated the development of new forms of care and social work. Some of the first adventure playgrounds, youth clubs, and comprehensive schools in Germany were in large outer estates. From the late 1960s onwards, resident groups in some estates spearheaded these early improvement programmes (Bodenschatz, 1987).

TECHNICAL PROBLEMS

Unlike the social problems which manifested themselves early, the technical problems of the outer estates were not even anticipated in the 1960s and early 1970s. The main defects of these residential buildings are on the outside surfaces (roofs, façades and balconies) and within the technical supply systems (water, sewage, heating, refuse chutes, and elevators). There are two main reasons for these defects.

First, inexperience with the new materials and construction processes of the large estates led to faults in the original construction. Also, the building labourers had been poorly supervised and trained in the rush to expand the country's housing stock. The second cause was the normal, but unanticipated, wear and ageing of the buildings' concrete surfaces, tiled façades, and pipes (Bauschadensbericht, 1988; Gibbins, 1988). The physical deterioration caught experts by surprise since they had forecast a much longer life span for the new technologies and materials.

In the end the technical problems became financial ones. The cost of keeping system-built tower blocks in good repair is about 150% to 200% of the amount allocated from the social rent for repairs expenses. The shortfall led to poor maintenance in many cases and ultimately to the need for massive repair investments. Not all building owners were able to keep up with the maintenance demands. Although all West German social housing is publicly subsidized, there is no mechanism for compensating housing companies with high repair expenses from the underutilized funds of companies with low expenses. Companies that possess a variety of buildings from different phases and in different locations can invest from their own reserves and concentrate their repair funds on the more urgent cases, and thus are able to keep their stocks in good condition. Companies that had their peak building activity in the 1970s are not likely to have the funds to do the necessary

97

maintenance work on their property. Generally, if a company has been able to continuously keep up with the minor repair needs, overall damages are kept marginal. But there have been cases in which well-maintained buildings have suffered a financial blow when major defects have evolved in the infrastructure that are extremely expensive to repair, such as cast-in pipes or prefabricated tile façades.

The first major repair problems seem to have emerged after 10 to 15 years of use. In the case of the systems buildings of the 1970s, the technical problems coincided with the letting problems of the mid-1980s. After the near bankruptcy of the housing giant, Neue Heimat, the emerging technical problems caused an additional shock to the West German social housing sector. The first call for public subsidies for the improvement of the post-war estates came from the federation of limited-profit housing companies. Nevertheless the technical problems and their economic consequences are not exclusively a problem of the outer estates, but of certain construction practices in the 1960s and 1970s, wherever the buildings are located.

THE INSTITUTIONAL FRAMEWORK FOR IMPROVEMENTS

In the early 1980s there was some discussion about demolishing or building back (demolishing the top storeys of tower blocks) large estates. A report on one experiment in Lövgärdet (an estate in Gothenburg, Sweden) drew widespread attention from West German experts (Irion and Sieverts, 1984). Even the federal Minister for Housing and Planning made some remarks to the media on inevitable demolitions. But a 1986 survey (Schmidt-Bartel and Meuter, 1986) revealed that the outer estate flats (constituting 16% of the social housing stock) contributed significantly to the F.R.G. total housing stock. The argument for building back ceased, and was replaced by a call for improvements.

In the F.R.G. improvement projects in outer estates can involve at least five different levels:

- the federal government,
- the *Länder* of the federation,
- the municipalities,
- the housing companies, and
- the tenants and other groups of users.

The federal government

The federal government is the legislative authority on planning procedures, the structural framework of direct housing subsidies, and tax regulations, which have assumed growing importance in the housing sector. The federation also gives some subsidies (in addition to the housing subsidies of the individual states) for special urban renewal and housing programmes and for research on housing and urban development.

Two federal programmes fund improvements in outer estates: the Experimental Housing and Planning Programme (Experimenteller Wohnungs- und

Städtebau), and the Urban Development Fund (Städtebauförderung). The latter is traditionally used for financing the unprofitable costs of urban renewal schemes. Ironically, funds from the former programme and its predecessor (Demonstrativbauvorhaben, or Demonstration Building Projects) originally helped finance many of the outer estates. Some of the largest estates (Chorweiler in Cologne, Langwasser in Nuremberg, and Osterholz-Tenever in Bremen) have been continuously funded by these programmes since their development, and continue to be funded since the start of the improvement programme. In 1988 these programmes funded projects in 26 estates: four were in the preliminary social survey phase (Table 1).

Table 1. Improvement action in outer estates subsidized by the federal government

Kind of measures	Number of cases
Improvement of the environment	
Landscaping	20
Traffic reduction	3
Improvement and physical repair of buildings	11
Additional new construction	
Housing	1
Infrastructure and private services	3
Energy saving	2
Miscellaneous	7

Source: Bericht (1988).

In addition to the projects being funded by the two federal programmes, various state and municipal funds are being used for the improvement of outer estates. It is difficult to estimate the total number of improvement projects in post-war estates in the F.R.G.

The states

The states have an important role in the actual development of housing. According to federal law, the *Länder* have the discretion to determine the conditions, structure, and allocation of grants and loans for financing social housing. Since 1984, when the federal government withdrew completely from subsidizing social housing, the states also determine the amount of funding for this purpose. Therefore, the *Länder* also determine whether and under what circumstances additional subsidies to reduce rents are to be allocated to the post-war social housing stock in general or to certain generations of estates (see below).

The approach to social housing taken by the various state governments differs not along party lines of the ruling majority, but also according to the area's demographic and spatial structure. The municipality states of Hamburg, Bremen, and West Berlin and the highly industrialized North Rhine–Westphalia area traditionally spent a great deal on social housing. In these *Länder* the government is considered to be responsible for the condition of social housing, and it is indeed more willing to react to problems in this sector. The *Länder* with a larger rural population are less engaged in housing policy and tend to react, if at all, on a smaller scale, or focus on a small number of problem estates, as shown below in the example of the Mettenhof estate in Kiel.

The municipalities

The municipalities are responsible for urban development planning and for public and social services. There are two legally fixed planning levels: the overall land-use plan (*Flächennutzungsplan*) covering the whole municipal area, and the more detailed development plans (*Bebauungsplan*) on the scale of an urban quarter or single block. Plans on either of these levels, which are developed according to a legally prescribed procedure, are not easily changed. Thus, problems tend to emerge if, for example, additional shops, industry, or services are proposed for estates located in areas reserved for housing.

The municipality usually runs the public transportation facilities and is responsible for social services such as childcare and schools, so improvements in these sectors are at the discretion of the local authority. Medical care (except hospitals), however, is privately organized in the F.R.G., so the city can only issue persuasive appeals to the local medical chambers to improve services.

In most cases, the city is shareholder of a large local housing company and thus indirectly an owner, often the most important one, of dwellings in outer estates. However, because the housing companies are independent firms, the local authority cannot directly intervene in particular management decisions, but can only influence the general policy of the housing company.

The housing company

The housing companies, because of their extensive rights as property owners, have the key role in the improvement of large estates. While the companies are restricted by the conditions of the finance and subsidies system, planning regulations, and housing market, it depends on their initiative whether improvements are made to an estate. It is almost impossible to force a reluctant housing company to do anything substantial to its stock. Also, all the information concerning the condition of an estate is in the hands of the housing company — rent levels, tenant turnover, vacancies, repair problems, the technical condition of the buildings, vandalism, and social problems on the estate. The housing companies can use rental income for improvements or draw additional funds from their own capital for such measures as technical repairs, employing additional personnel such as social workers, or opening a local management office on a problem estate.

The federation of housing companies is also an important participant lobbying the federal and state governments on behalf of the member companies. The federation also promotes among the housing companies innovative strategies (such as the intensive marketing of rental units, decentralization of housing management) to improve the social housing sector.

The most successful improvements to outer estates have occurred when a local housing company has organized and financed its own improvement project with the help of state subsidies and has solicited improvements of some municipal services.

Neighbourhood organization

In contrast to urban renewal procedures in inner city areas, the tenants in outer estates have rarely taken collective action to improve their situation or to put the problems of their neighbourhood on the political agenda. They tend to withdraw to the privacy of their own flats more than the residents of older neighbourhoods. Consequently, they tend to have fewer collective rights than people living in urban renewal areas, where participation procedures are legally codified and sometimes very lively. In some cases municipalities, commissioned planners, or housing companies have tried to activate the residential population through participation projects (see below).

FIELDS OF ACTION

This rather complex institutional structure results in a multiplicity of approaches to the improvement of outer estates. In contrast to the procedures for urban development and renewal, which were codified in a federal law in 1972 (*Städtebauförderungsgesetz*), there are no formal procedures for the improvement of outer estates, and no federal regulations concerning the availability of subsidies for this effort. Nevertheless, a *de facto* procedure has emerged, consisting of the following measures:

- building repairs and environmental improvements,
- rent limitations, and
- community work and improvement of social services.

Building repairs and environmental improvements

Programmes for the technical repair and improvement of buildings and their environment dominate in the federal and state-subsidized projects. The exact measures differ among estates, but the work usually includes, at least for high-rise buildings, the repair of roofs and walls and at least the cosmetic improvement of the entrance area. The latter is in response to the vandalism that has been rampant in many high rises. Damage to entrance and lift doors and graffiti on the walls of the often narrow and poorly furnished entrance halls have induced planners and managers of housing companies to see that these areas are improved and enlarged to encourage social control.

The grounds of large estates traditionally have much greenery, but the landscaping is often monotonous and designed for no more than easy maintenance. The grass and trees have been planted so as just to meet the building regulations relating to the open space between blocks. Projects for new landscaping sometimes accompany the improvements to the entrance area.

101

The landscaping plans are limited, however, when both public and private ground is involved, since subsidies are usually restricted to private recipients. Funds are therefore unavailable for improvement to municipally owned open space.

In general it is doubtful whether physical repairs and new landscaping will have a lasting effect. The housing companies, of course, are motivated to engage in thorough repairs to limit future operating costs. However, experts have observed that in the increased demand for concrete repair works, a plethora of firms have gone into business, many with little technical knowledge and experience. As there are no established, long-run state programmes for this kind of repair, it is unclear whether the rush to complete works before public funds are curtailed will result in sound structures. In addition, some of the technical problems of system building are difficult to eliminate (Grunau, 1984).

Rent limitation programmes

In terms of rental costs, the advantages of social housing have been shrinking since the mid-1970s, and since 1980 some rents have even been disadvantageous (see above). The preferred solution to the rent problem has been additional subsidies. Rent Care (*Mietenpflege*) or Hardship Compensation (*Härteausgleich*) are two programmes offered by most of the *Länder* to bring down social rents that were above market level. These programmes take the legally established 'equivalent rent' that may be collected in the private market as the maximum for social rents. In Berlin the programmes also take into account family income, household size, and building year, but North Rhine–Westphalia refused to take income into account because this could aggravate the market-induced segregation process.

In general, these rent limitation programmes of the *Länder* offer additional rent subsidies paid quarterly or low-interest state loans to replace high interest credits from the capital market. In some cases these subsidies are given on the condition that the owner of social housing renounces the interest on his own capital invested in the respective building for a period and so contributes to the rent limitation. In some cases municipalities also contribute additional resources in the form of direct grants or through their role as shareholders of municipal housing companies. Some programmes of this type are specially designed for difficult-to-let estates and are only applicable to these. There are so many rent limitation measures that even an official government report does not list them fully but gives examples (Bericht, 1988, p. 65ff.). Table 2 gives a brief survey of the state programmes, but municipal programmes provide additional diversity.

It is difficult to evaluate the effects of these programmes. The conditions under which they were started have changed considerably since 1987. As a result of the high birth rate in the 1960s, the number of households in the F.R.G. has started to rise, bringing a growing housing demand. The new immigration wave into the F.R.G. from the G.D.R. and Eastern European countries has also increased demand. These factors have accelerated the rise

Table 2. State programmes for rent rebates in post-war housing

Baden-Württemberg	additional interest rate reductions for state loans (dwellings built 1968–74)
Bavaria	replacement of market sector credits by state loans (dwellings built 1972–4)
Berlin	additional grants for post-war dwellings in relation to household income and family size
Bremen	additional grants for dwellings built 1972 or later in relation to income
Hamburg	additional grants to secure a fixed maximum rent per square metre
Hesse	additional grants in relation to household income and family size
Lower Saxony	additional allowances for tenants qualifying for rent allowances
North Rhine–Westphalia	additional grants for tenants qualified by income for social housing
Rhineland-Palatinate	no additional means
Schleswig–Holstein	no general regulation; additional grants for individual estates

Source: Die Förderungssystematik im sozialen Mietwohnungsbau, (1986).

of housing costs and rents in the private market. Furthermore the increase in housing demand has been accompanied by income increases with the economic recovery of the late 1980s. Today there are virtually no vacancies in either flats or houses, in the social or in the private sector, in rental or owner-occupied dwellings. Demographic processes probably did as much or more than public programmes to make even the flats in outer estates easy to let. This is true not only in high-growth regions like Munich, Stuttgart, and Frankfurt (where there are severe housing shortages) but also in Bremen, Kiel, Cologne, and the cities on the Ruhr.

Social programmes

Social approaches are few. Among the 22 projects in the two federal programmes there are social programmes in three estates in Hamburg, two in Bremen, and one in Berlin (a second is funded by the West Berlin government without federal funds), and one each in Cologne, Kiel, and Neunkirchen. The various social projects encompass a wide range of approaches. Additional social services were brought into the Chorweiler estates in Cologne (a kindergarten, a youth club, and an adventure playground), and a tenants' association opened a public advice office in a shop there. In the Osterholz-Tenever estate in Bremen a street market on a central square was started to enhance the supply of goods for everyday shopping and to stimulate social interaction and communication. In the West Berlin projects Märkisches Viertel and Gropiusstadt (see below) an advisory committee of experts and tenants' representatives met to discuss improvement plans (Bericht, 1988).

FRITZ SCHMOLL
COMPREHENSIVE APPROACHES

A few estates have advanced projects that offer comprehensive physical, economic, and social improvement measures. In this respect the most interesting projects, though still limited in scale, are in Kiel, Hamburg, and Berlin.

In Kiel's Mettenhof estate the municipal housing company faced vandalism and letting difficulties in two tower blocks and several adjoining four-storey blocks (altogether 550 flats), occupied primarily by families living on social security and assigned to their dwellings by the social office. Seventy children lived in one of the tower blocks. Forced inside on rainy days, they tended to litter and damage the staircases, lifts, and entrance hall. Rents were comparatively high, and because of the regressive subsidies system were rising yearly. Tenants living on social security had their rents paid by the social office, but many other families were driven out by the widening gap between price and quality. The vacancy rate rose to 25% (140 flats) in 1984. The company decided to renounce part of its rental income, and negotiated successfully with the state government of Schleswig–Holstein to halt the regression of rent subsidies. Rents were then lowered by 22–24% and kept constant for several years. Furthermore, the company took on a social worker to stimulate discussions among and participation by the tenants in planning improvements to the environment. Two projects resulted from this: the laying out and cultivation of allotments and the conversion of a two-storey car park into a community and youth centre. The voluntary self-help on the part of the tenants, particularly of the youths, was the core of both projects. Simultaneously the company began the technical repair and improvement of entrance halls and façades (Schultze, 1988).

A similar approach was taken in Hamburg. The Danner Allee estate, built in the early 1960s, is not very large but extremely monotonous in design and was lacking in facilities for children and the elderly. The basements of each of the four tower blocks were converted into clubs (for children, youths, the elderly, and a newly formed tenants' association). A kindergarten was enlarged by a newly built extension, and the environment was landscaped according to a plan discussed with the tenants. The conversion of the basements, the formation of associations to run the clubs, and some of the landscaping works were accomplished by tenant volunteers. A social worker employed by the housing company provided the initiative.

In both cases high tenant turnover and vacancy rates alarmed the proprietary housing companies. Their management took the initiative on several levels by negotiating with local and state authorities, hiring personnel to stimulate tenant involvement, and spending money on repair and environmental measures. It is this combination that made for relative success in both projects. Tenants who are engaged in the improvement projects either through working with their own hands, like the youths in Mettenhof, or through spending part of their leisure time in a tenants' initiative or participation group, tend to look after the buildings and the environment more carefully, exercise more social control, and feel more comfortable in their neighbourhood.

104

The Berlin projects in Gropiusstadt and in the Märkisches Viertel (the second and third largest estates in the F.R.G. with 18,000 and 17,000 housing units, respectively, housing more than 40,000 tenants each) are also to be mentioned in this context.

In the Märkisches Viertel almost the total stock of rented flats is owned by one company, the municipal GeSoBau, which possesses almost no property outside this estate. So the technical problems that emerged in the early 1980s in the mainly system-built blocks of flats soon posed a severe economic problem for the company. Furthermore, the Märkisches Viertel had been seen as a problem from the time it was opened. It was the most prominent negative example of an outer estate. Only for a short period once most of the teething troubles had been overcome did anyone believe that the estate could be normalized. The GeSoBau was very concerned that the technical problems were signalling a cumulative process of deterioration. The state government of West Berlin and the federation were approached for help, as was the local district authority of Reinickendorf. The West Berlin state created a new subsidies programme to cover part of the extremely high repair costs. The unaffordably high social rents had already been reduced by the state rent care programme. The federal government was persuaded to fund the costs of a new planning procedure through its urban renewal programme. Advisory committees were formed, a procedure based on certain experiences with participation projects in inner city urban renewal areas. However, as there has been much less activity and organization among the inhabitants of outer estates, the advisory committees have not really been tenant participation groups but rather project groups in which planners, housing company staff, representatives of the local and state authorities, outside experts, and a small number of tenants' representatives discuss improvement plans.

The project has emphasized the repair and improvement of single blocks, some of which are very large. A committee was installed in each block when planning began and disbanded when work was finished. (Only recently has a committee formed to consider general issues concerning the whole estate.) The block committees have been restricted in the kinds of decisions they can make. Finance problems, planning restrictions, and letting policies can be discussed but hardly influenced. In one of the committees most of the meetings were dominated by discussions about the shade of exterior paint. Broader initiatives for improvement came from the housing company in co-operation with the local shopkeepers: a newly built post-modern shopping gallery is the pride of the centre; and a promotion campaign was started with posters and decals advertising the slogan 'Das Märkische Viertel – in Berlin ganz oben' (the Märkisches Viertel – on the top of Berlin) referring both to the estate's location in the far north of West Berlin and to the predominance of tower blocks.

Recently the twenty-fifth anniversary of the completion of the first block was celebrated in the bright light of the estate's new and artificially created positive image. The GeSoBau proudly presented the results of a tenant survey showing that 18% were very contented and 55% were rather contented, though the methodological validity of the survey is dubious.

Political forces on the level of the Bezirk pushed the second West Berlin renewal project, Gropiusstadt, in a slightly different direction. Planned by the famous Bauhaus director Walter Gropius and his American team in the early 1960s, the estate was never viewed as negatively as the Märkisches Viertel. In its favour were better public services and transport facilities. The various companies and co-operatives that own parts of the housing stock at Gropiusstadt have felt the economic effects of the technical problems to a different degree. Some of the owners manage their buildings quite well and can cope with the repair claims.

The initiative for the improvement project in Gropiusstadt came mainly from the local council, the mayor, and the head of the building and planning department in West Berlin's Neukölln district in order to maintain the comparatively good image of this estate and planning policy in their district in general. The officials approached a planning firm and the concerned housing companies about launching an improvement project to be financed by the West Berlin state and the housing companies. The project emphasis here has been on environmental improvements (traffic, landscape, and recreation), in order to improve not only the estate itself, but to initiate a positive development in the adjacent areas in the south of West Berlin. Here, also, an advisory committee was formed, a single one in this case, since measures have been directed towards the area as a whole.

The procedures in the Märkisches Viertel and Gropiusstadt became models for renewal projects in other large and medium-sized estates built in the 1960s and 1970s in West Berlin. A subsidies programme for these efforts has become a regular part of the state budget.

The actions taken in the large West Berlin projects have mainly followed two courses: producing a positive image of the estates through public relations activities and attending to environmental enhancements of the public open space and technical repairs to the tower blocks. It is doubtful whether these measures will have a lasting effect, because of the wide range of problems—structural defects, the estates' isolated location, the relative social homogeneity, and the lack of cultural stimulation—that have not been fully addressed. Where work has been completed, the estates look more attractive and the reports in the media are less critical than before, but it is questionable whether the estates' more positive public image among the inhabitants and the general public is indicative of real long-term improvement.

POST-WAR ESTATES: A PARADIGM OF MODERNISM?

The housing market in the F.R.G. has changed so dramatically in the past five years that the problems of the outer estates seem secondary in the current situation of rising rents and building costs and increased homelessness in which more people are living in homes and hostels.

Evaluating the effects of improvement projects in outer estates is made difficult by general and long-term social developments that affect the living conditions in these areas in a specific way. In the 1960s and 1970s, outer estates provided not merely housing, but also conveyed the values of a modern life style. Housing reform was reform of a way of life. As early as the 1920s, housing companies and co-operatives were not only developing estates and supplying houses and flats, but also trying to teach the inhabitants, especially housewives, the values of modern living and housekeeping. This form of education figures prominently in Nazi propaganda. In the post-war period this behaviour conditioning through housing was more subtle but nevertheless effective: rising incomes and standards of consumption and the larger dwelling size and improved technical equipment of the houses made modern life in a modern flat desirable and its tenants predisposed towards modernism. Housing was one of the forerunners of the modernization of society, followed by the mass consumption of cars and technical equipment for the household. The production of durable consumer goods became a leading sector of the post-war economy and the foundation for its long-term growth. Consumption of these goods was possible not only because of rising personal incomes brought about by increased productivity, but also because of public subsidies and investments in such areas as social housing and road construction. The extension of the social security system further widened the market for consumer goods by lessening the financial risks for average working-class households.

Politically, the growth of the welfare state was partly an achievement of the trade unions, whose influence had been increasing since 1950, even when the conservative Christian Democrats were the majority party in the federal government. In the large cities the growth of social housing and facilities was associated with the Social Democrats, who were in power in most of West Germany's metropolitan centres in the 1950s and 1960s. When the Social Democrats came to power at the federal level in the mid-1960s, they further expanded welfare provisions in education, social services, and municipal infrastructure. It was the era of the planning and building of clinics, indoor swimming pools, comprehensive schools, and underground railways. It was also the era of a Keynesian economic policy, which promised a stabilized economy, ever growing wealth, and equal opportunities for everyone.

The consumption of market goods and the dependence on welfare state services and facilities are the most characteristic aspects of the new way of life in the outer estates. Previously intact structures of mutual and self-help within the family and among relatives and neighbourhoods broke down. By the 1960s these old structures seemed outdated.

The problems caused by this new way of life remained below the surface as long as the economy continued to grow and the welfare system to expand. As early as the mid-1960s, however, scholars were noting that some of the residents of outer estates were dissatisfied with the reduced choices and limited possibilities for social contact, communication, and spontaneous activities (Mitscherlich, 1965). Traditionally people's strategies for managing everyday life were based on personal relationships with friends and relatives. On the outer estates, residents now had to deal with impersonal officials and depend on the market to manage their lives. Most critics offered more of the same remedies: more or better institutions and facilities, a wider range and better choice of market goods.

It was not until the 1980s that criticism of outer estates as a housing form began to dominate political and cultural discourse (Schmoll, 1988). At present, technical problems are aggravating the social ones, at a time when additional facilities and services are being sacrificed to an austerity policy. Moreover, as the older social housing enters the private market, further segregation will be seen in the remaining stock of 1960s and 1970s buildings. In the face of these trends, the recent improvement actions seem inadequate in terms of quality, comprehensiveness, and extent, and of no lasting effect.

The political and cultural future of the outer estates is even more critical. The outer estates, strongholds of Social Democratic voters in the 1970s, have become areas where neofascist and extreme right-wing parties enjoy major gains. This is not a surprising development. The promises of modernism — the equality of opportunity and the growth of wealth — have failed, and have been replaced by new values of personal efficiency and individualism. These new values serve to fragment society, exacerbate cultural differences, and undermine the traditional values, priorities, and political attitudes prevalent in the working and lower middle class. Proponents of the counter-culture have advocated new political strategies, requiring involvement and participation and the ability to engage in intellectual and often confrontational discourse. Those living in outer estates, however, are generally not prepared for these strategies. Thus these groups can neither take advantage of the new participatory approaches or self-organized initiatives, nor keep up with the consumerism of the new middle class. Instead, they turn towards racism, nationalism, and a diffuse hatred of those on top. Thus, the traditional Social Democratic strategies have lost their integrative power.

For years the outer estates have been subjected to neglect and criticism. The residents see these negative views as an implicit criticism of their lives and values. This transference is at least partially responsible for the tendency for residents to adopt extreme right-wing political positions. We need to be aware that when we discuss the problems of outer estates we ourselves become part of the problem by defining criteria and values. We should be cautious that our views are not seen as absolute and we must avoid becoming cultural imperialists, imposing our standards on the life styles and attitudes of the residents, for this could contribute to the further deterioration of the outer estates.

NOTES

1. The most thorough in terms of methods and epistemology might be the study on the Gropiusstadt estate in Berlin in Becker and Keim (1977). See Keim (1979) for a critical account of social studies on outer estates.

2. For an impressive case study see Guggenheimer and Ottomeyer (1980).

REFERENCES

Bauschadensbericht (1988) *Zweiter Bericht über Schäden an Gebäuden.* Bonn: Der Bundesminister für Raumordnung, Bauwesen und Städtebau.

BECKER, H. and K.D. KEIM (1977) *Gropiusstadt: Soziale Verhältnisse am Stadtrand.* Stuttgart.

Bericht (1988) *Städtebaulicher Bericht: Neubausiedlungen der 60er und 70er Jahre — Probleme und Lösungswege.* Bonn: Bericht des Bundesministers für Raumordnung, Bauwesen und Städtebau.

BODENSCHATZ, H. (1987) *Platz frei für das Neue Berlin! Geschichte der Stadterneuerung seit 1881.* Berlin.

DURTH, W. (1988) *Deutsche Architekten; Biographische Verflechtungen 1900-1970.* Brunswick.

Die Förderungssystematik im socialen Mietwohnungsbau (1986) In: *Wohnungswirtschaft und Mietrecht,* vols 26 and 27. Köln.

FUHRICH, M. (1984) *Wohnungsversorgung als sozialer Auftrag — Gemeinnützigkeit im Wohnungswesen am Beispiel der Wohnungsbaugesellschaft Neue Heimat.* Berlin: Technische Universität; Arbeitshefte des Instituts für Stadt- und Regionalplanung.

GIBBINS, O. (1988) *Großsiedlungen; Bestandspflege und Weiterentwicklung.* München.

GRÜBER, W. (1981) *Sozialer Wohnungsbau in der Bundesrepublik; Der Wohnungssektor zwischen Sozialpolitik und Kapitalinteressen.* Köln.

GRUNAU, E.B. (1984) Betonschäden und -sanierung. In: *Baugewerbe,* Heft 16. Köln.

GUGGENHEIMER, M. and K. OTTOMEYER (eds) (1980) *Zerstörung einer Familie.* Reinbek.

IRION, I. and T. SIEVERTS (1984) Göteborg-Lövgärdet: Der kurze Lebenszyklus eines Stadtteils. In: *Stadtbauwelt* 24, p. 178 ff. Berlin.

KEIM, K.D. (1979) *Milieu in der Stadt.* Stuttgart.

MITSCHERLICH, A. (1965) *Die Unwirtlichkeit unserer Städte — Ein Pamphlet.* Frankfurt.

NIETHAMMER, L. (1979) Ein langer Marsch durch die Institutionen. Zur Vorgeschichte des preußischen Wohnungsgesetzes von 1918. In: L. Niethammer (ed.) *Wohnen im Wandel,* p. 363 ff. Wuppertal.

PFOTENHAUER, E. (1977) Nachbarschaft oder Bewohnerinitiative. In: Gronemeyer/Bahr (ed.) *Nachbarschaft im Neubaublock,* p. 259 ff. Weinheim.

SCHMIDT-BARTEL, J, and H. MEUTER (1986) *Der Wohnungsbestand in Großsiedlungen in der Bundesrepublik Deutschland; Quantitative Eckdaten zur Einschätzung der Bedeutung von Großsiedlungen für die Wohnungsversorgung der Bevölkerung und für zukünftige Aufgaben der Stadterneuerung.* Bonn: Bundesforschungsanstalt für Landeskunde und Raumordnung.

VON SALDERN, A. (1987) Die Neubausiedlungen der Zwanziger Jahre. In: U. Herlyn, A. v. Saldern and W. Tessin (eds) *Neubausiedlungen der 20er und 60er Jahre — Ein historisch-soziologischer Vergleich,* p. 29 ff. Frankfurt.

SCHMOLL, F. (1988) Das Image der Großsiedlung — Thesen zum allmählichen Aufstieg und rapiden Verfall eines funktionalistischen Leitbilds. In: Harms, Schubert *et al.* (eds) *Zukunft der Großsiedlungen — Ein Tagungsbericht.* Hamburg (TU Hamburg-Harburg).

SCHULTZE, J. (1988) Erfolgreich angepackt: Nachbesserung der Großsiedlung Kiel-Mettenhof. In: *Gemeinnütziges Wohnungswesen,* 1, p. 30 ff.

8 THE UPGRADING OF LARGE-SCALE HOUSING ESTATES IN THE NETHERLANDS

Hugo Priemus

After the Second World War, The Netherlands experienced a persistent housing shortage, which lasted longer than in most other Western European countries. While housing production declined elsewhere, The Netherlands continued to maintain a building programme of 100,000 to 120,000 dwellings a year in the 1980s. The combined effect of the post-war birth bulge, foreign immigration, and the thinning out of families led to a housing demand that persisted in exceeding forecasts. Despite the continuing shortages, a not inconsiderable vacancy rate has been noted in recent years. The striking feature of this is that the vacancies seemed to be concentrated in certain estates, whereas elsewhere within the same regional housing market excess demand manifests itself (Prak and Priemus, 1985).

Residents evidently perceive a housing and district hierarchy, which directs their demand towards housing estates with a favourable price/quality ratio. Price is determined by the basic rent as well as by the service charges, heating costs, and, where applicable, the housing allowance received by the occupant. Quality is determined by the physical characteristics of the dwelling and its surroundings and by such factors as the socio-economic status of fellow occupants, security around the home, and the degree of pollution and vandalism in the area. Vacancies tend to occur in those dwellings that rest at the bottom of the housing hierarchy.

This chapter begins by investigating the characteristics of large-scale housing estates with letting difficulties. The emphasis is placed on the price/quality ratio as an explanatory variable. There follows a survey of policy instruments that are available in The Netherlands for the improvement of post-war housing estates. Next, a successful approach to upgrading a post-war estate (the Gilliswijk) in Delft is discussed. The chapter concludes with comments on the evaluation of measures taken to upgrade post-war housing estates.

LARGE-SCALE HOUSING ESTATES WITH LETTING DIFFICULTIES

In The Netherlands most of the rented dwelling stock is owned by housing associations, which manage these dwellings on a non-profit basis with financial support from the authorities. Through the annual reports of these housing associations it is possible to determine in which housing estates loss of rent is concentrated. Earlier research (Priemus, 1986) has shown that the loss of rent in this sector is a reliable proxy for vacancy. An analysis has been made of post-war estates with at least ten dwellings and a vacancy rate of at least 5% (N5% estates). Table 1 presents a comparison of these N5% estates with the entire post-war stock of housing association dwellings at the end of 1985 by form of housing.

Table 1. Comparison of N5% estates with the entire post-war stock of housing association dwellings

Form of housing	N5% estates			Entire stock	
	Number of estates	Number of dwellings	%	Number of dwellings	%
Single-family houses	60	6,413	14.1	879,600	53.9
Blocks of flats	122	31,623	69.4	753,200	46.1
Mixed	30	7,545	16.6	–	–
Unknown	(2)	–	–	–	–
Total	212	45,581	100	1,632,800	100

Source: OTB and 1985/1986 House Demand Survey, adapted by OTB.

The N5% estates include both occupied and unoccupied dwellings; the 1985/1986 House Demand Survey covered occupied dwellings only. This makes the comparison less than exact. The mixed estates in the N5% collection also distort the picture. If we assume that these mixed estates are proportionately divided between the two categories (which means that a block of flats on a mixed estate runs just as much risk of vacancy as a block of flats on an estate consisting exclusively of blocks of flats), then we see that dwellings in blocks of flats are $(69.4 \times 100):(83.4 \times 46.1) - 1 = 81\%$ over-represented among N5% estates.

Table 2 is subject to the same reservation as Table 1. The over-representation of the number of N5% dwellings in blocks of flats higher than four storeys is $(52.9 + 12.8) \times 100: (21.2 + 7.6) - 100 = 128\%$. The over-representation of the number of N5% dwellings in blocks of flats higher than ten storeys is $(12.8 \times 100):(7.6) - 100 = 68\%$. The plausible assumption that vacancies would be greater in very tall residential buildings than in residential buildings with more than four storeys is not confirmed.

Swedish research has revealed that an estate's reputation declines the higher its number of dwellings (Liedholm et al., 1985). In the Bijlmermeer in Amsterdam this has possibly been the case among the twelve-storey blocks there. In addition to building height, dwelling size is a factor in vacancy. Housing estates with one- or two-room dwellings for young people have a relatively higher loss of rent. Finally, housing estates built after 1970 are more susceptible to vacancy than older ones, probably because of the higher housing expenses.

The effect of technical and physical building problems on the lettability of dwellings seems very slight. Occupants of subsiding or cracking blocks of flats see in these defects a reason for complaint, but not for moving out. The estates with concrete rot that were examined also remained fully occupied.

According to the Qualitative Housing Registration (a large housing survey

Table 2. Comparison of N5% estates with blocks of flats and the entire post-war stock of housing association dwellings (in blocks of flats) on 31 December 1985, with a breakdown by number of storeys

Number of storeys	N5% estates					Entire stock	
	Number of estates	%	Number of dwellings	%		Number of dwellings	%
1–4	68	41.2	14,194	34.3		531,900	71.2
5–10	78	47.3	21,876	52.9		158,800	21.2
11+	19	11.5	5,279	12.8		56,000	7.6
Unknown	(2)	–	–	–		(5,900)	–
Total	165	100	41,349	100			

Source: OTB and 1985/1986 House Demand Survey, adapted by OTB.

in the Netherlands), the technical state of post-war high-rises is better than that of single-family houses and medium high-rises. However, given the impact over time of wind loads on the top storeys of high-rises, it is questionable whether this difference in quality will continue in the long run; unpleasant surprises in the future are not out of the question. This expectation is based on investigations by Thijssen and Meijer (1988), who demonstrated that the technical standards for the construction of high-rise social housing were inadequate.

Finally, location factors, both interregional and intraregional, have considerable influence on the lettability of housing estates. The disappearance of regional employment or the presence of more attractive alternatives elsewhere fosters increased vacancy. Locally, unfavourable locations are to be found in city outskirts, in areas afflicted with noise or smells, and in neighbourhoods with negative images. Barriers such as motorways or rivers can reinforce among residents their sense of isolation. Location factors operate mostly as intensifiers of other drawbacks.

In general, we may conclude that housing estates with letting difficulties are those perceived by occupants as having an unfavourable price/quality ratio. The large-scale estates with letting difficulties are characterized by an isolated location, great uniformity, a large proportion of young people, a small proportion of families with children, and a higher than average share of ethnic minorities. These estates merely perform a housing function, offering few opportunities for employment and few amenities. Unemployment on such large-scale estates is high and average incomes are low. Residents with a weak position in the housing market, including entrants to that market, predominate on these estates.

POLICY INSTRUMENTS FOR UPGRADING POST-WAR DISTRICTS IN THE NETHERLANDS

The responsible body for improving post-war housing estates is the local authority, which uses numerous legal and financial instruments developed by the central government.

Legal instruments

The set of legal instruments that can be used by a local authority to manage post-war districts includes physical planning instruments, housing instruments, and other general laws and municipal by-laws.

Physical planning instruments

The structure plan. A structure plan reproduces future physical development as it relates to:

- the whole territory of the local authority;
- a part of it (e.g. only the built-up area or only the rural area); or
- parts of the territory of several local authorities (an intermunicipal structure plan).

Structure plans, although mentioned in the Physical Planning Act, are neither obligatory nor binding. The purpose of a structure plan is to present in a coherent fashion a broad outline of long-term physical planning policies. Structure plans at the neighbourhood or district level can provide the foundation for an integrated management policy for the larger area.

The land-use allocation plan. A land-use allocation plan is generally the best means for local authorities to give substance to regional planning and management. Such a plan prescribes land use within its geographic boundaries, outlining what is and what is not permitted at particular sites. While building at variance with the land-use allocation plan is forbidden, existing land uses at variance with the plan do not have to be terminated. A land-use allocation plan is obligatory under the Physical Planning Act (WRO) for rural and built-up areas protected under the Ancient Monuments Act. It is also allowed for other districts within the built-up area (Section 10 WRO).

The land-use allocation plan is the only physical planning tool that is directly binding. It offers the greatest legal security against developments that threaten an area's social climate and gives developers, town planners, and citizens the necessary clarity for planning the future. Therefore, many local authorities in The Netherlands are working on (or have already completed) land-use allocation plans that cover entire municipal areas.

There are disadvantages, however, to the land-use allocation plan. Many find it too detailed, expensive, and inflexible, which undermines its implementation. It requires lengthy preparation and attention to many procedures.

Because of this, the Physical Planning Act and Decree were amended in 1985. Now, shorter proceedings have accelerated the preparation of land-use allocation plans. In addition, flexibility has been introduced: it is now possible to compile less detailed plans for areas where no great changes are expected; the broad outlines can be filled in later.

Section 19 and the anticipation procedure.   Despite these changes, 75% of new house building comes under Section 19 or the exemption procedure. In an area where a new land-use allocation plan is being developed the local authority can grant an exemption for a given building plan from the provisions of the old land-use allocation plan (Section 19 WRO). The authority can also make a 'preparatory decision' (Section 21 WRO) to ban undesirable development or grant building permits in anticipation of the provisions of a new land-use allocation plan (Section 50, subsection 8, Housing Act). Sections 19, 21, and 50 allow municipal authorities to follow a dynamic and flexible policy, despite the protracted process of developing the land-use allocation plan.

The urban renewal plan.   The Town and Village Renewal Act (WSDV) of 1985 introduced the urban renewal plan. Unlike the land-use allocation plan, which is a form of admissibility planning, the urban renewal plan focuses on implementation. As important as the plan is the determination of a planning scheme, schedules for implementation, progress in time, costs, and community involvement in specific activities in the plan. An urban renewal plan can be instituted in post-war areas, and can designate areas for modernization or replacement (Section 32).

The environmental by-law.   The environmental by-law (LMV) has been introduced as part of the WSDV. Local authorities can use the LMV to save the environment from decay. With an LMV the authorities can deny a building or demolition permit if these activities are at variance with the LMV provisions. The authorities can also require that construction take place within a certain period of time after a building permit has been granted. In addition, temporary amenities (playing fields and playgrounds) can be instituted on empty lots.

The LMV is not obligatory, but it is a useful instrument when a site is between a land-use allocation and urban renewal plan, has outdated plans, or no plans. A great advantage of the LMV is its short procedures and rapid availability.

The LMV is not a popular measure, however. Few local authorities have instituted the by-law, because of its temporary nature. An LMV is valid for a maximum of five years, with a possible five-year maximum extension. Thereafter a different plan has to be drawn up, for instance a land-use allocation plan. This is why the LMV has often been described as a 'refined preparatory decree'.

The management plan.   Management plans, like urban renewal plans, encompass implementation procedures. At present, however, they have no legal status. Management plans may be appropriate for areas where large-scale changes in land use are not anticipated, as in the case of most post-war residential areas.

A management plan describes all existing plus expected problems in a certain area as well as the management measures to be taken to solve these problems and what these measures cost. The plan gives local authorities a vehicle for signalling problems early (passive management) and, even more important, solving them (active management). As a programme directed towards implementation of spatial measures it goes further than a land-use allocation plan or an environment by-law (LMV), which are aimed at averting undesirable developments through legal provisions.

Management plans can be drawn up for different levels. At the municipal level a structure plan might be developed outlining implementation and financial measures. Or a management plan can be developed for the whole local authority, including the municipality. On a smaller scale the municipality and the affected population can compile a neighbourhood management plan.

Housing instruments

Local authorities have an extensive set of housing instruments for the management of post-war districts. What follows is not an exhaustive, but rather a concise survey of these instruments.[1] Local authorities can develop a coherent and substantive housing policy through a housing plan in which the strategic housing policy choices are formulated and a housing information system is sketched with relevant data about developments on the housing market. Although these instruments have no legal basis, they are important as policy instruments.

Dwelling quality. Under Section 2 of the Housing Act every local authority is required to have a building by-law adopted by the municipal council. This by-law sets minimum standards both for future housing structures and for existing ones, and for land use and open space in the immediate vicinity of these structures. Numerous provisions in the building by-law regulate the urban landscape at the microlevel. The municipal executive is obliged to supervise the quality of the dwellings and to determine their suitability for occupation, requirements for additional facilities, and appropriate tenancy (Section 24, Housing Act).

If a dwelling is structurally unsafe, the municipal executive is obliged to order the owner to take the necessary steps to refurbish it (Section 25, Housing Act). If the owner refuses, the local authority must perform the repairs, but at the expense of the negligent owner. Dwellings that are unsuitable for occupation and cannot be improved by serving notice on the owner must be condemned as unfit for habitation by the municipal council (Section 33, Housing Act).

Dwelling improvement. The local authority receives subsidies for the improvement of rental dwellings according to quotas laid down by central government. The municipal executive then divides these quotas among social and private landlords. Improvements must be approved by the local authority. Large local authorities, which receive urban renewal funds directly from central government, must draw up a by-law describing the conditions under which owner-occupiers qualify for a home improvement subsidy. The local authority can also stand surety for loans on behalf of private dwelling improvement.

Housing distribution and use. The Housing Distribution Act of 1947, enacted to cope with the post-war housing shortage, is still in force in some three hundred local authorities. This law requires local authorities to draw up a housing distribution by-law to regulate the allocation of housing to those seeking accommodation. In these authorities it is prohibited to have in use or be given the use of dwellings without permission of the municipal executive (the housing permit). The Housing Distribution Act also offers the possibility of requisitioning accommodation (not only vacant dwellings) by the local government.

Because this act is territorially limited, local authorities can draw up municipal residence by-laws. These are used particularly in villages to give the original population priority over newcomers in the housing market. No one can use a dwelling without permission of the municipal executive (the habitation permit). The criterion for granting a permit is usually a tie with the village in question.

The Vacancy Act gives the municipal executive in all local authorities the power to requisition vacant housing. In 30 local authorities a permit from the municipal executive is required to divide dwellings into smaller units or to make dwellings non-residential.

Inspection and supervision of approved institutions. - The Housing Minister supervises housing associations on behalf of the central government (Section 59, Housing Act; and Section 32, Decree on Approved Housing Institutions). This supervision is directed towards ensuring that the local associations are meeting the housing objectives of the central government and towards monitoring the administration and finances of the institutions. The local authorities also have important supervisory tasks in line with their general responsibility for the management of the housing stock, since mismanaged housing institutions can pose financial risks for the local authorities.

Up to now both the central and local authorities have concentrated their supervision on financial matters. Recently more attention has been paid to the maintenance, lettability, and management of dwellings. In this respect, signalling and information systems can provide useful data on letting policy, new construction, and management of the housing stock.

General laws and municipal by-laws

Local authorities have other general laws and by-laws at their disposal that can play a part in the management of post-war districts. Some of these are mentioned here:[2]

- The Public Nuisance Act limits nuisances especially by businesses in the surrounding area.
- The Compulsory Purchase Act (Section 77) allows the local authority to purchase a dwelling in the interest of housing policy.

This occurs, for instance, if notice has been served on an owner under Section 25 of the Housing Act but the owner refuses to comply. The local authority can implement the notice itself or proceed to compulsory purchase.

- The ground lease allows the local authority, as owner of the land, to include management provisions in the contract or lease. These may relate, for instance, to the use, maintenance, purpose, or letting of the dwelling.
- The Municipal Priority Act gives local authorities the first right to purchase real estate in designated areas.
- A municipal parking by-law allows the local authority to regulate parking and parking permits.
- A municipal policy plan for traffic and transport (under the Passenger Traffic Act).
- A traffic circulation plan regulates traffic entering and leaving the city centre. A cycle track plan can also be developed in this context.
- A general policy by-law is aimed at the prevention and countering of nuisance, danger, and pollution. This instrument can be used in the control of vandalism.
- The Noise Nuisance Act and the Licensing and Catering Trade Act, which can be used to counter nuisance from cafes and bars.

Financial instruments

Management of the city and its post-war districts costs a local authority money — an expenditure not offset by much income. Good management, while not cheap, can save a local authority money.

Neighbourhood deterioration results in increased crime, vandalism, a fall in housing values, vacancy and great residential mobility, and the gradual disappearance of shopping facilities. These developments also carry an emotional price tag that comes with displeasure at living in the neighbourhood. These liabilities may be turned around if policy is directed towards preventing or eliminating deterioration.

A lesson can be learned from the classic forms of urban renewal. For a long time the pre-war districts did not receive the attention they required, resulting in a process of impoverishment and decay. In the short term, money was saved in these districts, but later huge amounts were spent on a drastic urban renewal process.

To finance measures, as part of a management plan, local authorities can tap various sources and subsidy schemes, especially if a district is tackled in its entirety. The local authority can exert an important role by co-ordinating the financing of these activities. Whether a management plan can be implemented depends on its financial feasibility. By creatively combining the finance sources, the local authority brings this a good deal closer.

The current budget. The general resources of the municipal fund and central government payments are earmarked for specific municipal sectors.

117

Examples of the latter are contributions under the Interim Soil Reclamation Act and the Noise Pollution Act. Budgets drawn up for only one sector eliminate the possibility of overall management. Overall management transcends the various sectoral interests.

The urban renewal fund. Large local authorities receive their urban renewal fund directly from central government. Other local authorities receive their funds indirectly from the province. The urban renewal fund has replaced 19 specific targeted payments.

Local authorities can choose how the urban renewal funds are to be used, since they are best aware of local needs. Local authorities can also utilize the funds for management activities to obviate drastic urban renewal measures in the future. The money can therefore be spent on post-war districts.

Financing of major maintenance of and improvements to post-war dwellings. An important part of district management is tackling deteriorating dwellings. This can be financed through three sources: an investment by the owner (landlord or owner-occupier), a rent increase, and/or a subsidy. A local authority is free to institute a subsidy scheme for improvements to owner-occupied dwellings.

For rental buildings, in addition to investments by the landlords and rent increases, maintenance and improvements can be financed through the Scheme for Financial Support to Provisions for Rented Dwellings enacted in 1987 (the MG 88–42; known as RGSVH'87). This scheme applies to rental dwellings owned by local authorities, housing associations, and private landlords. The improvements must be structural. In addition, subsidies are available for soundproofing installed at the same time as other provisions are made.

The size of the subsidy depends on the age of the dwelling, local construction costs for new dwellings, the type of landlord, and the overall cost of the measures. The subsidy is a percentage of the total improvement costs. For this a graded system is used in which in the higher brackets a lower percentage of subsidy is paid (Table 3). The total subsidy is the sum of the subsidies over the various brackets.

Each year a quota (a target number) is established of dwellings that can qualify for subsidies. In addition, a target subsidy determines the maximum average subsidy per local authority/province for improvements within

Table 3. Subsidies for housing associations

Costs of the accepted provisions as percentages of the costs of new construction	Lump sum contributions as a percentage of the costs of the accepted provisions for the year of construction categories		
	Up to 1 Jan. 1946	Between 1 Jan. 1946 and 1 Jan. 1968	After 1 Jan. 1968 but at least 15 years old
Bracket 1: 0–30%	80	40	20
Bracket 2: 31–60%	60	30	0
Bracket 3: 61–100%	40	20	0

each given year of construction category. Planned operations that do not fit within the improvement quotas cannot use the subsidies under RGSVH'87, although they can still be obtained for soundproofing, and costs for rehousing and refurnishing.

When the subsidies are for maintenance work only, there can be no rent increases. However, when improvements are also made (and the cost is more than 20% of comparable new construction) a rent increase must be passed on in accordance with the so-called '1, 2, 3, system', which will not be explained here. In dwellings where landlords have combined maintenance work with small, inexpensive improvements, tenants are usually faced with acceptable rent increases, in contrast to those tenants who have to pay high rent increases in buildings that have received massive improvements. Limited subsidies are available from the Ministry of Economic Affairs for energy-saving investments.

Investors and property developers. Private investment can be attracted to enhance the amenities and improve the infrastructure of post-war districts. A local authority, by making specific investments and offering financial incentives, can try to elicit investments by others.

Co-financing. Those who are directly involved in or affected by the management of a district are sometimes prepared to help finance matters for which they have no direct responsibility. Thus, shopkeepers are sometimes prepared to pay towards refurbishing their shopping street. Housing associations sometimes finance measures that lie outside the housing field, but relate to the maintenance or improvement of the district.

Urban adjustment. Good management can yield money. The privatization of public greenery, for example, brings in money and lowers maintenance and operating costs. Secondly, money can be obtained from land proceeds as a result of densification or demolition. Profits from these sources can be targeted for improvements in the same district in a process call 'urban re-adjustment' (van der Burg, 1985).

These various finance sources can be combined into a municipal management fund, which can be divided into district budgets.

Municipal management fund. A municipal management fund combines all the maintenance and management from the sectors involved in the local authority's improvement programme. Housing associations can also make contributions to this fund.

The management costs are of two kinds (Wuytswinkel, 1982): the costs of maintenance, to ensure continued functioning; and the costs of replacement or improvement if the economic or technical life of the property is at an end. Maintenance costs are largely covered by the municipal fund.

District budgets. A municipal management fund can be divided into district budgets to increase the supervision of resources and guarantee equity along social lines. Not all the management measures, however, should take place through the budget. Improvement subsidies for housing association dwellings, for example, or the financing of supradistrict infrastructure can be regulated outside the district budget. Maintenance funds, however, for greenery, roads, and minor public works can be combined and allotted to a district.

DECAY PERSISTS IN LARGE-SCALE HOUSING ESTATES

In spite of the numerous instruments available for the upgrading of post-war districts in The Netherlands, many large-scale housing estates have entered a spiral of decay. One example is the Gilliswijk district in Delft, where early steps were fortunately taken to reverse the decay and to make the district liveable again (see below).

The physical planning instruments — structure plan, allocation plan, Section 19, and the anticipation procedure — are commonly used for the development of new quarters. The urban renewal plan and the environmental by-law, in force since 1985, are applied almost exclusively to pre-war areas. The fact is overlooked that all these instruments can also be highly effective in post-war areas. The management plan is a new formula that offers great potential in The Netherlands for neighbourhood improvement. But the absence of management plans was at the root of the decay in post-war districts like the Gilliswijk.

Up to now the housing instruments that tend to dwelling quality and improvement have been interpreted exclusively in terms of the technical aspects of building. Too little thought has been given to adapting dwellings and their surroundings so as to increase personal safety. Until recently housing distribution was determined by highly formalized rules that often ignored the social climate in the districts and intensified local problems. Informal rules are also needed that respond to market developments, the preferences of those seeking accommodation, and the social environment. At present two new laws are being prepared concerned with the modernization of the Housing Act and the replacement of the Housing Distribution Act.

The financial instruments have been almost solely directed towards the development of new districts and the improvement of pre-war ones; very little money has been invested in post-war housing districts. Greater use of the available financial instruments in the post-war districts is an absolute necessity.

EXAMPLE OF A SUCCESSFUL APPROACH: THE GILLISWIJK IN DELFT

This case study considers the problems of degeneration, vandalism, and decay at a relatively new housing estate in Delft and how these problems have been addressed. Both the local authority and the managing housing association have been involved in efforts to reverse the decay. Funds were contributed by the Steering Group for Administrative Crime Prevention (SBPC), which was instituted by the ministers of justice and internal affairs. The results of these efforts are also discussed.

Situation sketch

The Gilliswijk was built in the early 1970s. The district consists of seven four-storey housing blocks, owned by the St Hippolytus Catholic Housing Association. Each block has a central entrance hall, containing a stairwell and a lift. On each floor the central hall leads to a balcony, on to which the front doors of the dwellings open. At each end of the block are smaller stairwells with a lift in one of them. The district has 523 dwellings, 86% of which have five rooms. On the ground floor of each block are 74% store-rooms and 10 four-room dwellings.

The Gilliswijk's design was a reaction against the monotonous mass buildings of the 1960s and was considered innovative. The greenery between the blocks and on the periphery of the district was intended as a recreational area, where children could play undisturbed and with little supervision. This green area of about five hectares is rather hilly. Dirt pathways have been worn in over time.

The development of problems

Soon after completion problems emerged at the Gilliswijk in the form of blocked rubbish chutes and civil disturbances. By the early 1980s, the problems and destruction had increased considerably and the district had degenerated greatly.

The interior public spaces had suffered most damage. Lifts were often out of order, there were many cellar fires, walls were covered in graffiti, break-ins occurred with great regularity, the lights were regularly smashed, mailboxes were torn down, and the windows were repeatedly shattered. The greenery was infested with large amounts of refuse because some tenants were not using their refuse containers and the containers were located where they invited use by non-tenants.

The park had become an impenetrable jungle; the vegetation was very dense and quick-growing weeds had taken over. Large stretches of the park could not be used because of poor drainage. Since the Gilliswijk maintenance system had always been insufficient, the maintenance fund had suffered a deficit in most years. Maintenance was highly intensive, but ineffective given the pronounced degeneration, the harassment of maintenance personnel, and the insufficient use of manpower.

The district acquired a poor reputation among those seeking housing in Delft. By the early 1980s, many applicants were refusing to live there. Only with great effort was the housing association spared acute vacancy problems. At the time, Delft was experiencing an influx of new residents. Through the stringent application of the housing distribution by-law large households were directed to the district. These incoming households, however, moved to the district only because they often had no alternative; they regarded the Gilliswijk as an intermediate stage. Occupants who could afford to do so left as quickly as possible, and because of this mobility, neighbourhood involvement was slight.

Children in the district became a source of some of the problems. The

121

young children who moved in when the district first opened became the young people of the 1980s; they represented the highest percentage of youth unemployment in Delft. Owing to the lack of suitable amenities, they tended to idle around the district and were seen as the perpetrators of the vandalism and disruptions there.

Early rehabilitation efforts

The problems in the district were too massive to be tackled solely by the housing association. The association, therefore, instituted an advisory group in late 1981. The group included representatives of the housing association, residents, police, peripatetic youth workers, school heads, and members of the housing, parks and gardens, welfare, and cleansing departments of the local authority.

Between 1981 and 1986 the housing association took the lead in a variety of rehabilitation activities, since it was the only body that was willing and able to make money available. Most of its efforts were directed to structural improvements. In this period nearly half a million guilders was spent on improving the property ('target hardening'), properly siting the refuse containers, and performing maintenance work to prevent vandalism. The association launched campaigns to encourage residents to paint and clean the blocks.

In spite of these efforts degeneration and petty crime increased. It became clear that technical measures were not enough. Efforts had to be directed towards the district's social climate. However, the local organization designed to attend to such measures either had no money because of budget cuts (such as youth workers), did not have the necessary instruments (the local housing department), or had other priorities (the local welfare department).

The local authority, at the time, was generally excluding post-war districts from its urban renewal efforts. Therefore, the municipal contribution to the Gilliswijk advisory group was confined to supplying information, signalling abuses, and seeking solutions within traditional frameworks and existing budgets.

A comprehensive approach

Two developments led to a different approach. First, eliminating vandalism became important in municipal politics. Second, the Gilliswijk advisory group became a co-ordinating group with independent powers in January 1987.

Combating vandalism in Delft. In 1985 the local authority began a co-ordinated anti-vandalism policy through the creation of the Steering Group for Vandalism Control. The members represent the welfare and education and culture service departments, the public works service, and the police. The group also includes representatives of private organizations affected by vandalism, such as the power company, the post office, the chamber of commerce, and the housing organizations. The mayor chairs the steering group.

The steering group is primarily an administrative organization directed towards comprehensive vandalism prevention. Each member of the steering group devotes attention to this effort with their own service or organization. In this way the steering group ensures that vandalism control is being given a central place in municipal affairs.

A Working Party for Vandalism Control has also been set up, consisting of representatives of the most closely involved municipal services (public works, welfare, education and culture, and police). The working party gives substance to anti-vandalism policy by making specific proposals to the steering group. In addition, it develops the ideas of the steering group into feasible plans. The steering group chose the Gilliswijk to spearhead its efforts. Various measures and experiments were applied initially in the Gilliswijk.

Two guidelines influence the efforts: the co-ordination of the anti-vandalism activities is conducted in such a way that these efforts are quickly expedited, so that the vandalism-sensitive period is of limited duration; and stock is taken of the possibilities with each service of combating vandalism.

The Gilliswijk project group. The initial Gilliswijk advisory group possessed little money and no powers, but it did at least give the initial impetus to refurbishing the district, in which the combating of vandalism was always one of the objectives. As the advisory group's plans became more concrete, a need arose for an independent co-ordinating group. Both the housing association and the residents' representatives began advocating the appointment of a municipal leader with a broad mandate.

When it became clear that there were financial commitments from the housing association, local government and central government, the municipal executive instituted a project group for the Gilliswijk in January 1987. The project group has the same composition as the advisory group, with the incidental participation of representatives of the Research Institute for Policy Sciences and Technology (OTB) and of the Steering Group for Administrative Crime Prevention (SBPC) in connection with the current experiments.

A municipal project leader from the Urban Renewal Project Bureau chairs the project group and is responsible for:

- co-ordinating the plans or wishes of the municipal departments, the residents, and the housing association;
- monitoring the planning;
- administrative feedback; and
- information and public relations.

The housing association is responsible for the group's administrative office and has the last word in conflicts over the estates's dwellings. Conflicts over residential environment are resolved by the local authority.

Concrete measures

Before 1986 the advisory group had made many plans, but because of the limited budget, the slow decision-making process, and other priorities, only a few plans were implemented. Now through the increased attention to the district's problems, the start of the project group, and, last but not least, the readiness to make financial means available, the problems can now be tackled more effectively. The following plans have been or are now being carried out:

- cellar segmentation;
- a new hall plan;
- flat division;
- appointment of seven caretakers; and
- a residential environment plan.

Cellar segmentation.   The large number of cellar break-ins and cases of arson, and the negative impact of the graffiti-covered walls, discouraged residents from using the basement. The residents found the cellar frightening as the area became a hang-out for youths. One of the group's first measures was to reduce access to the cellar passages. In each building twelve partition walls have been installed in the passages and an additional door has been made. Extra reinforcements have been fitted to the doors and frames. Each household has received several copies of a key for the outside, dividing, and cellar doors. The key cannot be copied, and replacements have to be ordered from the housing association.

The cellar segmentation costs (800,000 guilders) have been borne by the housing association, while the necessary adaptation of the pavement and greenery was paid for by the local authority (15,000 guilders).

The results have been highly positive: cellar fires no longer occur and break-ins have decreased by 85%. Supervision by the caretakers, however, continues to be indispensable; young people must still be sent away, and the graffiti, while less frequent, must still be painted out occasionally.

Hall plan.   The accessibility of the blocks' interior public spaces to outsiders and disruptive residents has been reduced through a new 'hall plan'. The back sections of the central halls opposite the balconies and the stairwells at the ends of the blocks have been closed off. The remaining sections of the central halls and stairwells have been completely refurbished, the walls have been tiled, hard-wearing linoleum has been laid, shatterproof glass has been installed, the ceilings have been dropped and fitted with vandal-proof lights, and surfaces have been painted. A caretaker's lodge has been installed in each block.

The front doors are closed in the evenings so that resident access is by key only. Visitors must announce themselves over a newly installed intercom; residents can admit them from their homes. The lock on the door in the central hall is fitted with a time switch; during the day the door can be opened by a pushing a button, so that children playing outside do not have to keep ringing the doorbell. The total costs of these changes were 1.4 million guilders, borne entirely by the housing association.

This plan, completed in late 1987, has completely changed the interior appearance of the blocks. Supervision and cleaning by the caretakers, however, are still necessary to counteract littering. Measurement of the results of all these changes began in late 1989 and are not yet available.

Flat divisions. Beginning in 1983 some five-room dwellings in the Gilliswijk have been split into one- and two-person units to allow for more demographic diversity in the district. This effort was reinforced by the local authority in 1985 when it allowed three-person households to occupy five-room flats in the Gilliswijk. This has partially abated the influx of large families into the district.

By late 1987 some 56 dwellings had been divided up. Unfortunately the smaller households that have moved into the Gilliswijk have tended to be young families who move out again quickly and are uninvolved in the neighbourhood. The proposal has been made in parts of the estate to divide every two dwellings into three and to offer them to elderly persons from the broader district in which the estate is situated. The hope is that these occupants will be more more tied to the district and an even more varied composition of residents can be achieved.

Caretakers. As early as 1985 the appointment of caretakers was considered but the costs were prohibitive. In 1987 a subsidy from the SBPC for the hiring of caretakers was made available as part of a crime prevention effort.

Since September 1987 seven caretakers have been employed, one for each block. Their work consists of cleaning the semi-public spaces, minor repairs, enforcing the rules of conduct, and giving the occupants general service (information, help with moving, supervision during holidays, first aid, filling in forms). During the evenings two caretakers are on duty patrolling the district.

The appointment of caretakers is experimental. Assessment began in January 1990 to determine the effects of having caretakers and whether they can be retained after the subsidy ends. SBPC made 523,000 guilders available, while the residents paid 22.35 guilders a month. The housing association paid for the counselling and training of the caretakers. Now, the residents and the housing association must come to an agreement on the apportionment of the costs. A contribution from the housing association's maintenance fund is envisaged. It has been suggested that some municipal tasks be included in the caretakers' job description so that the local authority can also make a contribution.

The first results of an evaluation survey indicate that the caretakers are serving a need. The relationship between the residents and the housing association has improved. Without the caretakers' supervision and cleaning of the semi-public spaces, the positive effects of the technical measures would be largely undone. The caretakers' success is influenced by the composition of the residents, whether the caretaker lives in the blocks, and the caretaker's ability to get along with people. If many children live in a block, the caretaker spends much of his time cleaning. The caretakers who live in the blocks are more aware of problems, but unfortunately they are constantly on the job.

Management plan for the residential environment.   In late 1985 the working party led by the Public Works Service instituted a management plan for the Gilliswijk. The urban planning department has been responsible for the content of the project; the parks and gardens and cleansing departments and the police have been intensively involved in the preparation of specific plans.

There have been two phases in the preparation of the plan: a broad urban plan for the whole district and a series of detailed new designs for the streets and the park in the district. Before drawing up the broad plan the urban planning department took stock of the district's main problems. Most of them had evolved because of deferred maintenance, which in turn encouraged vandalism.

Once developed the broad plan was discussed several times in the advisory and then in the project group and was presented to the residents in early 1987, first in a brochure and then at an information evening. The plan includes the following elements:

- complete repaving, including new pavements along all blocks and, where necessary, relocating parking places to allow for a better view of the cars;
- planting vegetation up against the blocks to prevent the daubing of walls;
- repaving the central halls more creatively using coloured tiles and materials;
- better location of refuse containers and replacement of containers;
- improved drainage and raising the level of certain parts of the park;
- uprooting trees and shrubs to obtain better sight lines;
- fewer but better play areas;
- better lighting at a limited number of places; and
- more varied greenery, through adding high-grade varieties.

In late June 1987 the Civil Engineering Maintenance Department began implementing the first part of the plan. The whole plan is scheduled for completion in mid-1989. The total cost of the residential environment plan was estimated at 1,495,000 guilders.

paving	488,000
greenery	616,000
play facilities	100,000
public lighting	120,000
drainage system	50,000
refuse containers	16,000
preparatory costs	105,000
Total	1,495,000

Since there are no special financial schemes for the improvement of post-war districts, various sources of funding have been drawn on:

municipal budget item for combating vandalism	300,000
contribution from urban renewal fund	268,000
subsidy from SBPC	153,000
municipal investment programme	264,000
various maintenance budgets	430,000
savings on future maintenance	80,000
Total	1,495,000

The measures for combating vandalism and increasing security are combined with the elimination of maintenance arrears. For the actual improvement of the residential environment approximately one million guilders is available; the remaining amount is intended for maintenance. The local authority pays 85% of the above budget; the central government contributes 15% in the form of the crime prevention subsidy.

CONCLUSION

A great deal of positive publicity concerning the Gilliswijk has appeared in the professional press in recent years. At a conference recently a video tape about the Gilliswijk approach was shown. The local press has begun to project a more positive image of the district. Delft residents no longer perceive the Gilliswijk so negatively. However, it is too soon for a thorough evaluation of the costs and benefits and effects of the renewal efforts. The benefits to the municipal departments will be difficult to chart, since there are no records of damage caused by vandalism. The municipality of Delft regards the Gilliswijk approach as experimental. Initially it was unclear whether the costs of the renewal efforts had to be borne completely by the general local budget or whether a modest contribution could come from the local 'urban renewal fund'. Only the costs of preparation and co-ordination of the projects were paid out of the urban renewal fund.

The Gilliswijk approach offers a model to other local authorities confronted with problems in post-war districts. A number of observations, however, should be made.

The above measures are directed mostly towards the built environment. Measures aimed at the social environment have been limited and poorly financed. The problems with young people are recognized, but because of cuts and other priorities only temporary measures have been taken. Counselling has been offered to young people above 16 years of age. The effects have been positive, but because of the age restriction, large numbers of youths continue to wander through the district.

Resident involvement also remains limited. The idea that home does not end at the front door is getting through to the residents with great difficulty.

A lesson can be learned from the earlier approaches to run-down pre-war districts. In the Gilliswijk a catch-up operation has been required to eliminate arrears and to refurbish the dwellings and residential environment and adapt them to changing needs. Although the expense is considerable, the level of investment is fortunately a good deal lower than what has been required in the post-war districts. Some housing associations are now experimenting with information and signalling systems on housing estates, so that operating problems can be observed early (Amory, 1988) and preventive rather than curative measures can be taken. A timely approach to the problems seems to keep costs under control. Our experience in the older districts also teaches us that it is not enough to improve the built environment alone. Social management should also receive attention.

EVALUATION OF MEASURES

The Netherlands possesses an arsenal of policy instruments for tackling problems on large-scale housing estates. The approach in the Gilliswijk in Delft shows that an approach that improves dwellings, the estate, and the residential environment simultaneously can be a success.

The Netherlands, however, has had little experience with the evaluation of measures aimed at the upgrading of large-scale estates. Scientific research is hampered by the development of a package of very different measures, the effects of which cannot be separated out for measurement. The most obvious approach is an evaluation in which the situation before and after the introduction of the measures is assessed. The most important single indicator is vacancy, but complaints, turnover of tenants, vandalism, and number of break-ins might also be considered.

It is advisable that both the short- and long-term effects be investigated. Often measures prove successful in the short term, but then problems return full blast. In addition to the pre- and post-assessment, the researcher must also take into consideration external factors that might have an impact on the estate being studied: improvement to competitive estates, new construction and urban renewal activities, changes in the housing and housebuilding market, and policy changes. To neutralize the effects of these variables, it is advisable to research estates in the same housing market to which different improvements have been made or control estates where no improvements have been made.

More evaluation research is required to register which therapies are effective. From the 1950s to the 1970s, a good deal of money was probably wasted on the construction of the wrong dwellings at the wrong rent for the wrong target group in the wrong place. Let us now try to avoid the wrong approach in confronting the operating problems. We have paid enough dues.

NOTES

1. For further information see other publications, such as *Volkshuisvestingsinstrumenten* (Housing Instruments), published annually by the Directorate-General of Housing, *Wonen bij de Gemeente Thuis; Instrumenten voor en Informatie over een Lokaal Volkshuisvestingsbeleid* (Living at Home in the Local Authority, Instruments for and Information on a Local Housing Policy), published by the Association of Dutch Authorities (VNG) (1984a), and *Volkshuisvestings- en stadsvernieuwingsrecht* (Public housing and urban renewal law) (Aussems, 1987).

2. For a more extensive survey see the VNG publication *Beheer van de Bebouwde Kom* (Management of Built-up Areas) (Association of Dutch Local Authorities, 1984b).

REFERENCES

AMORY, E. (1988) *Naar Beslissingsondersteunende Informatiesystemen voor het Non-profit Woningbeheer* (Towards Decision Support Information Systems for Non-profit Housing Management). Delft: Delft University Press.

Association of Dutch Local Authorities (VNG) (1984a) *Wonen bij de Gemeente Thuis, Instrumenten voor en Informatie over enn Lokaal Volkshuisvestingsbeleid* (Living at Home in the Local Authority, Instruments for and Information on a Local Housing Policy). The Hague: VNG.

Association of Dutch Local Authorities (VNG) (1984b) *Beheer van de Bebouwde Kom* (Management of the Built-up Area). The Hague: VNG.

AUSSEMS, TH. (ed.) (1987) *Volkshuisvestings- en Stadvernieuwingsrecht* (Public Housing and Urban Renewal Law).

BURG, A.J. VAN DER (1985) Stedelijk beheer; begrip, achtergronden, theorievorming, verdere ontwikkeling (Urban management; concept background, theory-forming, further development). *Stedebouw en Volkshuisvesting*, January, pp. 3–9.

Ministry of Housing, *Volkshuisvestingsinstrumenten* (Housing Instruments). The Hague: VROM, published annually.

LIEDHOLM, M., G. LINDBERG and A.L. LINDEN (1985) Housing Policy as an Agent of Social Welfare. Stockholm (unpublished paper).

PRAK, N.L. and H. PRIEMUS (eds.) (1985) *Post-war Public Housing in Trouble*. Delft: Delft University Press.

PRIEMUS, H. (1986) *Structurele Leegstand in de Naoorlogse Woningvoorraad* (Structural Vacancy in the Post-war Housing Stock). The Hague: Staatsuitgeverij.

THIJSSEN, C.C.F. and C.J. MEIJER (1988) *Bouwconstructieve Analyse van Naoorlogse Meergezinshuizen in de Non-profit Huursector 1946–1965* (Constructional Analysis of Post-war Blocks of Flats in the Non-profit Rented Sector 1946–1965). Delft: Delft University Press.

WUYTSWINKEL, L. VAN (1982) *Financiële Aspekten Stadsbeheer* (Financial Aspects of City Management). Platform stads- en dorpsvernieuwing in Noord-Brabant, September.

9 RENEWAL OF LARGE-SCALE POST-WAR HOUSING ESTATES IN SWEDEN: EFFECTS AND EFFICIENCY

Göran Carlén and Göran Cars

Many large-scale post-war housing areas in Sweden's metropolitan areas are facing severe difficulties. These problems are of a functional, physical, visual, and technical nature and have led to the low appeal of living in these areas. There is often an over-representation of households with poor resources and social problems living in these areas which has, in turn, led to high tenant turnover, vandalism, and a high proportion of residents who regard their living conditions as unsatisfactory.

With the growing awareness that these areas need renewal, municipalities during the last decade have launched a large number of improvement projects. A major problem in this renewal activity has been the discrepancies between the goals, the measures taken by the municipalities, and the results.

Studies of several projects—planned, ongoing, and completed—show that most of the financial resources have been directed towards improving the technical and physical aspects of the post-war estates. Despite ambitious goals and the large financial investments much of this renewal activity has yielded poor results. This has led to extensive criticism from government agencies, municipalities and affected tenants. There have been demands to develop guidelines for a new policy. The following problems have been observed:

- Renewal activities have led to positive changes within many of the renewal areas, but simultaneously negative changes sometimes emerge in adjacent areas. Problems seem to move from one area to another.
- Measures taken within an area sometimes do not have the intended effect because outside forces have an unpredictable (and sometimes contrary) influence on development.
- The results of many ambitious renewal programmes have been poor in the light of the large economic investments. The renewal activities have not solved the most urgent problems.

This paper analyses the effects and efficiency of several ongoing and completed renewal projects in Sweden. A description of national renewal policy and subsidies for this activity provides the context for our analysis of empirical results from evaluations of renewal activities. We conclude with suggestions for a revised renewal policy.

130

GOVERNMENT HOUSING POLICY AND IMPROVEMENT ACTIONS

Housing production

After the Second World War housing became one of the central economic and social issues in Sweden. Housing standards were inadequate, many people were living in overcrowded dwellings, and the shortage of homes was a serious problem. Parliament responded by making a number of important decisions on housing policy. A fundamental goal of post-war housing policy was to achieve a general improvement in housing conditions. Measures were not to be restricted to certain groups, such as households with poor social and economic resources, but were to apply to the whole population. The goal was to achieve social integration in all types of housing areas. Thus, public housing was to be given amenities that would attract higher-income households. This objective contrasted with policy in most other West European countries and previous housing policy in Sweden. To a large extent this policy was successful. The quality of the housing stock was improved, both with respect to space and standards.

With this new housing policy in place, Parliament enacted legislation to support a steady increase in housing production and to allocate resources for renewal. The most important measure implemented was the national government's financial contribution to new construction and modernization. Since the late 1940s, most housing production has been financed by state loans. Developers are free to build with market loans but the state subsidy is so large that private financing is unprofitable.

During the 1950s and 1960s the demand for housing grew even stronger with increased urbanization in Sweden, the growing population, and improvements in the standard of living. The demand was for more and larger flats of better quality. An extended housing programme became a priority policy issue.

Although housing production steadily increased, the shortages remained. In the mid-1960s Parliament adopted an ambitious housing construction programme called the Million Homes Program, which led to a significant increase in production. Parliament stated that 'society's goal for housing provision should be to provide the entire population with healthy, spacious, and functionally equipped housing of good quality at reasonable prices' (Sweden, 1967). Implemented over ten years, the programme raised housing standards and eliminated the housing shortage. This large increase in housing construction took place during a period of favourable economic development.

The construction of new dwellings peaked in the late 1960s and early 1970s with the production of more than 100,000 dwellings per year, which roughly corresponded to an annual increase of 14 dwellings per 1,000 inhabitants. Up to the 1960s a large proportion of the new flats were constructed by private persons or corporations. This pattern changed, however, during the Million Homes Program. Nearly 60% of all flats built in multi-family houses during the Million Homes Program were constructed by municipal housing corporations. In 1985 these housing corporations owned slightly more than 20% of all flats (Sweden, 1989a).

When the Million Homes Program was completed the demand for new housing construction was satisfied to a large extent and new construction began to decline. In 1987 the volume of newly constructed dwellings amounted to slightly more than one-third of the volume in 1970. Running parallel with the decline of new construction has been an increase in reconstruction activities. In 1985 investments in reconstruction were, for the first time, larger than investments in new construction. Reconstruction activity has continued to increase, both in absolute value as well as in relation to resources allocated to new construction.

Until the 1970s, rehabilitation mostly dealt with houses constructed before the Second World War. Housing policy was to a large extent aimed at the physical improvement of these houses to bring them up to standard, to maintain and improve their technical facilities, and to expand their floor plans (most flats consisted of only one or two rooms and a kitchen).

In the 1980s, the focus of renewal activity gradually changed to houses built in the 1960s and 1970s during the Million Homes Program. Despite the fact that we are now working with fairly new constructions, investments have not decreased, either in absolute numbers or in cost per dwelling (Carlén and Cars, 1988).

Some reasons why such extensive and expensive renewal is required in these relatively new and modern houses can be found in the conditions that prevailed in Sweden when the Million Homes Program was adopted. The political pressure for housing was so acute in the 1960s when the Million Homes Program was launched that the number of dwellings was a higher priority than the quality of housing. A new production technique, industrial prefabrication, was encouraged by the government and quickly adopted by the investors as a way to achieve the ambitious quantity goals. This technique was later shown to have considerable technical imperfections. The entire Swedish housing stock suffers from insufficient maintenance, but the problem is exacerbated in the housing stock from the 1960s and 1970s by insufficiently tested materials and construction methods. The technical problems involved are extensive and include leaking roofs, rotting window frames, insufficient thermal and noise insulation, radon radiation, and damage from abnormal wear and tear.

The construction methods introduced in the Million Homes Program also led to a degradation of the local environment. The residential landscapes are generally seen as artificial, which contributes to the negative impression associated with these areas.

The conditions for government subsidies encouraged such large-scale construction. Projects that included more than 1,000 dwellings received more favourable subsidies. The terms for subsidies also encouraged the large-scale production of cheap and prefabricated houses with little variation in design.

These deficiencies have led to social problems that inevitably take the dwellings into a vicious cycle of decay and neglect. Households with greater social and economic resources tend to move to more attractive areas. This leads to an over-representation of households with poor resources and social problems, which in turn lessens the appeal of these neighbourhoods. This creates a breeding ground for asocial behaviour. Vandalism and crime may spread, which further undermines the area's attractiveness (Cars, 1987).

An often neglected aspect of this process is that the general decline in status is followed by a corresponding decline in services. The area becomes less attractive to the private sector when the wealthy move and vandalism, crime, and general deterioration start spreading. But the same tendency can also be observed for public services. In many areas the standards of schools and day care decline as the area deteriorates (Carlén *et al.*, 1989).

The National Government Housing Improvement Program

In 1983 Parliament adopted a ten-year plan of action, the Housing Improvement Program, for the maintenance and rehabilitation of the housing stock. This action plan (Sweden, 1983/84) was intended to stimulate the urban renewal process. The programme's goal was to rehabilitate 275,000 flats in multi-family houses between 1984 and 1993. Municipalities had to develop renewal strategies for different types of areas: urban cores, urban areas built in the 1930s and 1940s, and newer suburban areas. Most dwellings to be improved already have modern amenities.

The Housing Improvement Program recognized the problems in unattractive areas as serious and stated that these areas were in need of both comprehensive action to improve general living conditions and better regular maintenance. The government provided the financial support for the programme through the creation of favourable financing conditions to stimulate improvements. These take the form of a variety of subsidized loans, and are described below.

Maintenance loans. This new type of loan was introduced to finance periodically required maintenance measures in the common parts of the building. The government provides subsidies for interest on non-priority loans obtained in the ordinary credit market by both the public rental and the co-operative sectors. Private owners of rental housing can also obtain interest subsidies if they forego the right to make immediate tax deduction for this expenditure. In 1988 these subsidies constituted about 30% of the discounted total costs.

Housing rehabilitation loans. More extensive measures that result in significant improvement to the building's technical or functional quality or to the residential environment can be financed with very favourable state housing rehabilitation loans combined with priority loans given by housing finance institutions. Both kinds of loan provide subsidies that initially keep interest costs very low and then gradually allow them to rise to the market level. In 1988 these subsidies accounted for about 60% of the total discounted capital costs.

Supplementary loans. In certain cases, special supplementary loans, free of interest and amortization for at least five years, are available. The conditions for each loan are reviewed periodically and such loans may be discontinued. The supplementary loans are available to correct problems caused by rot, mould, dampness, corrosion, radon, and other defects that affect health and safety. This type of loan can also be given to change the mix of flats in housing areas with many vacant flats or to improve the physical and social environment in areas suffering from poor social conditions.

All three types of loan can be combined. The level of subsidies, therefore, varies among projects. The system obviously includes thresholds: the more comprehensive the measures, the more favourable are the available subsidies.

Changes in the National Improvement Programme

The government evaluated the Housing Improvement Program in 1986 (Sweden, 1989b). The results of this evaluation stressed that the problems in many of the areas constructed during the Million Homes Program are so serious that they must be given special priority in future renewal activities. The evaluation also stressed that more attention must be paid to the improvement of social conditions, to the co-ordinating role of municipalities, and to strengthening tenant participation in improvement activities. This latter demand led to the stipulation that improvement measures must be approved by a tenants' organization before implementation. A new minor subsidy was also introduced to encourage renewal activities that include social programmes and improvements to municipal services.

During the same period the demand for housing and for office space began to increase rapidly, especially in larger urban regions. This increase has been so large that the construction sector has not been able to keep pace. Consequently, in 1989, Parliament decided to give priority to new construction and cut both the level of subsidies and the total sum available for housing renewal loans in the programme for housing improvement. Within the reduced budget, however, priority has been given to renewal activities in the large-scale housing areas from the Million Homes Program through the extension of resources available for supplementary loans. Thus, the cut will not affect these housing areas as strongly as older ones.

RENEWAL ACTIVITIES

What is being done?

It is impossible to describe renewal activities in a general way, since goals, ambitions, and measures vary so much among municipalities. There are, however, common features in many of the projects. We will summarize the variety of measures that have been taken. The description is based on a research project carried out in 1989, which studied ten areas that had been renewed or were undergoing renewal in Sweden's three largest metropolitan areas (Carlén and Cars, 1990).

Outdoor improvement. These measures were aimed at improving the outdoor environment through physical changes in the green areas, playgrounds, and other common facilities.

New management policies. The case studies noted that most of the management changes had two common features. First, improvement was sought in the delivery of daily services. A new service policy has been adopted by many housing corporations to improve their often very tarnished reputation, especially in municipal housing corporations. Second, the new management philosophy incorporates a tougher stance towards disruptive households by establishing strict rules for proper tenant behaviour.

Improvement of public services. A third approach to enhancing the appeal of various areas has been improving public services. Tenant demands have been met by raising the standards of schools, day care facilities, and other public services in the area. Standards have been raised both in terms of quantity and in quality.

Physical improvement. Technical improvements have included the repair of leaking roofs, and of rotting window frames, and improvements in thermal and noise insulation. Also, the layouts of dwellings have been altered; in some cases two smaller flats have been merged to form a larger one. Other physical improvements deal with the scale and monotony of design by rebuilding the exterior of houses.

In most of the areas included in the study, the different renewal activities were more or less integrated. There was, however, an imbalance in the costs of these measures. The outdoor improvement measures, new management policies, and the improvement of public services have been relatively inexpensive. The costs of changing the physical aspects of the housing estates, however, have been high. It is not unusual for up to 90% of the total renewal investment to be allocated to physical measures. The amount of resources put into the projects varies, of course, among different areas. The average investment per square metre in housing rehabilitation has increased over time. In the stock less than 30 years old, the increase has been particularly rapid. The average investment level for projects in this stock is now close to that for new construction (Carlén and Cars, 1990).

EVALUATION OF EFFECTS – USING A CASE STUDY

Through an examination of the comprehensive renewal activities in the housing district of Kroksbäck in the municipality of Malmö, we can form some overall conclusions about renewal programmes of large-scale post-war housing estates in Sweden.

Kroksbäck is a suburb about 5 km south of Malmö city centre. It was built between 1966 and 1968, and has 850 dwellings located in three- and eight-storey buildings. The area is owned and managed by the municipal housing corporation. Before renewal, this area suffered many of the problems mentioned above. The group of measures being applied to the area were also similar to those being used in other upgrading programmes.

Soon after it was completed, the area became unattractive as shown by the number of vacant flats, high tenant turnover, and social disturbances. In 1978 renewal planning began. This planning activity was conducted mainly within the municipal housing corporation. The plan for renewal included new policies for management and measures aimed at improving the outdoor environment. Physical improvements of the houses was a central point for renewal activities. The application for housing rehabilitation loans was granted in 1979 and renewal was carried out between 1980 and 1985. Only the eight-storey buildings were reconstructed. The investment per flat was about SEK 260,000 (the average cost, at that time, of new construction was approximately SEK 335,000 per flat) (Carlén and Cars, 1990).

Influence of upgrading activities on the renewal area

A mixed picture emerges at Kroksbäck. The study team did discover real and positive change. Before renewal, the proportion of vacant flats was four times higher than in the municipality as a whole. Today Kroksbäck has a vacancy rate similar to that for the rest of the municipality, and the migration rate (measured in moves per year) has declined from nearly twice that of the municipality toward the average of the municipality. The number of people living on social welfare is often used as a variable to describe the attractiveness of an area. In Kroksbäck this figure was, before renewal, five times higher than in the municipality. The figure has declined significantly, though it is still higher than the municipal average. Other welfare variables show a similar pattern. The renewal has led to the upgrading of Kroksbäck.

Despite this fact two questions emerge concerning the efficiency of the renewal activity. What were the consequences of the activities on adjacent residential areas? And, was the investment worth the effects achieved?

Effects in adjacent residential areas

Background of study. Two important facts underlie our investigations described in this section. First, the comprehensive rehabilitation programmes in the studied areas caused migration flows. Tenants had to move to another flat at least for a period. In most cases the tenants did not come back after renewal was completed. The reasons for this can be found either in the fact that the tenant preferred the 'new' flat to the old one, or that he was not accepted as a tenant by the housing corporation after renewal. This was not, of course, from the national government's point of view, an expected or desirable effect, because of the influence the movers might have on the receiving areas.

Second, the attractiveness of a housing area is generally gauged in relation to other areas in the housing provision region. This means that if the area that was worse off has gone through a rehabilitation project, some other area will take its place. Certain neighbouring areas risk inheriting the social problems that previously characterized the renewal area. The at-risk areas are those in which flats are the easiest to obtain. The number of households with social problems will increase in this area, especially as their immigration to the renewed housing area often is restricted by new management policies, including stricter rules for proper behaviour and income resources for tenants. These adjacent areas are probably the ones that are also receiving a large share of the movers from the area where renewal activities are taking place. Against this background, we have investigated the migration patterns and the changes in social indicators in adjacent areas.

Studies of moves. A starting point for analysis is observing the pattern of moves in the relevant areas. There are formal rules regulating the displacement of households during renewal. A household with a permanent lease has the right to an alternative flat and lease, secured either from the housing corporation undertaking the renewal or from a municipal board (if one exists) in charge of distributing flats in either municipal housing or in privately owned multi-family houses to tenants in need of housing. Households also have a formalized right to swap flats. Households that fail to pay their rent or exhibit disturbing behaviour may be evicted. Eviction is decided in court, after proposal from the housing corporation. Households that have been evicted have no right to demand a new flat.

Aggregated information on moves from Kroksbäck is presented in Fig. 1.

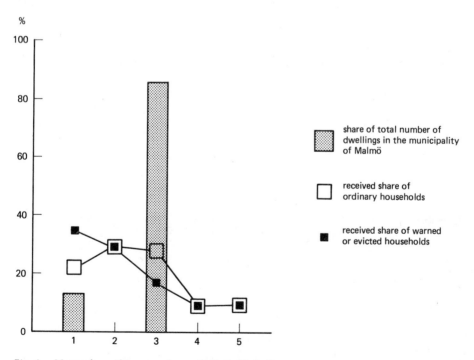

Fig. 1. *Moves from the renewal area in Kroksbäck. Key: 1, areas owned by the municipal housing corporation; 2, Kroksbäck eight-storey buildings; 3, rest of Malmö; 4, adjacent municipalities; 5, rest of Sweden/abroad.*

A large number of tenants moved within the renewal area, and of these a majority moved within the stock owned by the municipal housing corporation. The pattern, however, for ordinary households and warned or evicted households shows discrepancies. Warned or evicted households were more likely to move to flats owned by the municipal housing corporation. Ordinary households were more likely to move to private and co-operative flats. The pattern becomes even more striking when one takes into consideration the share of total Malmö dwellings in the various receiving areas. It becomes obvious that households with problems are not spread equally among the stock, which strengthens the assumption that renewal activity leads to declining attractiveness in some of the receiving areas.

To further our understanding of how migration flows have affected adjacent residential areas we studied the specific moves of households evicted because of disturbing behaviour. The study includes Kroksbäck, but also another area, Gullviksborg, that was renewed during the same period. The entire group included 65 households evicted between 1981 and 1987. Since they were evicted, these households made 119 moves within the municipality. (Note that the actual number of moves is larger than this number, since it was not possible to register in this study households that had moved out of the municipality.)

The result of this study, summarized in Table 1, serves as a starting point for an analysis of the social consequences of moves. We have chosen to

Table 1. Moves of households evicted between 1981 and 1987 from Kroksbäck and Gullviksborg, by receiving area, proportion of all municipal flats, and proportion of vacant flats

Area	Received share of evicted households	Average share of all vacant flats owned by the municipal housing corporation	Average share of all flats owned by the municipal housing corporation
Type 1			
Kroksbäck	23	14	5
Gullviksborg	16	5	4
Rosengård	11	35	8
Holma	9	17	7
Lindängen	11	14	7
All	(70)	(85)	(31)
Type 2			
Lorensborg	7	1	9
Nydala	2	1	5
Augustenborg	7	1	10
Bellevuegården	7	3	5
Sorgenfri	2	1	10
Segevång	5	2	6
Other areas	0	6	24
All	(30)	(15)	(69)
Total:	100	100	100

138

present moves only to flats owned by the municipal housing corporation, since these comprise the majority of moves of this population.

Table 1 breaks down the moves of evicted households to other municipally owned housing areas. In the first column the evicted households have been related to receiving areas. There are large differences among the areas, which become even more apparent when the receiving areas' share of the municipality owned housing stock is compared. In the second column the areas are compared according to their attractiveness, using vacancy level as an indicator.

A distinct pattern emerges from the comparative data. Type 1 areas received a high proportion of the evicted households, although these areas comprise only a minor share of the entire municipal housing stock, and are characterized by low attractiveness (with vacancy level as the indicator). In Type 2 areas the situation is reversed. These areas received few evicted households, although they include the major part of the municipal flats, and they have a high degree of attractiveness. We conclude from this pattern that there has been an export of problems from the renewal area to adjacent areas with relatively low attractiveness.

What happens in the receiving area?

Though upgrading has had a positive effect on renewal areas, the studies of moves indicate that this improvement can be partly attributed to the export of households with problems and poor resources to adjacent areas. This has without doubt led to a decline in the attractiveness of these receiving areas. We have chosen the receiving area, Lindängen, to document this process. Like Kroksbäck, Lindängen was built during the Million Homes Program and has 1,100 dwellings located in multi-storey buildings. The area is owned and managed by the municipal housing corporation. It is located approximately 3 km from Kroksbäck.

With the renewal and upgrading of Kroksbäck, concurrent decline has occurred in Lindängen. Before renewal activity in Kroksbäck began the proportion of vacant flats in Lindängen was about twice as high as in the municipality as a whole. When renewal was completed the rate was more than four times higher. The number of people living on social welfare also increased steadily in Lindängen during the renewal of Kroksbäck. In Sweden the level of participation is often used as a welfare indicator. While the level of participation in elections has increased in Kroksbäck the level has decreased in Lindängen. Other welfare variables show a similar pattern. It is not too surprising that a programme for the renewal of Lindängen has recently been adopted.

The development described for Lindängen can also be observed in other receiving areas.

FACTORS THAT CONTRIBUTE TO DECLINE

The impact of disturbing households

To find out whether households with social problems affect the stability of their surroundings we used our data on moves in the part of Kroksbäck that was not reconstructed. We compared parts of buildings housing warned or evicted households with parts of buildings that housed only ordinary households and discovered considerably higher degrees of mobility in the first category during the same period (30% as compared to 18% per year). This strengthens the assumption that areas receiving households with problems can be strongly affected.

Public services in the renewal area

The proximity of an area to services and work opportunities helps determine its attractiveness. This is often neglected in renewal analyses. The Stockholm region's 23 low-status areas are all located far from the city core and are therefore shut off from many conveniences and amenities (Stockholm Regional Planning Office, 1985).

The quality of public services in an area is as important as location to the attractiveness of an area. Surveys among residents in five renewal areas indicate that the quality of day care facilities and schools are of the utmost importance. A vast majority of residents affected by these services indicated in the surveys that they found them to be of poor quality and considered it essential to raise the standards of services to improve the attractiveness of the area.

Because of the importance residents gave these services, we studied the school situation from two aspects. First, we compared the school results of children from renewal areas with the results of children from other types of areas (Table 2). The attractiveness of the different types of areas has been indicated by the relative share of the social welfare population.

Table 2 shows a distinct difference between renewal areas and high-status areas as well as the entire region. In the renewal areas the proportion of people living on social welfare is high and the school results poor. This

Table 2. School results (1986) and share of the population living on social welfare (1985) by different types of area

Area	Living on social welfare (%)	Not accepted or have not applied to high school (%)	Accepted on 3- or 4-year theoretical high school programmes	Average marks after ninth form*
Average for 12 renewal areas	20	11	32	2.9
Average for 10 high status areas	2	4	66	3.6
Greater Stockholm as a whole	9	7	46	3.2

* The higher the score, the better the result. Five is maximum, one is minimum.

result may not be too surprising. In Sweden it is usually assumed that these differences can be explained by the poor economic and social resources of the households in the renewal area. However, this assumption provides only part of the truth; there are other reasons for these differences. In Table 3 we have compared the quality of the school environment in different types of areas. From this table we can see that deficiencies in the school environment probably contribute to the poor results among children from renewal areas. This indicates that public services should be included in the renewal strategy to a larger extent than has been the case.

Table 3. Some aspects of quality of the school environment in upper- and lower-class areas

	High-status area	Low-status area
Average number of years in the profession (class-teachers)	16	8
Number of pupils per weekly hour of school nurse	22	28
Number of books in the school library per pupil	15	6
Proportion of children that are newcomers to the class during first to third form (%)	16	30
Teachers without proper education	5	14

Source: Carlén and Cars (1990)

PUBLIC RESPONSE TO RENEWAL

An important aspect of analysing renewal activity is studying the wishes and needs of residents. Information about problems and suggestions from residents should form the foundation for an analysis of the effects and efficiency of renewal work. As a part of our research we conducted surveys among residents in five areas undergoing renewal. The pattern of needs and wishes that emerged in these surveys differs among areas, but some important features are similar.

A vast majority of the residents regarded important aspects of their living conditions as unsatisfactory. In all the areas social problems constituted the most important reason for dissatisfaction. Renewal measures that focused on reducing theft, vandalism, threats of violence, and problems with disruptive neighbours were given top priority by the residents. The need for a new management policy also was mentioned in several areas.

Many residents gave high priority to the improvement of services. Deficient commercial and/or public services was for many residents an important reason for feeling dissatisfied. A vast majority of these dissatisfied residents mentioned the need to improve the quality of day care facilities and schools.

When asked about physical changes, most residents considered improvement of the outdoor environment to be important. A large number of residents were sceptical, however, about the extensive rebuilding and redesigning of the houses. Questions about the importance of deficiencies in the dwelling and/or house showed that only a small portion of the

141

respondents placed value on these measures. This is surprising given the huge investments in physical change.

In conclusion, the surveys have shown that many residents are uncomfortable in their area. The reasons for this dissatisfaction vary but a pattern can be seen. According to the residents the most urgent problems require measures with a social focus. Renewal measures with a physical focus are generally given a lower priority. It is obvious that the residents' priorities diverge significantly from what has actually been done in renewal projects. This discrepancy will be analysed in the next section.

EVALUATION OF EFFICIENCY

What has been said about the effects of renewal measures may suggest that these measures have not been effective. This depends, however, upon the definition of the word effective. To analyse efficiency, it must first be defined from the points of view of the various actors involved in renewal. A measure that one actor might judge to be important and leading to an efficient solution to the problem, another might consider less important and inefficient.

In the simplest terms, efficiency is often reduced to the question of whether the measures fulfil the formulated goals. We find this definition incomplete since it does not consider whether the measures are economically reasonable. We have used the following criterion for determining efficiency: a measure can be identified as efficient if a corresponding or better result cannot be achieved by another measure or a combination of measures at the same or lower cost.

Below, we identify the main actors in the renewal process and discuss efficiency from each perspective. We conclude with a summary analysis. The four important actors in Swedish renewal are the state government, the municipalities, the municipal housing corporations, and the residents.

National perspective

The analysis of efficiency from a national perspective must take into account the national housing goals. The basic goal, stated in the programme for the improvement of the existing housing stock, is that every inhabitant has the right to a flat with high standards and an outdoor environment of good quality (Sweden, 1983/84). This programme, however, also includes goals directed to conserving energy and increasing employment within the construction sector. All these goals must be considered when analysing efficiency in renewal activities from a national perspective. With this in mind, we see that the results are mixed. If the focus is on employment as well as on housing quality, the results achieved through physical improvements can be judged as efficient. If, however, the focus is on improving living conditions in the renewal area, the measures taken must be considered inefficient. Other measures would have better met the residents' needs and wishes, at a lower cost.

Municipal perspective

The municipalities' renewal goals are to achieve social stability and a general improvement in the attractiveness of the area. If these goals are compared to what has actually been done, efficiency is questionable.

From the municipal point of view the allocation of most of the financial resources to physical measures represents efforts that do not correspond to the most urgent needs in the area. Other measures, without being more costly, would have led to a better result. This indicates that the renewal activity could be regarded as inefficient from a municipal point of view. This might, however, not be the case. The discussion of efficiency must also take into consideration that the physical improvement measures are mostly financed by state subsidies.

This means that the municipality is in a situation where, on the one hand, it can choose to focus the renewal on physical measures, knowing that state subsidies can be used to finance these activities, but also knowing that these measures do not meet the areas' most urgent needs. On the other hand, the municipality can choose another set of measures that more directly meet urgent needs, but have to be financed without state support. Another aspect of efficiency from a municipal perspective is that renewal can lead to the exportation rather than the solving of problems. If this is the case, efficiency is questionable.

However, the question of efficiency, from a municipal perspective, incorporates both positive and negative aspects and, thus, cannot be answered in a general way. How the municipality assigns values to various aspects of renewal determines the overall analysis of efficiency.

The municipal housing corporations

The housing corporations, like the municipalities, wish to improve the attractiveness of the area and to achieve more social stability. The housing corporations, however, have one additional goal that, even though it is not often officially acknowledged, is vital. This goal concerns maintenance of the buildings, which is often neglected. Housing companies, therefore, find it attractive that renewal is focused on physical improvement, since it helps them solve their problems of neglected maintenance and provides them with state subsidies to finance these investments.

On the other hand, the housing corporations could benefit from other measures that would have a more positive impact on the attractiveness of the area. Increased migration flows have a negative impact on efficiency, especially when problem households move from the renewal area to other areas owned by the corporation. For the housing corporations the question of efficiency cannot be answered in general terms. The overall judgment is determined by the relative value the corporation assigns to various aspects of renewal.

The residents' perspective

Our comments here focus on the community of residents remaining in the renewal area after completion, rather than on those who had to leave during the renewal process or who live in adjacent areas influenced by renewal.

For residents in the area, the measures have led to positive changes according to their preferences. However, these measures, according to the surveys, correspond poorly to those judged by the tenants to be the most urgent. The residents have also been subjected to inconvenience costs caused by the reconstruction activities, including temporary moves out of flats and noise disturbances. For the residents remaining in the renewal area other measures would have had a more positive impact on the area's attractiveness, at lower cost.

A STRATEGY FOR RENEWAL

Since the 1980s subsidies for renewal activities have been increasingly redistributed from pre-war housing to flats constructed in the 1960s or later. The primary problems in pre-war housing were substandard conditions and physical maintenance, but the most urgent needs in the post-war housing stock have to do with social problems. Despite this difference, the requirements for state government subsidies for renewal have remained the same. The current subsidy system does not meet the most urgent needs in the post-war housing stock and, in fact, encourages renewal activity at a very high cost.

On the basis of our findings we would like to present an alternative approach to the renewal of these residential areas. The strategy includes measures on various levels and with a somewhat different focus.

The renewal area

Though renewal activities have led to positive changes, they have been achieved at high costs and have failed to solve some of the most urgent problems of the area. In terms of efficiency there is little correlation between the needs and wishes of the tenants and the renewal measures. A better outcome could be achieved by assigning different priorities to the various renewal activities.

An inevitable conclusion, based on results of various evaluations (Ehn, 1989; Danemark and Ekström, 1989), is that the absence of public participation explains the discrepancy between needs and wishes on the one hand and measures on the other. If the tenants' perspective is taken into consideration it seems clear that the focus of the renewal activities must shift to resolving the social problems that the residents have identified as underlying the unattractiveness of the area.

A broader perspective

In addition to analyses of the renewal area, studies of its surroundings should be carried out to determine whether changes there might help solve problems in the renewal area. This has generally not been done. Our findings strongly indicate the importance of including these 'outside' factors as part of the renewal strategy. These outside factors emerge on two levels.

Near (or even within) the housing area to be renewed services are usually offered that are of vital importance to the tenants. Our surveys indicate that many of the residents consider an upgrading of services to be of vital importance for enhancing the attractiveness of the residential area (Carlén and Cars, 1990). Schools and day care facilities are especially important. Many of the tenants judged these services to be of poor quality and contributed greatly to their dissatisfaction. Many of the households that had the resources to move to another residential district cited these deficiencies as an important reason for the move.

On a regional level, external factors also have a vital influence on the attractiveness of a renewal area. These factors include the accessibility of the workplace, the quality of commercial and public service provision, and transportation facilities. Access to these facilities is important for an area to function and for the residents to feel satisfied. Our conclusion is therefore that factors outside the area must have a high priority in renewal strategy. Factors outside the residential area must by analysed to ascertain their impact on the attractiveness of the renewal area. This analytical work is complicated, because it usually involves a large number of planners and decision makers on different levels and because problem resolution requires long-term planning and implementation. We stress the importance of developing a planning and decision-making organization that includes actors from the renewal area, the municipality, and the region. It is of extreme importance that programmes and plans for renewal be co-ordinated. Changes in the area must correspond to changes in external conditions.

Adjacent residential areas

The relationship between the renewal area and its surroundings can be seen from two perspectives. The renewal area, and the activities taking place there, influence adjacent residential districts. At the same time the renewal area is influenced by its surroundings.

Many adjacent areas have declined as the renewal area has been upgraded. The impact of the renewal activity on adjacent residential areas leads to the conclusion that the focus of the renewal strategy must be widened to include the affected residential districts near the renewal area. All renewal activity must include plans for the mitigation of long-term negative effects. This strengthens our conclusion that actors at the municipal and regional levels must be more involved in renewal activities.

THE FUTURE

In conclusion, we feel that our research strongly indicates the necessity of using comprehensive measures in order to solve the problems that characterize many large-scale areas from the Million Homes Program. However, when looking at what has been done so far, we conclude that current measures have not met the most urgent needs of residents in the affected areas. We also observe that the renewal activity has often had an unwanted impact on adjacent areas.

The national subsidies are currently being revised. A first draft, in which financial support is proposed for both reconstruction as well as for social programmes, has already been presented. Renewal ought never to be seen as an arsenal of one-shot measures aimed at solving an isolated problem. Rather it is an ongoing process that involves and influences the renewal area and its surroundings.

REFERENCES

CARLÉN, G. and G. CARS (1988) *Renewal of Large Scale Post-War Housing Estates—Effects and Efficiency*. Paper presented at the Regional Science Association's 28th European Congress, Stockholm, August 1988.

CARLÉN, G. and G. CARS (1990) *Förnyelse av Storskaliga Bostadsområden*. (Renewal of Large-scale Housing Estates). Stockholm: The Swedish Council for Building Research, Rapport R31:1990. In Swedish.

CARLÉN, G., G. CARS and U. CARLSON (1989) *Enkätsammanställning—Barnhushåll i Hjällbo, Göteborg* (Inquiry—Households with Children in Hjällbo, Gothenburg). Stockholm: Royal Institute of Technology, Department of Regional Planning. In Swedish.

CARS, G. (1987) *Renewal of Post-War Housing Areas in Sweden*. Stockholm: Royal Institute of Technology, Department of Regional Planning. Paper presented at the IFHP seminar on Deterioration of Housing Estates, Coventry, U.K., May 1987.

DANEMARK, B. and M. EKSTRÖM (1989) *Rosta i Örebro—erfarenheter från ett utvecklingsarbete i samband med ombyggnaden av stjärnhusen i Rosta* (Rosta in Örebro—Experiences from the Rehabilitation of the Rosta Neighbourhood). Örebro, Sweden: University of Örebro. In Swedish.

EHN, S. (1989) *Rinkeby i Stockholm—18 Hushålls syn på Ombyggnadsplaner och Evakuering* (Rinkeby in Stockholm—18 Household Perspectives on Renewal and Relocation). Stockholm: Royal Institute of Technology, Department of Building Function Analysis. In Swedish.

Stockholm Regional Planning Office (1985) *Sketch '85 (Skiss '85)*. Stockholm: Sketch of a new Regional Plan for Stockholm. In Swedish.

Sweden (1967) Angående riktlinjer för bostadspolitiken mm (Government proposal. Guidelines for the housing policy). Stockholm: Regeringens proposition 1967: 100. In Swedish.

Sweden (1983/84) *Program för Förbättring av Bostadsbeståndet* (Government proposal. A Program for Improvement of the Housing Stock). Stockholm: Regeringens proposition 1983/84:40 bil 9, BoU 11, rskr 63. In Swedish.

Sweden (1989a) Official statistics of Sweden. *The Annual Report Yearbook on Housing and Building Statistics 1989*. Stockholm: National Bureau of Statistics.

Sweden (1989b) The Parliament's Auditor's report. I. Carlman and K. Maunsbach. *1983 års Bostadsförbättringsprogram* (The 1983 Housing Improvement Program). Stockholm: Riksdagens revisorer, rapport 1989/90:2. In Swedish.

10 PLANNING AND IMPLEMENTATION OF ISRAEL'S PROJECT RENEWAL: A RETROSPECTIVE VIEW

Rachelle Alterman

Israel's 'Project Renewal' is one of the most ambitious programmes for neighbourhood regeneration in the world in terms of scale and scope. At its apex in the mid-1980s Project Renewal encompassed some 90 neighbourhoods. In Israel, a small country, this has meant that most cities and eligible towns have had at least one neighbourhood in the project, and that 700,000 people have been included — approximately 16% of the country's population of 4.5 million. By the late 1980s, the project had spent some $800 million. In scope, the project was consciously comprehensive, offering programmes in housing and infrastructure improvement, educational enrichment, welfare, community and cultural activities, improved health services, and in later years, some modest beginnings in economic development and job training. Project Renewal was to involve neither the relocation of neighbourhood populations nor gentrification. It was an attempt to draw from international resources on the very latest in how to achieve neighbourhood regeneration. To some extent, Project Renewal was modelled after the then already defunct American Model Cities Program (Frieden and Kaplan, 1987–1988), but has persevered longer and is larger relative to country size.

A project of this magnitude could succeed only by changing institutions — altering their modes of decision making and empowering the local residents. After all, government action, and inaction, were responsible for the formation of most of the neighbourhoods needing renewal, as is shown below. Government policies are often part of the problem of declining neighbourhoods, as reflected in these neighbourhoods' increasing dependency on government services and their reduced leveraging power (Alterman, 1988). Implementation analysts have been arguing for over a decade that as good as a proposed programme might be, implementation cannot be assumed to work simply on the strength of the proposed new policy.[1] One author in the field has even gone so far as to title his book *Why Government Programs Fail* (Larson, 1980). The question is especially apt for neighbourhood regeneration programmes, because they seek to deal with what planning theorists have called 'wicked problems' or 'meta-problems', whose attributes, extent, and possible cures are not fully understood (Rittel and Webber, 1972; Cartwright, 1973).

Without necessarily adopting such a pessimistic view, this chapter focuses on the implementation of Project Renewal, and asks three questions: To what extent have the operational principles of the project been met through

147

the institutions created and the decisions made? Have they operated well enough to enable the project to produce outputs that can reasonably be expected to lead to the desired outcomes? And to what extent can the changes produced in institutional structures or modes of decision making be regarded as substantive outcomes in their own right? This chapter looks at Project Renewal's planning, implementation, and outputs (budgets and programmes delivered), while Chapter 11 looks at the project's social and physical outcomes.

But first, we shall provide a brief introduction to Israel's land policy, housing, and planning systems, which are related to the formation of the neighbourhoods now in need of regeneration.

ISRAEL'S LAND POLICIES AND THE HOUSING PRODUCTION PROCESS

Public land policy and the housing system

The vast majority of neighbourhoods included in Project Renewal are located on public land and were established through public initiative. A few are located in inner cities, are old or privately built (only one of the 10 neighbourhoods in our research sample). Yet not all neighbourhoods developed through public initiative are in distress; on the contrary, a large part of Israel's population resides in viable housing constructed on public land. It would therefore be useful to discuss Israel's land policy and housing systems to understand the formation of distressed neighbourhoods and the context within which revitalization efforts take place.

Israel presents an interesting mix of public and private involvement in land development and housing (Alterman, 1990a).[2] About 93% of Israel's total land area of approximately 20,000 km^2 is publicly owned. With municipal land banking almost unheard of in Israel (Alterman et al., 1990), most public land is centrally administered by the Israel Lands Authority. Private land, however, has played a much more significant role than this statistic implies because it is, for the most part, concentrated in the larger cities. A few of the neighbourhoods in Project Renewal are located in inner cities, on private land.

The Lands Authority leases land on a long-term basis either to public bodies or to private developers (Borukhov, 1980).[3] Leased land, however, behaves in the marketplace much like private land. During the state's first two decades, when most Project Renewal neighbourhoods were built, the overwhelming majority of housing starts were classified as 'public'. In the 1950s some 80% were public, by the 1970s about 65%. These included housing constructed directly by the Ministry of Housing,[4] as well as housing constructed by various quasi-public bodies such as the General Trade Union (the Histadrut), the Jewish Agency for Israel, and associations related to political or religious movements. These agencies or companies received either direct government budgets or substantial subsidies in land and financing. (I call this housing 'publicly constructed' to differentiate it from 'public housing' in the American sense, where only the very poor, virtually captive population lives.) Most of these units were 'purchased' by their residents. Because the Lands Authority does not sell public land, the transfer has always been done through long-term leases, but the public regards these as tantamount to ownership and popularly calls them so.

Most Israeli families start off with some government aid in the form of a subsidized mortgage towards the 'purchase' of their first apartment or house. The categories of eligibles include, in addition to young couples, new immigrants (currently with enhanced loans), families living in overcrowded conditions, and recently, also bachelors over a certain age. Project Renewal has added a new category of eligibles — residents in project neighbourhoods, whether otherwise eligible or not — and has offered them attractive loans for enlarging their apartments.

For the past two decades, Israel's housing policy has been undergoing a gradual trend towards privatization. From Israel's establishment in 1948 until the late 1970s, all eligible families, except those in need of rental housing, had to purchase their housing unit directly from one of the approved public agencies to qualify for a subsidized mortgage or grant. Since 1979, eligible households can usually use their loans to purchase an apartment on the open market in any city or location they prefer, whether from a public or private developer, on public or private land. The terms of the loans are graded by distance from the country's centre in order to encourage population dispersal.[5]

This change of policy is expressed in the figures on the share of publicly constructed housing units, which, before the wave of mass immigration began in 1990, nosedived to 17% (Israel Central Bureau of Statistics, 1987). Some public construction has remained in development towns and in distressed rural areas, but virtually all public construction in the metropolitan areas has ceased, except in some Project Renewal neighbourhoods (mostly for housing expansion rather than new units). The current wave of mass immigration is reintroducing public sector construction to accommodate the housing needs of immigrants. But although the public sector's share is rising, it is unlikely that there will be a comeback of its domination in new construction.

Israeli housing policy has always encouraged ownership (or long-term leasehold) of housing units, mostly condominium apartments, and increasingly in the 1980s, town houses and single-attached or detached homes. At least 70%, and probably more, of Israeli families own (or long-term lease) their homes.[6] The high cost of borrowing in Israel has made it uneconomical for private developers to construct rental housing and until 1990 there were no public policies to encourage that. Rental units are to be found mainly in publicly constructed housing and have always been intended to house the very poor. The general population wishing to rent housing must rely on apartments or houses of private individuals who might be temporarily out of the country or might own a second home.

The public housing companies that manage public rental housing have for a long time been encouraging residents to purchase their apartments, and have legally been able to do so even where not all the residents in an apartment block are willing to do so. As might be expected, neighbourhoods in

149

Project Renewal usually have a greater share of rental public housing than other neighbourhoods, but even poor neighbourhoods often have a substantial population of apartment owners. Among the neighbourhoods in our sample, the average percent of owner-occupied units prior to Project Renewal's entrance was 46% (ranging from 32 to 92%),[7] and has increased by several points through the project's policies (Carmon, 1989, p. 114).

Urban policy and the creation of distressed neighbourhoods

Urban development and housing policies in Israel's formative years were, to a large extent, responsible for the creation of distressed neighbourhoods. During the pre-state period, the ideological emphasis was on rural development and a utopian form of living to symbolize the return of the Jews to their land. Yet the factual reality has always been that the majority of residents (above 80% even in pre-state times) preferred urban life (Alterman and Hill, 1986). Urban areas did not receive much attention from planners and were not equipped to absorb mass immigration. Yet, the war-stricken state established in 1948 was faced with the need to house masses of immigrant refugees — survivors of the Nazis and refugees from Arab countries — several times the size of the 1948 Jewish population of 650,000. Planners had to shift their attention to mass housing.

The result was the establishment of some 30 new towns in all parts of the country, many in outlying areas. These development towns may have been perceived as a compromise with the rural ideology. In addition, new neighbourhoods were constructed at the outskirts of cities where immigrant transit camps had been located. These were all constructed on national land by government or other public agencies. The housing was characteristically composed of uniform blocks of apartments designed by central government architects, with little regard for consumer diversity, and with little attention to differing landscapes, so that a new town in the green and empty hills of Galilee would be planned at a density similar to a neighbourhood in Tel Aviv.

The apartments were at first very small — 28 to $32\,m^2$ per family (and many families were large) — but with running water and bathrooms. The average size of publicly constructed housing rose quickly in the 1950s and 1960s, reaching $86\,m^2$ in the late 1980s (Carmon, 1989, p. 9).[8] The public standard, however, could not compete with the still higher standards set by the private sector, which since the 1980s has been concentrating almost exclusively on large apartments and town houses. Meanwhile, architectural preferences and styles in the private sector became diversified, allowing more consumer choice than for publicly constructed units. Thus, publicly constructed housing tagged many neighbourhoods as future candidates for regeneration through public intervention.

Indeed, most of today's neighbourhoods in distress included in Project Renewal are the creation of public policies and government construction. Built mostly during the country's formative decades, from the 1950s through the mid-1970s, the housing and land allocation processes were stamped by central government control. However, not all publicly constructed

neighbourhoods were to become distressed. Some have drawn private investment and have undergone a process of improvement through private action.

What factors explain the difference? Naturally, location has been important. Some neighbourhoods within or close to metropolitan areas have never
declined, while a few have undergone a natural gentrification process.
Another factor explaining the decline of some neighbourhoods has been their
large scale and the lack of diversity in housing sizes and styles. The major
factor, often related to the others, has been social. In many neighbourhoods,
whether in development towns or in metropolitan areas, a negative selection
process has occurred: populations of greater mobility left these neighbourhoods at the earliest opportunity, leaving the less mobile, poorer population
behind. This process has been especially marked in development towns,
some of which have been included in Project Renewal in their entirety.

Planning controls: their obliviousness to neighbourhood regeneration

Israeli law supplies a wide range of planning controls and requires a permit
for every construction or demolition. But as in most countries, these tools
have proven to be suited more to new development than to upgrading existing development. Planning controls did not succeed, nor perhaps were they
ever considered, as tools for preventing the construction of neighbourhoods
destined to become targets for renewal.

Israel's planning and development control system is highly centralized and
strict. Statutory plans are obligatory and binding, containing land use
(zoning-like) designations and other development regulations. Every plan
originating at the local level, whether big or small, requires the approval of
a committee of central government ministries, and can in effect be vetoed
by the Minister of the Interior. At least on paper, the system calls for a
co-ordinated and consistent hierarchy of plans from the national, through
the district, down to the local levels. A national plan for population distribution controls the establishment of every new town, and, ostensibly, the
maximum permitted population of every existing town as well (Alexander
et al., 1983; Alterman and Hill, 1986).

Until 1965, however, when the Planning and Building Law[9] repealed the
planning legislation inherited from the British, these planning controls did
not apply to government bodies. The new law required all government
jurisdictions to abide by land-use regulations and procedures, except for
defence-related land use. Thus, construction by the Ministry of Housing had
to go through the same procedure as construction by a private developer. By
this time, however, all the new towns and most neighbourhoods now in Project Renewal had already been established and public construction activity
was starting to ebb. A hypothetical question is whether planning controls
over government construction of housing would have altered the character
of these new towns and neighbourhoods. The answer to this question is probably very little.

In Israel, as in most countries, statutory plans, enhanced as they might be
in legal powers, are not equipped to prevent the construction of housing
destined to become distressed neighbourhoods. Some reasons for this lie in

the passive nature of most planning controls, their focus on new construction, and their physical bias. Other reasons pertain to institutional relations: regulative planning in Israel is the responsibility of the Ministry of the Interior, which is weaker and poorer than the powerful Ministry of Construction and Housing, which is entrusted with initiatory planning. And finally, regulative planning agencies in Israel are notorious for the slow pace of their decisions and their chronic bottlenecks (Alterman, 1989).

Thus Israel's land-use planning system has not proven effective in preventing the creation of distressed neighbourhoods or in providing the initiative for renewal. Neighbourhood regeneration, as in most countries, has needed a special public policy, and sometimes legal, boost from outside the planning system. And so Project Renewal was proposed as a comprehensive programme to do what regulative planning cannot or will not do.

The emergence of project renewal

Project Renewal was conceived by Prime Minister Begin shortly after the nationalist Likud Party came into power in 1977, and was directed at one of the party's most devoted electorates—residents of poor neighbourhoods, mostly Jews of North African or Mid-Eastern origin. The project started operation in 1979. The first batch of neighbourhoods was selected from a preexisting list of 160 neighbourhoods considered to be in need of renewal. While a declaration of general national goals was made at the outset, the operational goals remained largely unstated and evolved with time. In Israel, a government programme of this kind requires no special legislation, except for the standard annual budget approval by the Knesset (Parliament). The actual design of the project was left largely in the hands of planners and other urbanists, with relatively little direct political input in the project's formative stages. The programme as a whole had no termination date, but each neighbourhood was to benefit for only several years, as a 'booster shot' towards regeneration.

EVALUATION OF THE IMPLEMENTATION PROCESS OF PROJECT RENEWAL

Method of analysis and evaluation

The study on which this paper is based focuses on a sample of ten neighbourhoods of various sizes in different regions and towns. The study is part of a comprehensive evaluation conducted by the author and colleagues (Alterman et al., 1984, 1985). The field work was carried out from 1982 to 1984, the project's most active years.

The analysis of the implementation process was carried out by the author and a colleague (Alterman and Hill, 1985). The method used combined observation with a more structured evaluation: each neighbourhood was assigned a field researcher who participated in meetings and events, followed official decisions, and became personally acquainted with the decision makers and the neighbourhood leaders. To structure the evaluation, the field researchers

152

were given a uniform set of guiding questions that served as criteria for evaluation. In their written responses, they relied, in addition to their own observations, on interviews with key informants whom they judged to be reliable, on budget documents, protocols of meetings, and on other formal and informal documents, as required.

The project's six principles of implementation[10]

To implement its ambitious goals, Project Renewal had to create institutional machinery that could carry the load. The project also had to shake up existing modes of doing government business. This implied a need for innovation. Successful implementation of the project's goals would depend on the degree to which six major operational principles were fulfilled:

- relying on existing agencies for service delivery within a clear and effective organizational structure;
- decentralizing authority to the neighbourhood level and encouraging resident participation;
- maintaining good relations with the local authorities;
- creating an effective planning process within each neighbourhood;
- ensuring adequate interagency co-ordination to enable integrated action; and
- minimizing the substitution of Project Renewal funds in existing programmes.

Let us look at the degree to which each of these principles has been implemented.

Reliance on existing agencies.   The designers of Project Renewal were aware of the unmitigated failure of Israel's Urban Renewal Agency of the late 1960s, established by the 1965 Law for Reconstruction and Clearance of Renewal Areas. As a new agency, it turned out to be powerless against existing government agencies (Alexander, 1980). Therefore, the project's designers declared their intention that the project would rely on existing agencies for service delivery, adding only a modest superstructure for planning, co-ordination, and evaluation. Even this, however, meant that project implementation depended on a complex structure composed of the existing agencies, plus the superstructure. The implementation machinery needed to be equipped with good hierarchical integration and clear rules for decision making (Mazmanian and Sabatier, 1983, p. 27).

In practice, the institutional structure that evolved was neither clear nor free of conflicts. Much of the complexity was due to the dual-track structure of the project, which required the co-operation of two 'in-laws': the Israel government and the Jewish Agency for Israel (JAI). Together, they ran the major decision-making body on the national level, the Inter-Organizational Committee (Fig. 1).

153

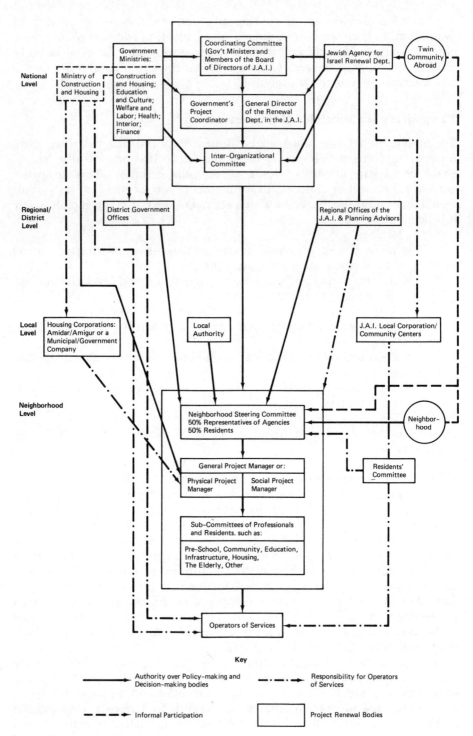

Key

───────────▶ Authority over Policy-making and
            Decision-making bodies

─ ∙ ─ ∙ ─▶ Responsibility for Operators
            of Services

─ ─ ─ ─▶ Informal Participation

☐ Project Renewal Bodies

Fig. 1. Organizational chart of Project Renewal.

154

The Jewish Agency is an international organization, which since pre-state times has been aiding Jewish communities in distress in various parts of the world (of late, in Ethiopia and the U.S.S.R.). In Israel, the agency has always shared selected responsibility with the government for social services, especially immigrant absorption and rural community development, playing a role similar to that of national or international agencies for technical co-operation and assistance, such as USAID or UNESCO. Urban neighbourhoods were a new area for the agency. Both sides of the partnership had considerable power, and shared the financial burden through a cost-sharing agreement.

To add to the complexity, the Israeli government was not monolithic. Five major government ministries were involved, with only a modestly powerful co-ordinator to orchestrate among them. Reliance on existing personnel for service delivery raised some problems of allegiance and subordination.

Interestingly, excluded from the government agencies involved in the project was the Israel Lands Authority, the landowner of most of the neighbourhoods and development towns included in Project Renewal. This reflects the agency's traditionally passive role in the upgrading of existing development, usually restricting itself to administering the leases. The Lands Authority has allowed the Ministry of Construction and Housing almost a free hand in determining what is to be rehabilitated, and has usually co-operated willingly when its authorization as a landowner has been needed.

Meanwhile, the Jewish Agency developed a special institutional structure of its own for planning, budgeting, and evaluation, which, to some extent, dipped into service delivery as well. Built-in contradictions in role definition plagued the role of the neighbourhood project manager, one of the crucial officers for project implementation.

Had these problems with the institutional structure gone unmitigated, it is doubtful that the project would have succeeded to the extent that it did. Several forces, however, helped smooth out some of the friction in the institutional machinery. First, commitment, that *sine qua non* for successful implementation (Bardach, 1977, p. 268; Mazmanian and Sabatier, 1983, p. 28), was available to a high degree among the central decision makers on both sides of the marriage. Apparently, they succeeded in instilling a good measure of commitment in many field personnel. Second, it turned out that the institutional structure of the Jewish Agency served as a powerful engine, pulling the project along and supporting innovation. The agency's Project Renewal department was a brand new institution without ossified modes of operation in urban neighbourhoods; also, the agency as a whole had a special source of commitment to the project through its web of financial and political obligations. Third, the project's unique structure of twinning with Jewish communities abroad provided volunteer professionals interested in the project's success who often served as watchdogs to oversee implementation at the central level. In those neighbourhoods where the twinned community representatives were active, this watchdog function also operated at the local level.

Decentralization of authority and citizen participation. One of the major innovations introduced by Project Renewal was the delegation of responsibility for decision making to neighbourhood steering committees. The degree to which decentralization was realized should be assessed against Israel's highly centralized structure. We concluded that decentralization was achieved to a significant extent, but with compromises (Alterman, 1988).

First, let us look at the format of the institutions created. At the central level, local residents had no direct representation. On the local level, the structure of the neighbourhood steering committees represented a compromise between centralization and decentralization: half their 22 members were residents, but the other half were representatives of each of the relevant central government offices, the Jewish Agency, and local government. Our findings indicate that the requisite number of local residents had been met in all the sample neighbourhoods, and that, unexpectedly, the representatives of most government agencies did indeed come 'down' to meetings within the neighbourhoods, an important innovation (Churchman, 1985, 1987–88).

In practice, the degree of discretion allotted to the local committees was never formally clarified. In the absence of legislation, a vacuum was left that allowed the central bodies to determine the division of authority. We determined the degree of discretion actually allowed at the neighbourhood level by comparing the number of programmes and budgets requested by each neighbourhood steering committee with those actually approved by the Inter-Organizational Committee. No neighbourhood was found to be totally free of central intervention. Such intervention, however, declined markedly with time. In the formative years until about 1981, the Inter-Organizational Committee sometimes vetoed entire programmes and occasionally added some. After 1982, the correspondence between programmes requested and approved rose significantly, reaching near overlap.

Another question initially left unclear related to the division of labour between the central and neighbourhood levels. Our findings showed that the delegation of authority to the local level was viewed by the central agencies, and by most of the neighbourhoods, as being limited to planning decisions, that is, to determining the package of desired programmes. Notions of empowerment in the form of responsibility over budgets and service delivery, to be found in some Western European and North American countries (Susskind and Elliott, 1983), were quite alien to the decision makers. Decentralization was rarely expressed as *devolution*, whereby central government transfers functions to agencies with autonomous legal powers (Rondinelli, 1983; Alterman, 1988). Rather, it was a combination of mere *deconcentration*, expressed as the requirement that government officials sit at the neighbourhood level, along with partial *delegation of authority* over planning decisions, while programme responsibility ultimately remained with central government.

The following story highlights how alien the notion of empowerment through citizen-based service delivery was to the decision makers. In one neighbourhood (unique to the project as a whole) the local community leaders demanded direct control over part of the budget, and wanted to be responsible for running a few small services. This behaviour was termed a 'revolt' by almost all personnel at all levels. That neighbourhood became known as the black sheep of the project and officials responsible for it were apologetic and angry, and at times virtually punitive. The local leaders were viewed as self-serving. In 1984 new elections finally brought in more conciliatory leaders and full co-operation was resumed on both sides. The central agency officials were not malevolent. Simply, the devolution of responsibility for budgets or service delivery required such a major departure from regular modes that it could not be considered.

Decentralization did have a tangible impact on service delivery, not through devolution, but through simple deconcentration. Some programmes were made more accessible to the residents, including housing loans, welfare, and even the notoriously inhospitable building permit process. Determination of educational curricula, traditionally planned centrally down to the last textbook, became more open to residents' input. Personnel were assigned to keep office hours in the neighbourhoods, and higher-level decision makers became more accessible and more aware of the neighbourhood's problems through their service on the local steering committees. Although these changes did not empower residents directly, they were some of the most tangible changes that decentralization brought about for the residents at large, not just the activists.

How sustainable is the experiment in decentralization likely to be? A positive omen are several cases in which the organizational structure of Project Renewal has been copied, almost 'automatically' in non-project neighbourhoods. Some housing agencies have become more accessible (Carmon and Oxman, 1986). In some local authorities, the procedure for obtaining building permits according to the planning and building law for self-help construction financed through Project Renewal has been made more user-friendly. If these new modes persist, government operation in several areas may have taken a permanent turn toward deconcentration.

Maintaining good relations with local governments. Project Renewal's official guidelines speak of securing the goodwill of the local governments on which the project depends for delivering many of its programmes. Yet a look at the project's institutional structure indicates that, ostensibly, local authorities had little to gain. Decentralization in Project Renewal did not vest local governments with greater authority; their formal involvement was limited to representation on the local steering committees alongside the more powerful central government ministries. Project Renewal thus turned local governments into service delivery agents without granting them greater authority, and introduced central involvement in several areas that previously were free from it. The project was in danger of further weakening Israel's already feeble local governments.

Yet, despite these effects, the score for local governments was positive. The best indicator was the strong pressure placed by towns wishing to be included in the project, and the virtual absence of cases where they wished to be excluded. Local governments seemed to savour the opportunity of having more budgets pass through their coffers, thus freeing some funds from existing services (contrary to declared project policy, see below). They also seemed to like the possibility of showing politically marketable improvements in the community, and these apparently were ample compensation for the loss of some control. In most of the sample neighbourhoods, a reasonably good working relationship with local government was secured, even though particular local officials at times felt bypassed.

The project also seeded an alternative model for central and local government co-operation over service planning and delivery. The neighbourhood steering committees created a structure for ongoing dialogue between central government offices and local government over the delivery of central government services. Previously, the exchange was dependent largely on lobbying by the mayor, or on separate exchanges among low-level bureaucrats or professionals within each service area. The precedents created by Project Renewal coincide with changes that are occurring in local government in general, which is becoming more professional, self-assured, and less dependent on central government than it was in the past.

Creating an effective and comprehensive neighbourhood planning process. The project's goals were to pull the neighbourhoods out of the social structure, economics, and infrastructure of poverty. Because each neighbourhood had a different profile or perception of its problems, successful implementation of the national project goals thus hinged on success in designing a suitable tailor-made strategy for each neighbourhood, i.e on comprehensive planning. This was no easy task, given that the existing social programmes had each had similar goals in their separate areas for a long time. The planning process thus had to be different to make a difference. It had to reflect some comprehensive view and to tackle the 'wicked problems' that previously had eluded solution. The planning task was formally assigned to each neighbourhood steering committee.

A comparison of the packages of programmes requested by each steering committee with the neighbourhood's central problems shows that the majority of the programmes, especially in housing quality and crowding, infrastructure, community organization, welfare, and to a lesser extent educational enrichment, did address high-priority problems. There were many programmes, however, that dealt cosmetically with problems, relying on the provision of cultural services, equipment purchases, and face-lifts of housing façades, which proved to be of little value in the long run. In the absence of employment retraining or economic development in the project at that time, and with little structural change in the education system, few programmes attempted to tackle the root causes of poverty.

The planning process enjoyed mixed success. Positively, in all the sample neighbourhoods, the planning process yielded the annual decisions that the central agencies expected. Yet in most neighbourhoods the planning process was lacking in many ways: the database was grossly inadequate for determining the extent of problems; there was a tendency to cut off prematurely the possibilities for adding programmes or terminating unsuccessful ones; little attention was paid to identifying and evaluating alternative strategies and programmes; and in most neighbourhoods, there were few attempts to take an overview of the neighbourhood's problems to determine priorities.

It is not easy to pronounce judgment on whether the planning process was a positive link in the programme-to-resources-to-outputs-to-outcomes process. Ideal planning processes are hard to come by anywhere, as planning theorists have long recognized (Hudson, 1979; Alexander, 1984). The project's achievement was that a planning process was institutionalized at the neighbourhood level for the first time in Israel. Long-term positive effects of this innovation lie ahead if local governments use this precedent to improve neighbourhood planning. Meanwhile, the bottom line is that the neighbourhood planning process is responsible for both the good and the missed shots in finding solutions to neighbourhood problems.

Interagency co-ordination for integrated action. Project Renewal, unlike existing social and housing services, was to be an integrated programme — a concerted onslaught on the social, educational, health, and physical problems of poor neighbourhoods. This meant that government offices would have to overcome their genetic tendency towards separate action, and would have to learn to co-ordinate. Formation of an *ad hoc* committee or appointment of a co-ordinating officer, previously tried in Israel for the co-ordination of other programmes (with limited success), would not do for a neighbourhood programme: here there had to be long-term co-ordination on a large scale, entailing scores of neighbourhoods spread all over the country. Of all the project's operational principles, this one required the greatest departure from traditional behaviour.

Co-ordination was achieved, but not to the desired degree. Instead of *co-ordinated* action, in many neighbourhoods the project achieved *concurrent* action. Also, there were differences between the sectors: co-ordination between the two major sectors of activity, the social and the physical, was weaker than within each sector. Thus, co-ordination between social and educational programmes, for example, was better than between social programmes and housing.

On the positive side, even concurrent activity in a wide array of physical-improvement programmes along with social, educational, and community programmes is an impressive achievement. Most significantly, the project's organizational structure supplied a forum for eight or nine government and quasi-government agencies to sit together on a routine basis, focus jointly on a particular neighbourhood, and decide, at least formally, on a set of programmes. Also notable are the attempts to create, from scratch, norms of co-operation among service delivery personnel.

No doubt, better co-ordination would have made the project's implementation process more effective. Yet this may not have been feasible, since good co-ordination is notoriously hard to achieve. Despite its shortcomings, this precedent could serve as a model of an improved organizational format for co-ordinating government services in distressed neighbourhoods.

Adding services rather than substituting funds. What often happens during implementation of public programmes is a game of tug-of-war that pulls the process in unplanned directions (Bardach, 1977). If a programme is well

funded and is perceived as a success, this 'game' may take the form of participants substituting the new programme's funds for their own and shifting
their own funds to other purposes or sites. Such a process could occur either
as a conscious policy on the part of some of the participating agencies, or as
gradual slippage.

To what extent did Project Renewal actually add to existing services, as
its goals implied it should, rather than simply change the budgetary address
for some services? This is a tough question methodologically because it
involves second guessing. This issue, popularly called in the project's jargon
'budgetary escape', was one of the most sensitive implementation questions.
Neighbourhood residents and bureaucrats alike were keenly aware but
inaccurately informed of this issue. The method we developed to measure
the extent of displacement did not use actual budgets; inflation was too high
for that at the time. Rather, using expert judgment, we classified each of the
programmes delivered as either net addition, partial substitution, or full
substitution.[11]

The findings indicate that about 40% of the programmes involved *partial*
or *full* substitutions, but the percentage of funds concerned was considerably
smaller. Not all the agencies in Project Renewal undertook, or allowed,
substitution to the same extent. Table 1 shows that, contrary to popular lore,
local authorities were not the only, or the major, culprits to benefit from
substitution: 23% of local authority-delivered programmes had some
substituted funds in them, while as many as 35% of Ministry of Education
programmes benefited from substitution. Some of the latter were internal
substitutions of Project Renewal funds for existing Ministry of Education
programmes.

Which agencies 'paid' for the substitution by financing programmes that
substituted for existing programmes? (Recall that Project Renewal was
financed both by the Jewish Agency and by specific ministries of the Israeli
government.) The Jewish Agency was the most 'generous' of all the institutions in allowing substitution: as many as 58% of the programmes it
financed were at least partial substitutions for existing programmes. The
Ministry of Education allowed 26%. The two other financing ministries had
low displacement rates. It is difficult to assess whether the large chunk of
'generosity' displayed by the Jewish Agency reflected a conscious policy of
allowing indirect subsidies of Israeli government operations, or a 'natural'
process of bandwagoning onto a new source of financing.

The degree of substitution varied by type of programme (Table 2). Formal
education, postnatal, and toddler programmes were highly susceptible to

Table 1. Percentage of social programmes with some displacement by benefiting agency

Benefiting agency	Percentage	Benefiting agency	Percentage
Ministry of Education	35	Local governments	23
Ministry of Labor	13	Religious and cultural institutions	24
Ministry of Health	5		

Source: Alterman and Hill (1985, p. 148).

Table 2. Percentage of social programmes with some displacement within each programme category

Programme category	Percentage	Programme category	Percentage
Postnatal and toddler	59	Employment	14
Formal education	53	Health	0
Youth and sports	46	Senior citizens	37
Community	31	Planning and admin.	0

Source: Alterman and Frenkel (1985, p. 76)

displacement, because of our expectation that some of these would have been delivered anyhow, without project financing, as they were in some non-project neighbourhoods. The youth and sports category also showed high displacement. Programmes that were totally new to Project Renewal, such as planning, or were highly innovative, such as neighbourhood-based job training and special health services, naturally showed no displacement.

Substitution undoubtedly weakened the net outputs of the project to some extent, especially in the areas of formal education, and what might be regarded as informal education—youth, sports, and community programmes. Many of these informal programmes were financed by the Jewish Agency. But in view of the fact that the figures presented above included many programmes of only partial substitution, we estimate that the extent was not enough to jeopardize the possibility of a causal connection between project-financed programmes and possible outcomes. Some substitution is inevitable in any programme with budgets, political support, and a large number of institutional participants. From this point of view, the substitution that occurred in Project Renewal could be regarded as an indicator of success. We found insufficient awareness, however, among the project's decision makers of this phenomenon and few attempts to prevent it.

THE PROJECT'S OUTPUTS: PROGRAMMES AND BUDGETS

Total budgets and investments

Although budget figures by themselves may not be useful for cross-national comparison, the change in investment levels over time and the relative allocations for the different programme areas could be of interest.

The total investment[12] in Project Renewal from its inception to 1987 was $756 million, ranging annually from about $75 million in 1980 and 1987, to a high of about $125 million in 1981 and 1982, the years of maximum investment per neighbourhood. Of these sums, 32% was invested in social, education, and cultural programmes (henceforth, social programmes), 45% in housing and infrastructure (excluding mortgages to residents), and 23% in public buildings such as sports facilities and community centres (Carmon, 1989, pp. 47–48; Hovav, 1988). The extent of investment in individual neighbourhoods has declined markedly with time and with the increase in the number of neighbourhoods, from a high of $1.8 million in 1982, to $800,000 in 1987.

161

Could this level of investment make a significant difference? Carmon (1989, pp. 51–52) analyses Israel's total budget for social, education, housing, and health services, and comes to the conclusion that in Project Renewal neighbourhoods, the additional budgets constituted a 22–34% supplement to the per capita public expenditures for these services. Project Renewal's policy was to invest most of these budgets in the community, through enhanced housing and social services. Only a small proportion was given directly to the residents in the form of loans or scholarships.

Programmes delivered in the research neighbourhoods[13]

The range of programmes delivered in each of our sample neighbourhoods reinforces the fact that Project Renewal's strategy was to carry out many programmes simultaneously, covering a wide scope of intervention. In view of the differences in budgeting social and physical programmes, we shall discuss each of these categories separately.

On the average, 40 specific social programmes were carried out in each neighbourhood in a given year (during the project's peak). The areas of intervention included, in all sample neighbourhoods, postnatal and toddler programmes, education, youth and sports, community activities, and services for the aged. In some neighbourhoods, there were also enhanced health services and job training (in four of the ten neighbourhoods). In our ten sample neighbourhoods, the average social budget for 1982/83 was $747,000 per neighbourhood, as against an actual expenditure of $461,000. Table 3 presents the distribution of social programmes by subject category, and the percentage of total expenditures for each type of programme.

Table 3. Percentage of social programmes and of expenditures, by subject category, 1982–83

Subject category	Percentage of social programmes	Percentage of expenditures
Toddlers	17	13
Education	25	33
Youth and sports	25	23
Community	20	23
Employment	1	0.4
Health	2	3
Old age	10	4
Total	100	~100

Source: Alterman and Frenkel (1985, p. 9).

In addition, physical-improvement and housing programmes were carried out. These do not lend themselves to a meaningful quantitative count by number of programmes delivered because their budgets varied widely. Table 4 presents the average percentage renewal budget invested in our research neighbourhoods in each of the three major areas of physical improvement: housing, infrastructure, and public buildings and facilities. It is shown that

Table 4. Percentage of the average budget allocated to physical programmes, by category (the dollar value is in thousands of dollars; 1981–82 and 1982–83 averaged out)

Physical programmes	$	%
Housing	656	23
Infrastructure	290	11
Public facilities	784	26
Total/physical programmes	1,730	60

Source: Alterman and Frenkel (1985, p. 19).

60% of the budget on average in the two budget years studied was allocated to physical programmes. Of these, public facilities received the largest share, housing the next largest, and infrastructure the smallest.

This chapter will not evaluate the extent to which these investments achieved social and physical change in the neighbourhoods, since this is the focus of Chapter 11. In terms of implementation, the data in Tables 3 and 4 indicate a robust programme of expended budgets (though not always in full) and the delivery of a large number and variety of programmes to local neighbourhoods.

Target populations

One of the indicators of effective implementation is the degree to which programmes reach the target populations. Project Renewal scores well on this count. In our research neighbourhoods, we found that programmes of formal education (including baby-care and toddler programmes) had the widest reach, as might be expected: 51% of the children from birth to 17 years of age had participated in one or more of the education programmes financed by the project. This percentage varied by age group, as shown by Table 5.

Formal programmes reached the majority of children. Informal programmes, such as youth clubs, adult education, cultural programmes, and community organization, where attendance is voluntary, had a lower rate of outreach, but still managed to attract a sizeable chunk of the population — one-quarter of the adults and one-third of the children. These figures are on the conservative side, because they are averaged over all the neighbourhoods.

Table 5. Average percentage of residents reached by project renewal, by age group, 1982–83

Age group	Formal education programmes	Informal programmes
0–2	12	14
3–5	75	12
6–11	92	33
12–17	15	29
18–64	—	22
65+	—	39
Average	51	26

Source: Alterman and Frenkel (1985, p. 38).

If we include only those neighbourhoods where a specific programme had been offered, the rates are higher by some 5 to 10%.

In the area of physical improvement, we cannot present equivalent figures because the reach of these programmes is cumulative and takes a long time, whereas we studied the neighbourhoods only for a limited period. In general, though, for all the neighbourhoods, physical improvement programmes eventually covered most of the housing units and some of the infrastructure and streetscape. The extent of intervention, however, varied a great deal, from simple façade face-lifts supplemented with pipe improvement, to innovative architectural designs for the expansion of entire apartment blocks for which Project Renewal has become renowned. There is no question that the latter were the more durable and meaningful outputs, creating a substantial alleviation of crowding and, if the housing unit was in private 'ownership' (usually long-term leasehold), also adding a significant asset to the family's finances. While almost all households enjoyed some improvement in housing, apartment expansions were less frequent.

Are these degrees of reach high or low? The rates for the voluntary social programmes are probably quite high, when we consider the problems of reach encountered by equivalent programmes in other countries, but parallel data are not easily available. The rates for physical improvement are high in terms of coverage, but vary in terms of depth and endurance of the change. The assessment of success would depend on the outcomes achieved, which are not the subject of this paper. In terms of capacity to deliver programmes that would reach the target populations, Project Renewal seems to have been quite successful.

ASSESSING THE DEGREE OF SUCCESS IN IMPLEMENTATION

How successful has the implementation process of Project Renewal been? I shall discuss success on two levels: implementation as a means – the degree of effectiveness in delivering the programmes and services planned by the project – and, implementation as an end in itself – the degree of change achieved in the modes of decision making in government programmes.

Although the implementation process presents a somewhat ambivalent picture, one conclusion is clear-cut: Larson's pessimism concerning why government programmes fail does not hold in the case of Project Renewal. Project Renewal will probably never be judged a failure. But there will likely be a lively debate about its degree of success.

If judged solely as the link between programme and outcomes, the implementation process was like a sieve with some plugged-up pores. Its shortcomings in the neighbourhood-based planning processes, interagency co-ordination, and the partial substitution for existing services slowed down the project's capacity to achieve its goals. Not all ostensible outcomes can be attributed to the project: some, probably a minority, are the result of pre-existing programmes, either continued as before or financed with substituted project funds. Other outcomes are the result of social and economic change occurring in Israeli society in general, which the project reflected and from which it benefited.

Yet the project did deliver an impressive array of additional services. Thus, despite the shortcomings enumerated above, the neighbourhood-level planning processes, the institutional alignment, resource allocation, and project outputs were significant enough to underwrite the project's capacity to produce social and physical changes in the neighbourhoods (discussed in Chapter 11). Thus, investigation of the implementation process leaves no doubt that many of the programmes under the project's name can indeed be credited to it.

How successful has the implementation process of Project Renewal been in producing administrative institutional change? One of the factors proposed by Sabatier and Mazmanian (1981) for assessing success in implementation is the degree of behavioural change. If one considers the major departure from Israeli administrative structures and norms that the project called for, its implementation process can be seen as a qualified success. For residents of poor neighbourhoods, greater accessibility to government services through decentralization and public participation, better co-ordination among central and local government agencies, and the establishment of a precedent for neighbourhood-level planning can all be counted as substantive outcomes.

THE CHALLENGES OF THE 1990S

In retrospect, Project Renewal will likely be seen as Israel's major social and housing programme of the 1980s. By the end of the decade, the project had been phased out of many of the neighbourhoods. Although several new neighbourhoods were taken on in the late 1980s, and the project has not been officially terminated, by the early 1990s the project had lost its important place among public policies and its budgets were cut. The 1980s saw a general bridging of the ethnic cleavage between Jews of European origin and those of Asian–African origin (about 50% of Israel's Jewish population). The mainstreaming of the latter group is best expressed in its rising political representation on both the local and the national level. This bridging had been the social motivation behind the project and is now less of a burning issue.

The 1990s will likely be marked by new national goals in urban development and by new social processes. Mass immigration from Eastern Europe is expected to reach 200,000 in 1990 alone, and possibly one million (or more) over the next few years – to be absorbed into Israel's Jewish population of only 3.7 million. The immigrants are encouraged to occupy rental units in their first year while they attend language education and seek employment. In 1990 there was already a shortage of market-rent apartments, and it is expected to worsen over the coming years. New immigrants, whose educational level is considerably higher than the Israeli average, are already seeking accommodation in some of the distressed neighbourhoods, especially in the country's centre and in some of the peripheral development towns that have seen no newcomers for many years.

Meanwhile, the panic-stricken central government is formulating plans for stimulating the construction of new housing to reduce the huge anticipated gap in housing availability. From the vantage point of late 1990, the contours of the new policies are still sketchy.[14] Faced with a private construction sector that by 1990 has shrunk to a mere 14,000 housing starts, the government is tempted to consider a resumption of public-sector domination. In mid-1990, the Ministry of Housing issued tender for the first batch of 60,000 new housing units, over and above what the private sector was expected to construct. The Ministry also began the construction of infrastructure for temporary and prefabricated 'emergency' housing sites to meet the time gap in housing starts. At present, the government seems committed to a policy of relying mostly on the private construction sector, while providing public subsidies and incentives to speed up the process and reduce developers' risks. However, centralized planning is back in action as government planners hurry to identify possible sites for large new neighbourhoods and several new towns in various parts of the country (all within Israel proper).[15] Many sites are on the periphery of existing cities where land is more available.

The lessons of Project Renewal should be heeded at this time. The overwhelming majority of neighbourhoods needing regeneration were the result of public design and construction. It was the emphasis on quantity rather than quality, reliance on central government agencies, location in peripheral areas, and obliviousness to market preferences that created neighbourhoods in distress in the first place. Israeli land and housing policies have changed over the past two decades in that, one would hope, the repetition of earlier mistakes and the extent to which they were committed will be avoided. One important difference is apparent: today's new immigrants will insist on making their own decisions and expressing their market preferences. So far, the government seems committed to a policy of allowing immigrants to exercise freely their market preferences, using the subsidized mortgages available to them. To avoid the creation of the next decades' candidates for Project Renewal, public policy should not be tempted to resume large-scale initiatives for public-sector construction. Central planning should restrict itself to creating a more responsive planning and permitting system, to strategic planning, and to the provision of subsidies and other incentives. Public construction should be limited to sites where the market is not robust enough on its own, and to 'emergency housing'. The housing should exhibit diversified designs. Will Israeli public policy be able to resist the temptation of recentralization in meeting this new emergency?

NOTES

The empirical research on Project Renewal was carried out under the auspices of the S. Neaman Institute at the Technion, with joint financing by the Institute and the Jewish Agency for Israel. Some parts of this chapter are modified versions of selected parts from three articles previously published by the author (Alterman, 1987–1988, 1988, 1990b).

1. The pioneering work in the field was by Pressman and Wildavsky (1973). Major subsequent contributions are by Bardach (1977), Sabatier and Mazmanian (1981), and Barrett and Fudge (1981). For the author's analysis of approaches to implementation analysis, see Alterman (1982, 1983, 1987–1988, 1988).

2. For a comparative description of land policies in several other countries see Hallett (1988).

3. Most of the information here on land policy is based on the author's cumulative knowledge and her ongoing research in the field. There are as yet few publications available in English.

4. That ministry's name has changed many times in Israel's history, in various combinations with other ministries. Today it is called the Ministry of Construction and Housing.

5. The attractiveness of the loans has fluctuated depending on the centrally controlled level of interest for these loans and the relationship between average income and the cost of living index, to which these loans have been linked since the late 1970s. During the 1980s, the ostensibly subsidized loans have in many parts of the country turned out to be a quicksand trap, since the index rose more than the value of the apartment and faster than the family's salary. A new grassroots organization of citizens with onerous mortgages has recently emerged. It has successfully raised serious grievances against government mortgage policies and government insensitivity to the trapped families who received 'eligibility' public mortgages. See media coverage, such as the daily newspaper *Ha'aretz*, 6 April, 1990, p. B4.

6. This latest available statistic is from the Central Bureau of Statistics, Survey of Housing Conditions (1978). One can assume, however, that this statistic is somewhat higher today, given the policies encouraging purchase from the public housing companies, as well as the rising standard of living and the desire of most families to own equity. See Cannon (1989, p. 114).

7. This average is calculated for nine of the neighbourhoods, and excludes an inner-city Tel Aviv neighbourhood that is atypical because it was not created through public action.

8. The European or American reader should remember that average family size in Israel is considerably larger than in most European countries, at 3.3 in the Jewish sector and 5.6 in the Arab sector (Israel Central Bureau of Statistics, 1988).

9. Laws of the State of Israel, 1965 (available in English).

10. For the full discussion of the methods of analysis and the findings for each of these six principles, see Alterman and Hill (1985).

11. In each neighbourhood, each programme was classified as an outright substitution for an existing programme (a minority of cases), a partial substitution, or a full addition. A major conceptual problem concerned those programmes that were not actually in existence when the project entered the neighbourhood, but which would have likely been added in the normal course of events as they were in non-project neighbourhoods. This classification was based on a judgment of probabilities. It was not possible to analyse actual budgets owing to difficulties in following the accounting in a situation of high inflation and budget transfers. See Alterman and Hill (1985), Part 7.

12. Because of the different reporting systems of the agencies involved in Project Renewal, the numbers presented are actually a mixture of budgets and investment. Because the budgets were not all spent in full, the figures for actual investment are somewhat lower.

13. The full data are presented in Alterman and Frenkel (1985).

14. The information in this section is based on the May 1990 Government Decision on the Program for Immigrant Absorption, which, although not published, received extensive press coverage. Further information was provided by Uri Shoshani, Director of the Planning and Engineering Authority with the Ministry of Construction and Housing. This author is a member of the *ad hoc* national advisory committee on housing for new immigrants created in May 1990.

15. To date, all these new units have been within the borders of Israel proper; official policy is that none are to be constructed in the West Bank or Gaza Strip.

REFERENCES

ALEXANDER, E.R. (1980) Neighbourhood renewal in Israel: history and context. Working Paper no. 8, Samuel Neaman Institute for Advanced Studies in Science and Technology, Technion, Haifa.

ALEXANDER, E.R. (1984) After rationality, what? A review of responses to paradigm breakdown. *Journal of the American Planning Association*, **50**, 62–69.

ALEXANDER, E.R., R. ALTERMAN AND H. LAW YONE (1983) *Evaluating Plan Implementation: The National Planning System in Israel*. Progress in Planning monograph series, Vol. 20, Part 2. Oxford: Pergamon Press.

ALTERMAN, R. (1980) Decision-making in urban plan implementation: does the dog wag the tail or the tail wag the dog? *Urban Law and Policy*, **3** (1), 41–58.

ALTERMAN, R. (1982) Implementation analysis in urban and regional planning: toward a research agenda. In: P. Healey, G. McDougall and M. Thomas (eds) *Planning Theory: Prospects for the 1980s*, pp. 225–245. Oxford: Pergamon Press.

ALTERMAN, R. (1983) Implementation analysis: the contours of an emerging debate, review essay. *Journal of Planning Education and Research*, **2** (3) 63–65.

ALTERMAN, R. (1987–1988) Opening up the 'Black Box' in evaluating neighbourhood programs: the implementation process in Israel's Project Renewal. *Policy Studies Journal*, **16** (2), 347–361.

ALTERMAN, R. (1988) Implementing decentralization for neighbourhood regeneration: factors promoting or inhibiting success. *Journal of the American Planning Association*, **54** (4), 456–469.

ALTERMAN, R. (1989) Shortcomings in Israel's planning and building law, and ways of correcting them. Working paper published by The Center for Urban and Regional Studies, Technion—Israel Institute of Technology, Haifa. In Hebrew.

ALTERMAN, R. (1990a) Developer obligations for public services in Israel: law and social policy in a comparative perspective. *Florida State University Journal of Land Use and Environmental Law*, **5** (2).

ALTERMAN, R. (1990b) Implementation analysis of a national neighbourhood program: the case of Israel's Project Renewal. In: N. Carmon (ed.) *Neighbourhood Policy and Programs—Past and Present*. London: Macmillan.

ALTERMAN, R. and A. FRENKEL (1985) *The Outputs of Project Renewal: Services Delivered and Populations Benefited*. Vol. 3, Part II of *Comprehensive Evaluation of Israel's Project Renewal*. Research directors: R. Alterman, N. Carmon, and M. Hill, collaborating with A. Churchman. The Samuel Neaman Institute for Advanced Studies in Science and Technology, Technion—Israel Institute of Technology, Haifa. (Hebrew and English versions).

ALTERMAN, R. and M. HILL (1985) *Evaluation of the Institutional Structure, Planning and Implementation of Project Renewal*. Volume 1 of *Comprehensive Evaluation of Israel's Project Renewal*. Research directors: R. Alterman, N. Carmon and M. Hill, in collaboration with A. Churchman, M. Shechter and A. Frenkel. Final Report. The Samuel Neaman Institute for Advanced Studies in Science and Technology, Technion—Israel Institute of Technology, Haifa.

ALTERMAN, R. and M. HILL (1986) Land use planning in Israel. In: N. N. Patricios (ed.) *International Handbook on Land Use Planning*, pp. 119–150. Westport, CT: Greenwood Press.

ALTERMAN, R., N. CARMON and M. HILL (1984) Integrated evaluation: a synthesis of approaches to the evaluation of broad-aim social programs. *Socioeconomic Planning Sciences*, **18** (6), 381–389.

ALTERMAN, R., N. CARMON and M. HILL (1985) *Comprehensive Evaluation of Israel's Project Renewal*. The Samuel Neaman Institute for Advanced Studies in Science and Technology. (Hebrew and English versions).

ALTERMAN, R. et al. (1990) *Municipal Land Policy in Israel: Does It Exist?* Center for Urban and Regional Studies, Technion. In Hebrew.

BARDACH, E. (1977) *The Implementation Game*. Cambridge, MA: MIT Press.

BARRETT, S. and C. FUDGE, eds (1981) *Policy and Action*. London: Methuen.

BORUKHOV, E. (1980) Land policy in Israel. *Habitat International*, **4** (4/5/6), 505–515.

CARMON, N. (1989) *Neighborhood Rehabilitation in Israel — Evaluation of Outcomes.* Haifa: Samuel Neaman Books, Technion.

CARMON, N. and R. OXMAN (1986) Responsive public housing: an alternative for low-income families. *Environment and Behaviour*, **18** (2), 258–285.

CARTWRIGHT, T.J. (1973) Problems, solutions and strategies. *Journal of the American Institute of Planners*, May, 179–187.

CHURCHMAN, A. (1985) *Resident Participation in Project Renewal.* Vol. 2 of R. Alterman, N. Carmon and M. Hill (1984) Integrated evaluation: a synthesis of approaches to the evaluation of broad-aim social programs. *Socioeconomic Planning Sciences*, **18** (6), 381–389.

CHURCHMAN, A. (1987–88) Issues in resident participation: lessons from the Israeli experience. *Policy Studies Journal*, **16** (2), 290–299.

FRIEDEN, B.J. and M. KAPLAN (1987–1988) Model cities and Project Renewal: adjusting the strategy to the 1980s. *Policy Studies Journal*, **16** (2), 377–383.

HALLETT, G., ed. (1988) *Land and Housing Policies in Europe and the USA: A Comparative Analysis.* London: Routledge.

HOVAV, H. (1988) *Project Renewal: Implementation Report for 1987.* Jerusalem: Ministry of Construction and Housing and the Jewish Agency for Israel.

HUDSON, B. (1979) Comparison of current planning theories: counterparts and contradictions. *Journal of the American Planning Association*, Oct., 387–397.

Israel Central Bureau of Statistics (1987) *Construction in Israel.*

Israel Central Bureau of Statistics (1988) Annual Report.

LARSON, S. J. (1980) *Why Government Programs Fail: Improving Policy Implementation.* New York: Praeger.

MAZMANIAN, D. and P. A. SABATIER (1983) *Implementation and Public Policy.* Glenview, IL: Scott, Foresman.

PRESSMAN, J. and A. WILDAVSKY (1973) *Implementation.* Berkeley, CA: University of California Press.

RITTEL, H.W.J. and M. M. WEBBER (1972) Dilemmas in a general theory of planning. Working Paper 194, Institute of Urban and Regional Development, University of California, Berkeley.

RONDINELLI, D.A. (1983) Implementing decentralization programmes in Asia: a comparative analysis. *Public Administration and Development*, **3**, 181–207.

SABATIER, P.A. and D. MAZMANIAN (1981) The implementing of public policy: a framework of analysis. In: P. A. Sabatier and D. Mazmanian (eds) *Effective Policy Implementation*, pp. 3–35. Lexington, MA: Lexington Books.

SUSSKIND, L. and M. ELLIOTT (1983) Paternalism, conflict and coproduction: learning from citizen action and citizen participation in Western Europe. In: L. Susskind, M. Elliott *et al.* (eds) *Paternalism, Conflict and Coproduction: Learning from Citizen Action and Citizen Participation in Western Europe*, pp. 3–32. New York: Plenum Press.

11 PHYSICAL AND SOCIAL CHANGES ACHIEVED BY ISRAEL'S PROJECT RENEWAL

Shimon E. Spiro

Evaluations of social policies and programmes may be directed at many different questions but ultimately policymakers and the public want to know about outcomes. The most important questions for them are: Did the programme make a difference? Did renewal programmes improve the quality of life in the neighbourhoods and the life chances of their residents? Have processes of decline and deterioration been reversed?

These questions are not easily answered. Urban policy is made and implemented under rapidly changing conditions. The neighbourhoods that are the targets of these policies are subject to many powerful, often conflicting, influences. In the words of an observer of England's inner city policies:

> Even detailed studies of particular localities find it hard to establish either the direct impact of intentional urban policy, the unintended consequences of other policies, or the effects of national trends upon local areas. (Stewart, 1987, p. 136)

Similarly, an observer of American neighbourhood policies notes:

> It is often difficult to establish causal linkages between federal aid and improved neighborhood status. Exogenous events, like a change in the prime lending rate, an increase in the price of world oil, a decline in the trade balance, an increase in regional or metropolitan economic health, and related variations in migration rates have profound effects on the health of neighborhoods. (Kaplan, 1988, p. 5)

The same is true for Israel's Project Renewal and for similar programmes elsewhere.

The evaluation of outcomes has two distinct components: the measurement of change and the assignment of causality. The first involves the repeated application of social indicators as valid representations of the goals and objectives of the programme (e.g. residential density, migration balance, unemployment rates, school achievement levels). The availability of such indicators depends on the ongoing collection of data by government agencies. This, as is well known, is limited. Data on objective social indicators are often supplemented by the findings of opinion and attitude surveys to ascertain subjective change in the neighbourhood residents' sense of well being.

When evidence of subjective and objective change is available, the problem

170

remains of estimating the contribution of renewal to observed changes. Some evaluators compare data from programme sites with those from non-programme sites or with regional or national averages. Others attempt to link outcomes to implementation through case studies. The problems and limitations of these approaches are discussed in greater detail elsewhere in this book. The discussion that follows, however, shows that cautious assessments of outcomes may be feasible in spite of the limitations and difficulties.

Comprehensive neighbourhood renewal programmes have two types of expected outcomes: (1) changes in composite measures that reflect overall changes in the situation of the neighbourhood, such as expressions of neighbourhood attachment and in- and out-migration rates; and (2) changes in specific conditions or behaviours, such as housing conditions, school achievement levels, or delinquency rates.

Using Israel's Project Renewal as our case in point, we shall present and discuss findings of evaluations dealing with a number of composite measures, such as migration trends, population characteristics, and residents' self-image and expressions of satisfaction and attachment, and outcomes in two specific areas — education and housing.

CHANGES IN POPULATION COMPOSITION

One of the main goals of Project Renewal was to stabilize the neighbourhoods and reverse trends of selective out-migration. Changes for the better in the demographic characteristics of the population can be taken as evidence that the renewal neighbourhoods have become more attractive to the stronger population — to families who in the absence of renewal would have migrated to 'better' areas of their cities.

The most reliable source of demographic data is the decennial census. Baron et al. (1988) compared population characteristics in renewal areas in 1983 with the same characteristics in 1972. (Project Renewal was declared in 1977 and started in 1979.) The study included only neighbourhoods that had been part of the project as of 1981. Table 1 shows the marked 'upgrading' of the population between 1972 and 1983. In 1983 the residents of renewal neighbourhoods lived in smaller households, were better educated, enjoyed higher incomes, and more of them worked in prestigious occupations. On the other hand, the proportion of the elderly grew considerably.

These changes can be attributed to any one or more of three possible processes: (1) direct effects of education and income-enhancing programmes that were part of Project Renewal; (2) indirect effects of the project through the enhanced attractiveness of the neighbourhoods to residents with smaller families and higher socioeconomic status; and (3) intergenerational changes and other demographic and economic trends characteristic of the country as a whole, such as declining family size, better schooling, and rising incomes.

From Table 1 we see that trends among the Jewish population of Israel were similar to those recorded in renewal neighbourhoods. Furthermore Baron et al. (1988) compared renewal areas with other areas that in 1972 had similar characteristics. In Table 1 we see that the improvement in control

Table 1. Socioeconomic and demographic characteristics of renewal and control neighbourhoods and of the Jewish population of Israel, 1972 and 1983 (percentages and percentage change)

	Renewal areas			Control areas			Jewish population		
	1972	1983	Change	1972	1983	Change	1972	1983	Change
Households with six persons or more	25.1	14.1	−43.8	24.5	15.6	−36.3	14.1	9.7	−31.2
Elderly (65+)	6.5	9.4	+44.6	7.3	8.4	+15.1	7.7	10.1	+31.2
Adults (15+) without formal schooling	18.8	14.3	−23.9	17.4	12.0	−31.0	13.1	9.0	−31.3
Academic, technical and managerial occupations	10.1	13.1	+29.7	10.6	18.6	+75.5	19.9	27.1	+36.2

Sources: Baron *et al.* (1988), Central Bureau of Statistics (1975, 1985).

neighbourhoods was, on the whole, not less than the improvement in renewal neighbourhoods. The study concludes that Project Renewal had no effect on population composition and that the changes must be attributed to other economic and demographic developments.

This conclusion is not necessarily warranted. We note that in 1972 the 'control' neighbourhoods were, on the average, slightly better off than the renewal neighbourhoods. It is quite plausible to assume that between 1972 and the beginnings of Project Renewal in 1979 the gap between the two groups of neighbourhoods widened, and that precisely for this reason the control group was not included in the project. It might well be that Project Renewal did have a positive impact on the neighbourhoods, that it reversed processes of deterioration, and prevented a larger gap between renewal and control neighbourhoods, and that the positive effects of the project have compensated partly for the negative developments in the years immediately preceding it. Thus, all we can say is that the comparison of 1972 and 1983 census data provides evidence for positive change, but does not allow us to attribute this change to the effects of the project.

MIGRATION BALANCE

More direct evidence of the possible effect of Project Renewal on the attractiveness of the neighbourhoods comes from migration data based on the 1983 census, which included a question about change of address since 1978. Baron *et al.* (1988) analysed responses to this question and found that during this period, renewal neighbourhoods, as a group, lost 3.7% of their population, while the control neighbourhoods remained stable. Furthermore, they found that in both renewal and control neighbourhoods the migrants, both those moving into the neighbourhood and those moving out of it, represented a stronger population than the stable residents. They had better education, held more prestigious occupations, were younger, had smaller families, and enjoyed higher incomes. In control neighbourhoods there was no difference in the characteristics of in- and out-migrants. In renewal neighbourhoods those who left were slightly 'stronger' than those who moved in.

Again, we can only guess as to what the migration trends would have been in the absence of Project Renewal, but the least we can say is that the statistics provide no basis for the claim that the project made the neighbourhoods more attractive to strong families.

ATTITUDES TOWARDS THE NEIGHBOURHOOD

The residents of renewal areas may be the best judges of the impact of renewal efforts. Thus, one way to measure outcomes is to issue public opinion surveys asking residents to evaluate the neighbourhood: its conditions, amenities, and services. When such surveys are repeated over time, changes in findings may reflect the impact of the project (unless, of course, there are other, more plausible explanations for them).

A series of public opinion surveys conducted in renewal areas throughout Israel in 1983, 1986, and 1989 allows us to follow changes in attitudes over time and attempt to relate them to Project Renewal. The samples interviewed were quite large: 2,462 and 2,173 in 20 neighbourhoods in 1983 and 1986, respectively; 3,962 in 15 neighbourhoods in 1989. Sampling methods and the wording of questions differed among surveys, but these differences had only a minor effect on the findings (Spiro and Feit-Stern, 1990).

The 20 neighbourhoods surveyed in 1983 included 15 that had been part of Project Renewal from the beginning and five that were added in 1982. Work had progressed considerably in the veteran group, but had hardly started in the newer group. Differences in attitudes and opinions between these two types of subsamples may be taken to represent project effects. Table 2 presents a few examples from among dozens of questions designed to elicit feelings of attachment to or alienation from the neighbourhood, as well as satisfaction with public services and different aspects of life in the neighbourhood.

On almost all items residents of veteran renewal areas expressed higher levels of satisfaction and stronger feelings of attachment to their neighbourhoods than respondents in new renewal areas. A more detailed analysis

Table 2. Changes (in percent) in expressions of neighbourhood attachment among residents of Israel's renewal areas, 1983, 1986, and 1989

	1983 New	Veteran	Total	1986	1989
Satisfied with neighbourhood	46	62	59	58	50
Satisfied with schools	41	50	49	48	48
Satisfied with flat	52	53	53	67	69
Plan to stay in near future	72	79	77	78	80
Stay, even if had a choice	45	51	50	46	*
Area enhances prestige	8	9	8	9	9
Area reduces prestige	28	28	28	29	36

* This question was not included in the 1989 survey.

showed that differences in location and demographic characteristics between the two types of neighbourhoods could not account for the differences in attitudes and that the most plausible explanation of these differences would be the impact of Project Renewal (ICEPR, 1984).

The cross-sectional analysis in Table 2 is supported by a longitudinal local study conducted in five renewal areas in Tel Aviv by the Municipal Center for Economic and Social Research (Harpaz *et al.*, 1983). An attitude survey administered to a city-wide sample in 1977 was replicated in five renewal areas in 1983. Harpaz *et al.* report that, compared with 1977, the 1983 renewal respondents tended to be more satisfied with their housing conditions, with the quality of public services, and with the neighbourhood in general. Similar, but much weaker, changes occurred in two 'control' neighbourhoods and in the city as a whole.

The positive effects of renewal were only partly sustained over time (Table 2). We note that expressions of the neighbourhoods and attachment to them declined between 1983 and 1989. We know, however, that thanks to Project Renewal, the quality of life in most of the renewal neighbourhoods improved during this period. The most plausible explanation for these findings is that the initial achievements of Project Renewal raised expectations for change that were only partly realized. Thus, in 1986 and 1989 neighbourhood conditions were evaluated by yardsticks more severe than the ones used in 1983. Be this as it may, the best interpretation of the findings presented in Table 2 would be to say that Project Renewal had an immediate positive impact on resident satisfaction with various aspects of the neighbourhood and attachment to it. The positive changes, however, were not reinforced over time.

One of the main failures of Project Renewal was its inability to enhance neighbourhood prestige, as seen by the residents. The survey question was: 'When you meet strangers and tell them where you live, do you feel this adds or detracts from your standing in their eyes?' The proportion feeling that their address added to their prestige remained constant and very low, whereas the proportion of those who felt that it detracted grew from 28% in 1983 (with no difference between veteran and new renewal areas) to 36% in 1989. Again, changes in sampling cannot account for the decline (Spiro and Feit-Stern, 1990). The most likely explanation is that either the label 'renewal area' may have some stigma attached to it or the project raised the consciousness level of the residents and made them more aware of the low status of their neighbourhoods.

HOUSING CONDITIONS

Housing improvement is one of the main goals of neighbourhood renewal programmes. In Project Renewal a large share of resources was devoted to a programme of home enlargement loans to owner-occupiers. Evaluations of the home enlargement programme (Lerman, 1988; Spiro and Laor, 1988) reported high rates of participation and considerable gains in space, comfort, and property values. Lerman, in a study in three renewal areas, found that before enlargement 67% of the participating households lived at a density of

Table 3. Housing conditions in renewal and control neighbourhoods and among the Jewish population of Israel, 1972 and 1983 (percentages and percentage change)

	Renewal areas			Control areas			Jewish population		
	1972	1983	Change	1972	1983	Change	1972	1983	Change
Living in small flats (two rooms or less)	50.5	30.6	−39.4	51.4	26.8	−47.9	39.6	24.5	−38.1
Density of 2.5 or more persons per room	24.3	5.2	−78.6	25.4	5.4	−78.7	12.7	2.6	−79.0
Owner-occupied flats	42.0	54.0	+28.6	*	58.6	*	63.8	72.9	+14.3

* No information for 1972.
Sources: Baron et al. (1988), Central Bureau of Statistics (1975, 1985).

17.5 m^2, or less, per person. After enlargement only 22.1% of the same families reported such density.

We know, from various studies in Israel (Carmon, 1989) and elsewhere (Seek, 1983), that households invest in home enlargement with and without public assistance. The question is whether the number of home enlargements and the ensuing improvement in living conditions were greater than might have been expected without the intervention of the project. Again Baron et al. (1988) shed some light on these issues. They compared census data for 1972 and 1983 and found considerable improvement in three key indicators: the proportion living in small flats (two rooms or less), the proportion living under crowded conditions (2.5 or more persons per room), and the proportion owning their apartment (Table 3).

Once again, their findings raise doubts as to the impact of the project. While housing conditions improved in renewal neighbourhoods, they improved even more in the control neighbourhoods. In both types of neighbourhood, at least some of the improvement can be attributed to country-wide trends — a general rise in the standard of living, home improvement assistance available to all citizens, a country-wide campaign to sell flats located in public housing estates to their residents, decline in family size, and a move away from multi-family or multi-generational households.

The lack of any advantage of renewal over control neighbourhoods can be explained in a number of ways. One would be the inevitability of home improvement. If loans and subsidies provided by the project had not been available, residents might have used their own resources or applied to universal assistance programmes to achieve the same level of improvement.

Another explanation refers to the possible diffusion of programme effects, mostly through resource displacement, an inclination on the part of government agencies to transfer some of their resources from renewal neighbourhoods to distressed areas that are not part of the project. Alterman and Hill (1985) estimated that in 40% of the programmes that were carried out under Project Renewal some resources were transferred to other areas (see also Chapter 10). If this is true, it means that at least some

175

of the improvement in 'control' areas can be attributed to indirect effects of Project Renewal.

Finally, there remains the possibility (to which we referred above) that in the absence of Project Renewal the negative trend that had characterized the neighbourhoods would have continued and consequently residents would not have found it worth their while to invest in home improvement. According to this view the fact that the achievements in housing in renewal neighbourhoods were similar to those in the slightly better-off control areas (see Table 1) can be seen as a success of Project Renewal.

EDUCATION

Unlike housing, where one finds a direct link between inputs and outcomes (home enlargement equals reduced crowding), in education the relationship between inputs and outcomes is much more tenuous. Longer school hours, more teachers, and modernized facilities do not necessarily lead to better achievements and enhanced life chances.

Evaluations of Project Renewal documented a high level of investment in neighbourhood schools, so that the inputs into schools in renewal areas now surpass those enjoyed by typical middle-class schools. The project corrected long-standing educational deprivation in low-income areas (Carmon, 1989). Higher inputs included smaller classes; longer school days; more counselling; more extracurricular activities; computer-aided instruction; and improved libraries, laboratories, and sports facilities. All of this meant a real improvement in the pupils' quality of life, reflected in growing satisfaction with the local schools as expressed in attitude surveys (see Table 2).

Periodic standardized achievement testing is only now being introduced into Israeli schools. Occasionally such tests were conducted locally but the results were usually not available to evaluation teams. Thus, we do not have reliable data on changes in achievement levels, and must rely on the opinions of experts. Those evaluating Project Renewal concur that the educational inputs were not well enough targeted and focused to create a real difference in achievement levels and in the life chances of pupils (ICEPR, 1984).

More recently, two small towns that were part of Project Renewal participated in an experiment designed to turn the local elementary schools into 'effective schools' (Bashi et al., 1990), an educational programme organized not around inputs but around outcomes — carefully specified learning objectives in key areas such as reading, comprehension and arithmetic. The authors report significant gains in achievement tests at the conclusion of the experiment, and evidence of continued momentum one year later. Additional studies are needed to assess the long-term effects of this programme, but the results seem to indicate that the objective of enhanced school achievement is obtainable.

IMPACT ON NEIGHBOURHOODS

Did renewal change the neighbourhoods? It would seem that Project Renewal achieved more than some critics are willing to admit, but less than the ambitious goals declared at the initiation of the project. The project's massive investments in physical infrastructure (parks, pavements, street lighting), in public amenities (community and day care centres), in the improvement of public services (computer-aided instruction in the schools, home care for the elderly), and in home improvement undoubtedly enhanced the quality of life in renewal neighbourhoods. Data collected in a number of local case studies (Carmon, 1989) lend credence to the argument that much of the improvement would not have occurred without the project.

On the other hand, it is almost impossible to detect the expected effects of Project Renewal through the analysis of changes in objective or subjective social indicators. The analysis of changes in population composition and in housing conditions showed impressive progress in renewal areas, but similar (in some respects even greater) progress occurred in other low-income areas that were not part of Project Renewal. We have offered a few alternative explanations for the findings reported by Baron et al. (1988), but we have to accept the fact that the expected impact of Project Renewal is not reflected in the available social statistics.

Furthermore, although in the short run the project seemed to have a positive effect on the residents' attitudes towards their neighbourhoods, these effects were not maintained over time. Residents of renewal areas may be caught in a trap. A number of studies have shown that the negative attitudes of residents in low-income areas towards their neighbourhoods are determined more by the low opinion they hold of their neighbours than by the neighbourhood's physical appearance or the quality of services (Yuchtman-Yaar et al., 1979; Spiro and Laor, 1988). Thus, the real achievements of Project Renewal would not be reflected in the feelings and self-image of the residents, as long as the project does not change the composition of the population. This change, however, would be contrary to the mandate of Project Renewal (and similar programmes), which is the improvement of neighbourhood conditions without removal and replacement of the population. We may have to accept the fact that no amount of improvement will change the low prestige and self-image of residents of renewal areas.

The results of attitude surveys may also reflect a gap between the emphases of the project and the priorities of the residents. Unemployment increased in Israel considerably during the 1980s and some of the renewal areas were affected most severely. Project Renewal invested only a minor part of its resources in attempts to upgrade the local labour force and improve employment opportunities. Neighbourhood boundaries are largely irrelevant to employment issues, and neighbourhood-oriented programmes may not be the right instruments to deal with them. This failure to address employment problems may explain some of the decline in satisfaction and self-image.

Furthermore, Project Renewal was unable to solve problems for which no effective social technology is available, such as delinquency and drug abuse. Lack of progress in these areas may offset real gains in physical appearance and in the quality of services.

Project Renewal, far more than other neighbourhood rehabilitation programmes in various countries during the last three decades, has been extensively studied and evaluated. The findings of various published and unpublished evaluations have provided us with an opportunity to formulate a balanced evaluation of the achievements of the project. Many questions are still unresolved and will remain so until more extensive local and international data become available. As with so many other ambitious social programmes, the reader will have to consider the evidence and decide whether the Project Renewal glass is half full or half empty.

REFERENCES

ALTERMAN, R. and M. HILL (1985) *Evaluation of the Institutional Structure, Planning and Implementation of Project Renewal.* Volume 1 of *Comprehensive Evaluation of Israel's Project Renewal.* Research directors: R. Alterman, N. Carmon and M. Hill, in collaboration with A. Churchman, M. Shechter and A. Frenkel. Final Report. The Samuel Neaman Institute for Advanced Studies in Science and Technology, Technion – Israel Institute of Technology, Haifa.

BARON, M., U. BAR-ZION, N. CARMON, and H. GAVISH (1988) *The Influence of Project Renewal on SocioEconomic Gaps and on Migration Trends.* Haifa: The Samuel Neaman Institute for Advanced Studies in Science and Technology, Technion – Israel Institute of Technology, Haifa.

BASHI, J., Z. SASS, R. KATZIR and I. MARGOLIN (1990) *Effective Schools – From Theory to Practice.* Jerusalem: The van Leer Institute.

CARMON, N. (1989) *Neighborhood Rehabilitation in Israel – Evaluation of Outcomes.* Haifa: Eked Shmuel Neaman. The Samuel Neaman Institute for Advanced Studies in Science and Technology, Technion – Israel Institute of Technology, Haifa. In Hebrew.

Central Bureau of Statistics (1975, 1985) *Census of Population and Housing Publication.* Jerusalem 1975 and 1985.

HARPAZ, H., M.HADAD and M. FADIDA (1983) *The Effects of Project Renewal in Tel Aviv–Yafo on Residents' Change of Attitudes.* Tel Aviv: Tel Aviv-Yafo Municipality Center for Social and Economic Research.

ICEPR (The International Committee for the Evaluation of Project Renewal) (1984) *Report for 1983.* Tel Aviv.

KAPLAN, M. (1988) American neighborhood policies – mixed results and uneven evaluations. Paper presented at the 25th European Congress of the Regional Science Association, Stockholm, 23–26 August.

LERMAN, R.I. (1988) Project Renewal's home enlargement program – its rationale, utilization, costs and benefits, *Megamot. A Behavioral Science Quarterly,* **31** (3–4), 409–427. In Hebrew.

SEEK, N.H. (1983) Adjusting housing consumption – improve or move. *Urban Studies,* **20** (4), 455–469.

SPIRO, S.E. and G. LAOR (1988) Effects of home improvement on residential mobility and family life. Discussion paper 34 4–88. Tel Aviv: The Sapir Center for Development, Tel Aviv University. In Hebrew.

SPIRO, S.E. and S. FEIT-STERN (1990) Selected Issues in Project Renewal – Equity, Power and Prestige (unpublished). In Hebrew.

STEWART, M. (1987) Ten years of inner city policy. *Town Planning Review,* **58** (2), 129–145.

YUCHTMAN-YAAR, E., S.E. SPIRO and J. RAM (1979) Reactions to rehousing – loss of community or frustrated aspirations? *Urban Studies,* **16**, 113–119.

12 THE UPGRADING OF LARGE-SCALE HOUSING ESTATES IN HUNGARY

Anna Gáspár and Peter Birghoffer

Following the Second World War, changes in industry and agriculture and the ensuing population migration set an extraordinary task for the Hungarian building industry in terms of the construction of large industrial facilities, agricultural buildings, and, primarily, for mass housing and town planning. Both the state-owned design companies and the contractors were unable to cope with the quantity of buildings needed and the new building technologies that had to be learned. This situation was typical in other Eastern European socialist countries.

Although the provision of housing was considered a state task up to the end of the 1960s, the government at the time was not much involved in the construction of single-family houses in agricultural areas, where privately financed building dominated new construction (Table 1). Direct state intervention provided only one-third of the newly built housing; state subsidies were concentrated on council flats, co-operative flats, and houses built for state workers. In the mid-1960s, factories emerged for the production of prefabricated system-built units, which resulted in a very centralized building industry with a monopoly in large-scale state housing construction.

The post-war building activity in housing can be characterized by the dominance of two, extremely different building forms: flats in high-rise estates and single-family houses. Today's Hungarian homes (building stock)

Table 1. Distribution of dwellings (all types of housing) by age

Year built	Hungary No. of dwellings	%	Budapest No. of dwellings	%
Up to 1899	411,000	12.3	123,000	15
1900–19	378,000	9.6	105,000	12.9
1920–44	669,000	17.1	173,000	21.1
1945–59	482,000	12.3	54,000	6.7
1960–69	637,000	16.2	99,000	12.0
1970–79	889,000	22.7	154,000	18.9
1980–87	381,000	9.9	107,000	13.0
Total	3,923,000	100	816,000	100
	777,000 belong (rented) to the state		412,000 belong to the state	
	3,146,000 are private		404,000 are private	

are of three forms: new dwelling estates (built since 1950), private one-family houses or apartments (built since 1960), and 50–100-year-old blocks of flats in towns, especially in the capital, Budapest.

About 50% of the Hungarian building stock (1.8 million flats) was built before 1960. Of this, approximately 800,000 buildings are obsolete; they belong to the state, and are rented mostly by lower-income tenants. These flats (400,000 in Budapest), found mainly in urban areas, are mostly in very poor physical condition. According to state housing policy, these old flats constitute a necessary low-rent housing provision for a segment of the population, but low rents and state ownership together in reality mean inappropriate and derelict housing conditions. (Almost all renewal efforts towards this housing have been made through private initiatives and funding.) The government acknowledged that many of these buildings were unsafe, and in 1978 restoration activity was initiated in Budapest, taking into consideration the financial, technical, and social aspects of the problem.

STATE HOUSING ACTIVITY

Housing conditions in Hungary have improved during the past 30 years. Through direct state support and intervention, different technologies and styles were introduced. The newer housing stock ranges from the semi-traditional 'socialist–realist' style to the products of the prefabricated, system-built technologies. The new blocks of flats have greatly improved the general quality of the dwelling stock: all the flats are supplied with amenities, modern heating, and most have two rooms (Table 2).

With the introduction of prefabricated elements in the 1960s came, according to Hungary's first 15-year plan in housing, a change in housing location. The new estates were concentrated in the underdeveloped outskirts of towns and cities. Of Hungary's total of four million dwellings, a quarter are of new construction, having been built after 1950. Half of these are on housing estates.

The basic principles involved in the planning of the housing estates aimed at providing alternatives to and overcoming the problems of the older urban dwellings. In older urban districts the quality of the housing stock (as originally built) varied considerably from building to building. By contrast, uniformity of quality and value has been sought in the new estates. New construction regulations were introduced to eliminate the ventilation problems found in the older urban districts where dwellings were not properly sited. The environmental problems found in the older districts because of the proximity of houses to various economic functions (small trade, goods transportation, delivery) have been avoided by guaranteeing that the dwelling function is predominant in the vicinity of housing estates.

In spite of these efforts to avoid traditional urban housing problems, a multitude of other difficulties have arisen as a result of the failure to maintain the traditional values of the older urban areas. This has proved to be a serious error.

Many of the residents of the new housing estates have not been able to adapt either physiologically or psychologically to their dwellings and

Table 2. **Distribution of dwellings (all types of housing) by number of rooms and by infrastructure**

	1949	1960	1970	1980	1988*
Number of dwellings (thousands)	2,467	2,758	3,122	3,542	3,923
Dwellings with					
1 room	1,739	1,729	1,440	973	741
2 rooms	606	900	1,348	1,720	1,887
3 rooms or more	122	129	334	849	1,295
Total number of rooms					
(thousands)	3,480	4,067	5,120	7,065	8,657
Average number of rooms per					
dwelling	1.4	1.5	1.6	2.0	2.2
Inhabitants per 100 rooms	265	245	202	152	122
Ratio of dwellings (%) supplied					
with:					
water conduit	17.0	22.7	35.1	62.7	78.1
flush toilet	12.6	16.1	26.4	51.4	67.8
gas-tubing	7.0	10.6	16.0	25.1	30.2
sewage conduit	–	–	36.8	65.4	79.4
public drainage	–	–	26	35	39
bathroom, wash-basin					
alcove	10.1	17.0	30.8	58.5	74.2
Location of dwellings					
(thousands) with above					
amenities					
Budapest	–	536	626	727	816
Other towns	–	–	919	1,218	1,479
Villages	–	–	1,977	1,600	1,628

immediate environment. Because the residents did not regard the buildings as their own, they could not be persuaded to do anything to make their environment more pleasant and home-like.

The estates were erected under pressure of an acute housing demand (and the 'show-window' policy of socialist society), but in conditions of limited financial support. These huge buildings were constructed according to strict guidelines regulating materials, technology, and implementation. The flats were planned with the sole aim of housing what was considered to be the typical family (a young couple and two children).

Because of the uniformity of this new construction, settlements lost their individuality and the inhabitants lost their faith in contemporary estates. By the late 1970s, as the failure of the housing estates became a much debated topic in the press, the government began to consider long-term measures for the reconstruction, maintenance, and revitalization of urban areas, paying particular attention to the upgrading of large-scale housing estates. These measures were based on the physical, technical, and social aspects of urban housing problems and the housing experiments of the previous 30 years.

ANNA GÁSPÁR AND PETER BIRGHOFFER
TECHNICAL AND SOCIAL PROBLEMS OF HOUSING ESTATES

By 1989 there were nearly 500,000 prefabricated flats in Hungary, housing 12–14% of the country's population. Calculated at present prices, their gross value is approximately Ft 500 billion (Ft 64 is approximately equal to U.S. $1). The majority of these flats have been built in the past twenty years, though 33,700 are older. Two-thirds of the flats are privately owned; one-third are owned by councils.

This housing affects the appearance of Hungarian towns, sometimes determining it. Thus, the operation and maintenance of these dwellings have become an important part of the district's management. Local government is responsible for organizing and financing the operation and maintenance of these houses. Generally, the current state of most panel houses, which compares unfavourably with the ideal, has had a negative impact on public morale.

Domestic and international experience, research measurements, and tests have proved that after 10 to 20 years of use, these buildings suffer physical deterioration and their inhabitants social decline. From 1990 the renewal of some 12,000 to 25,000 panel flats and building units will be necessary every year. Mass housing, which aimed at the elimination of shortages, has had many problematic consequences. Unfortunately the resources are not available at present for the continuous development and maintenance of these housing estates.

Technically, these buildings are plagued by failures in the panel joints and flat roofs, leaks resulting from cracked panels and other causes, mould growth inside the dwellings, lack of heat and sound insulation, and the poor installation of vents, pipes, and fittings.

The negative social impact of these dwellings has many causes. The flats are small, especially the kitchens, relative to the usual number of occupants, and they cannot adequately accommodate large families or extended families of several generations. There is a uniformity in their external appearance. Public areas are neglected and parking areas are few. The occupants are overwhelmed by the size of the buildings and are inconvenienced by the lack of services. Located in the urban outskirts, these estates pose transportation problems for their occupants. The lack of adequate sound insulation threatens the occupants' privacy and tranquillity.

Any attempts at ending the decline must address both internal and external conditions on the estates. The individual flats can be transformed internally through layout changes, the linking of flats, and the modernization of fittings. The buildings can be improved through the addition of lofts, high-pitched roofs, and shops, and the improvement of façades. Services must be adjusted according to changing needs. Improvement requires additional parking, parks and garages, and living space for invalids and others with special needs.

POSSIBLE APPROACH TO THE UPGRADING OF HOUSING ESTATES

The Hungarian government has initiated a programme to renovate many of

182

these deteriorating buildings over a 25-year period, from 1990 to 2015 (Fig. 1).

Although the renovation and improvement in the quality of the housing estates is only in its preliminary phase, important results have already been achieved. A conference in Budapest in October 1985 of the International Federation for Housing and Planning (IFHP) dealt with the subject of redeveloping housing estates built in the post-war period. At this conference, Hungarian urbanists presented the rehabilitation efforts of the housing estate at Landorhegy, Zalaegerszeg.

It is planned that within a 25-year overall renovation cycle on the estate, the dwellings are to be overhauled every 5 years with all necessary repair work being carried out. The heating system, lifts, and other items of architectural engineering are to be carefully examined for repair. The order of repairs should be determined by the urgency of the work.

Attention was paid to the janitorial staff and their efforts to make the lives of tenants more comfortable. Regarded as the providers of community services, the janitors have free accommodation. Their tasks include collecting the rent, cleaning the buildings, and locking up for the night. They generally have a good relationship with the tenants. They try to see to the tenants' complaints, as well as make the tenants observe the basic rules of coexistence.

Built-in television antennas were installed on the buildings. These not only provide better programme reception, but also make it possible for the repair team to have a system control panel in their office. In this way, breakdowns in the water, gas, or electrical supply or faults with the lifts can be signalled immediately.

Other plans for improving the living conditions at the Landorhegy housing estate included: converting storage areas into hobby rooms, using the flat roofs as additional common space, turning unused space into recreation areas, and helping the population organize local cultural centres.

On the basis of research on Hungarian housing, a national competition entitled 'Upgrading of New Housing Estates' was announced in 1985, requesting complex solutions to the urban, architectural, infrastructural, and operational problems that have been the source of social decline on the estates. The competitors were directed to consider all aspects of the rehabilitation of buildings and flats as they related to two characteristic housing estates in Budapest and Gyor. The results of the competition were popularized through the publication of a summary and a design reference book.

Proposals for improving the buildings' ground included:

- the transformation of the barren, unused areas between the buildings into multi-purpose areas or gardens;
- the introduction of hillside planting and security systems and the establishment of 'stressed' points;
- the maintenance of outdoor areas through determining the correct proportion of the different proprietary forms: the private areas (mainly ground floors) belonging to the flats, the half-community

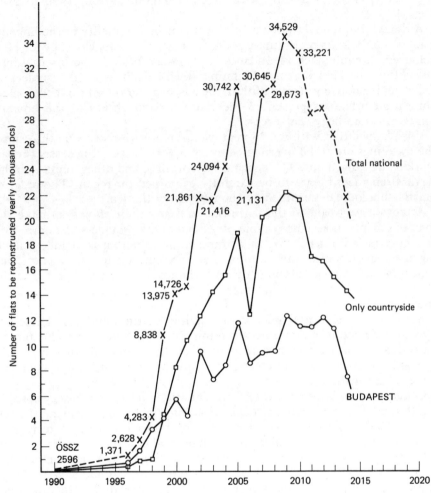

Fig. 1. Number of flats built using panel technology scheduled for reconstruction between 1990 and 2015 in Hungary.

areas handled by the different groups and societies, and the common areas belonging to the whole housing estate, to be managed by a town management organ; and the

- expansion of parking areas through the construction of multi-level or partly green-belt parking garages and the transformation of the traffic system by building new roads for mixed communication (i.e. combination for pedestrian and car traffic use).

Proposals for improving the buildings' exteriors included:

- changing the function of, or enlarging, the lower levels to accommodate small shops and catering units on the entrance side of the buildings;

- increasing the square footage of the flats by building in front to allow for the widening of kitchens, the making of winter gardens, or the enlarging of terraces and private gardens;
- accentuating the buildings' entrances;
- raising the roofs of the buildings to accommodate roof gardens, enlargement of the top flats, and the development of community areas; and
- further improving the appearance of buildings through the use of heat-insulating covering, colouring the façade, and accentuating doors and windows.

The flats themselves could be improved by:

- restructuring the living space (typically two-room flats) to diminish the homogeneous flat structure through reorganizing inner rooms, connecting certain rooms between flats, and flat-joining so that the units could accommodate multi-generation families; and
- enlarging the living space by building in front of the façade or by building on at roof level.

The ideas and solutions proposed by the winning entries redirected the attention of experts; for example, suggestions for raising roofs, establishing small shops on the ground floor, etc. They began to consider the issues of differentiated management, the technical questions of renewal, the relationship between inhabitants and designers, the enlargement and transformation of flats, the connection between housing policy and the housing market, the relationship of the estates to their townscapes, and the new developments emerging from changing ownership patterns.

It is difficult, however, to determine a uniform upgrading policy for all housing estates. It has become clear that the interrelationship of dwelling units, families, and the larger social and urban environment differs and this affects the changes that must be introduced. At the same time, however, we are planning standardized improvements to the heating, lighting, water, and drainage systems of those buildings constructed by industrialized building methods because of the uniformity of their original design.

Current housing policy is also a part of the renewal process. Only some of the flats in housing estates can be enlarged. It is clear today that the standard $50\,m^2$ flat is suitable for four people only when the family has small children. These small units can meet the growing demand for housing among recently married couples with low incomes. The small, fully equipped flat can also provide comfortable accommodation for the retired, for whom homes for the elderly are suitable only in extreme situations. It is more natural for the elderly to live among the younger generations.

Another variable that must be taken into consideration when launching a rehabilitation effort is the question of ownership—whether the units are state-owned rental flats, co-operatives, or owner-occupied flats—and how these ownership patterns affect attitudes toward the housing estate. Rehabilitation efforts must begin by asking inhabitants about their needs and encouraging their helpful participation.

Thought must also be given to the transitional accommodation of residents during rehabilitation. Temporary flats can be built attached to the existing medium-high and multi-storey buildings.

Uniformity among the estates can be achieved in the upgrading and maintenance of the buildings technical systems irrespective of the ownership patterns. By contrast, the renewal of the interior, the rehabilitation of façades and grounds (streets, roofs, play areas, parking places, resting areas), and the creation of service or public areas on the ground floor should and must be determined according to local demands and financial means and with the help of the residents.

CONCLUSIONS

State involvement in housing policy has undergone massive changes since the Second World War. After the war the government was heavily involved in building new residential estates, while neglecting the existing building stock and discouraging private building activity. In the early 1960s the government permitted private building activity and from 1970 subsidized these efforts for the country's growing population. In 1978, attention was first paid to the renewal of the old, neglected building stock. In 1983 the government reduced its involvement in new construction and began supporting the social aspects of the population's housing needs. Private construction was encouraged more than in the past. In the 1990s the government will mostly cease building large estates and will gradually reduce its support of the renewal, reconstruction, and upgrading of the new estates because of economic constraints. Private initiatives are expected to increase in the light of the real need for improved housing.

PART **II** DILEMMAS OF
EVALUATION AND
TRANSFERABILITY

13 EVALUATION OF NEIGHBOURHOOD SOCIAL DEVELOPMENT POLICY[1]

Jean-Paul Tricart

The evaluation of social policies has become fashionable, if the speeches at professional gatherings are any indication. Use of the word, however, has led to many misunderstandings. The reason why the word 'evaluation' is used so much, to the point that it has become the key word of social policy in the 1980s, is that its significance remains imprecise and can encompass a whole range of diverse meanings corresponding to the many expectations and concerns of these social policies. Beyond fashion and beyond the ideological controversies about the legitimacy of the welfare state, the interest in evaluation corresponds to the doubt or disenchantment that has developed concerning the efficiency and relevance of social policies. The lasting economic crisis of the 1980s resulted in increasing poverty, insecurity, and marginalization for broad parts of the population, and therefore revealed the failure of the doctrine and know-how of traditional institutions in charge of social problems. These failings and uncertainties have undoubtedly transformed evaluation into a challenge for administrators, political leaders, and intervention professionals.

While it is necessary and legitimate to assess the efficiency and relevance of social policies, it is undeniably a difficult task because of the complexity and opacity of these policies, but also because of the limited methodology and practical experience in this field.

This chapter reports on attempts made in France during the last few years to promote the evaluation of neighbourhood social development policies as a way of identifying usable approaches. Within this context, the chapter first establishes a working definition of 'evaluation' to avoid from the outset false debate and confusion; secondly, it considers the problems inherent in the evaluation of local social development programmes; and finally, it discusses the propositions that have been advanced and the experiments that have been initiated in evaluating social programmes.

WHAT WE MEAN BY EVALUATION

'To evaluate a policy is to recognize and measure its own effects' (La Documentation française, 1986a). This definition, from a recent administrative report, stresses three elements. It is a definition that insists on the integration of evaluation within a scientific approach; that insists on the clear identification of the policy that is being evaluated; and that stresses that statistics constitute only one dimension of the evaluation process. Let us examine these three elements.

The evaluation of a policy entails a commitment to a scientific approach. This should be obvious. Many of the debates, however, on the evaluation process centre more on the particular circumstances under which an evaluation is being commissioned, produced, or used, rather than on the rigorous rules integral to a scientific approach. The scientific approach is ignored when a comparison of the relative advantages of self-evaluation or outside evaluation is based not on which approach will yield the best information but rather on which approach will endorse the expert's position or invalidate external criticism. This is also the case when the debate focuses solely on the ordering of the evaluation, the use of its results, or the uses that could be made of it, rather than on the accuracy of the adopted methodology. This definition does not prejudge the ordering, production, or use of an evaluation; by the same token it clearly states that the rigour of the approach is the element that distinguishes the scientific evaluation from all the spontaneous evaluations or all types of control or assessment that are otherwise used and have their own internal logic. This does not deny the importance of discussion on the political issues involved in the conditions of ordering, producing, or using an evaluation; these issues provide the actors with a forum for the expression of their scientific deontology as well as their special interests and specific strategies. Rather, this definition makes an important distinction between the debate of political issues and the debate on evaluation as a scientific practice.

In order to evaluate a policy it must be clearly identified. Again, this appears obvious. Experience shows, however, to do so is not always easy. First, the boundaries of the particular policy must be set, but these are often elusive. Some policies do not necessarily include an administrative or financial procedure, or a whole set of easily noticeable means, which makes delimitation through procedure or means quite difficult. Delimitation through objectives is all the more elusive since these are often too broad to specify the particular policy in any concrete form. Thus, we can only evaluate a policy if we have first made it 'evaluable'—if we have built or rebuilt it as such.

An evaluation will not be able to determine the effects of a particular policy unless the policy has been clearly identified. Ideally an evaluation approach should introduce rationality and accessibility to the policies studied. We know, however, that social policies are often irrational or, to be more precise, they emerge from a combination of several often diverging or contradictory theories. Still, if we cannot say unequivocally what specifically the policy is, it will be impossible to evaluate. This does not endorse the positivist or technocratic illusions of rationality, but rather is a reminder that the evaluation must entail a logical and rigorous construction to qualify as a scientific endeavour.

Policy evaluation is not only or primarily a statistical process. It should be obvious that figures never 'talk' alone and that not everything can be measured. Many debates on evaluation, however, deal exclusively with the availability of information, its collection, and quantification, while measurement is only one aspect of a global process. The essence of statistics lies in their interpretation. Correct research requires that we devote as much time and means as necessary to each stage: the definition of a research plan, data collection, analysis of information, and writing of conclusions. To forget this means that we accumulate pieces of information not knowing what to do with them or having the time to analyse them. If we lose perspective on how to conduct good research, we tend to expend our energies looking for 'the perfect number' through the creation of new pieces of information, instead of critically and judicially using the existing data, even if imperfect, to arrive at results that are not significantly different or of lesser quality.

As already stated, these comments do not pretend to be original. Rather they identify the context within which evaluation, in general, is considered here, and within which, in particular, the evaluation of the neighbourhood social development (NSD) policy is presented below.

PROBLEMS IN EVALUATING NEIGHBOURHOOD SOCIAL DEVELOPMENT

The difficulties in evaluating NSD are related to the characteristics of this policy. NSD, launched in late 1981, mainly consists of an extensive volunteer effort in urban neighbourhoods identified as deteriorated or disadvantaged. It was hoped that the programme would produce positive neighbourhood change through the mobilization of local actors and through the simultaneous establishment of interventions covering all aspects of public policy (employment, housing, education, etc.). This programme first dealt with 16 and then 22 experimental sites, and was then extended to some 120 to 150 neighbourhoods throughout France.

Though NSD is a national programme, it acknowledges and relies on the support of local initiatives. Local programmes are the responsibility of the mayors of the targeted communities, who mobilize all the partners who can intervene in a given area. This policy is both comprehensive and transverse: it strives at integrated neighbourhood development through the convergence of multi-sectoral efforts and through the establishment of durable partnerships. Finally, this policy is pragmatic: it does not endorse a specific doctrine as to exactly what social development must be;[2] rather, it admits that local actors are the ones who have to define priorities according to the characteristics of the local context. The policy acknowledges that the adopted programmes will be diverse and encompass experimental aspects.

Local programmes exhibit huge disparities. Some programmes deal with very small neighbourhoods; others relate to huge housing estates with tens of thousands of inhabitants. In some programmes, the city council is actively involved; in others it assumes a distant role. Some programmes stress job training and employment; others urban planning and housing renovation. In addition to the disparities among the sites is the heterogeneity of the local programmes. Many of them consist of separate measures that have not been organized through the identification of priority objectives. This heterogeneity has partly evolved from the principle that interventions must be initiated in multiple fields and with multiple actors; but it also reflects the difficulties at the local level in building a consensus on how to develop a coherent programme and the impossibility of avoiding compromises between distinct, and sometimes contradictory, approaches. NSD, therefore, does not consist of a whole set of simple interventions whose possible effects could be easily defined. This also means that NSD is not a policy that is normatively defined at the national level with local applications that can be easily followed.

These characteristics explain the difficulty encountered in evaluating NSD and the scarcity of effectively implemented evaluations. We shall first consider the methodological problems we met in evaluating the policy. According to the above definition of evaluation, these problems deal, on the one hand, with the identification of the policy and, on the other hand, with the locating of its results.

The national NSD policy consists of local programmes that are dissimilar and heterogeneous. If most neighbourhoods face the same social and urban problems (i.e. unemployment, school failures, deterioration of housing estates, etc.), the local programmes may grant either higher priority or greater resources in treating some of them. Still, the evaluation of the national policy can only be a synthesis of the evaluations of local programmes (or of a sample of local programmes).[3] At the local level, however, we meet the already mentioned methodological difficulty that NSD is both a procedure and a policy. Local programmes often consist of a set of measures whose unity or convergence is determined only by very general objectives without operational objectives or clear guidelines.

Since NSD does not incorporate a theory of social development that would explain the chain of processes and results, it is impossible to determine *a priori* the mechanisms through which social development could be implemented. How can we then examine the impact of NSD? Methodologically, policy evaluation has recourse to comparisons between the places where the programme has been implemented and those where it has not, or between the conditions of the place before and after programme implementation. Uncertainties as to the comparable character of NSD and non-NSD areas forbid the first choice and oblige one to adopt the second, although it has its own difficulties. While it is possible to identify some immediate effects of an isolated action (e.g. the setting up of specific equipment), it is difficult to determine the less immediate results and, especially, the composite effects of a combination of several actions. In fact, even the analysis of the immediate effects (within time and space) is sometimes difficult.

These methodological difficulties alone do not explain the scarcity of evaluations of NSD. In fact, no political impulse for a permanent evaluation procedure was given at the outset of the NSD programme, although the intention was expressed to provide the policy gradually with a doctrinal foundation based on interpretations of the experiences at the initial sites. Two reasons explain this situation. First, the interest in evaluation was less acute in the early 1980s than it is today, and second, implementing the policy rather than evaluating it had primary importance at the local level. It is also certain that the actors involved in NSD were hesitant to commit themselves to a rigorous evaluation process, fearing that it would become a means of national control over the local initiatives. They feared that a formal evaluation would undermine fragile local consensus or that it would be controlled by those with the most political influence or technical expertise. It is thus not surprising that at the local level empiricism and impressionistic balance sheets reigned. This approach, of course, reveals some social truths, based on observations of tangible solutions to problems and the disappearance of evidence of blight. Neither is it surprising that on a national level, examination of the NSD policy first consisted of the exchange of experiences and ideas among the areas rather than a rigorous examination of the long-term effects of the policy.

In late 1984, however, the General Commissariat for Planning set up a working group to try to overcome these earlier methodological difficulties and to promote a scientific approach to evaluation that could be recommended to the local authorities. The reflections and analysis that appeared in this framework are presented below.[4]

ATTEMPTS TO EVALUATE NEIGHBOURHOOD SOCIAL DEVELOPMENT

The working group on the evaluation of social policies at the local level was made up of social science researchers and administrative representatives. The working group had a double mission: first, to suggest an evaluation approach that might be used to examine the social development policies; and second, to improve the suggested approach based on conclusions drawn from its implementation in precise areas.

Presented in a report in late 1985 (La Documentation française, 1986b), the recommended approach took these problems into consideration. Since the working party could not make up a 'ready-to-use' methodology for all circumstances and all programmes, the group searched for a 'ready-to-build' methodology to be tailored to the specific needs of the operations to be studied. That is why we talked of a 'research approach', rather than presenting a list of technical formulas. We endorsed a classical approach to evaluation: identifying objectives, listing the means to realize these objectives, identifying results, and measuring and explaining them. We stressed the dangers of a mechanical application of social indicators, which would make the evaluation too narrow in its scope. In order to make it possible to evaluate the NSD programme, our approach focuses on the questions to be asked rather than on the measurements to be taken. This would require local actors to face the difficult task of formulating concrete definitions of their objectives, rather than leaving them vague and general, as is often the case.

To determine what effects a policy has had on neighbourhood development the report suggests a central methodological approach: to choose for each area, according to the concrete contents of the launched programme, a whole set of variable elements, quantitative ones if possible, which might yield information on results. This approach emerges from the following observation: while it is difficult to evaluate each of the multiple concrete actions that make up a local programme, and especially to make a synthesis of the detailed examination of each of these measures, it is possible to characterize the neighbourhoods by some variable elements related to the fields in which the programme is thought to have had some impact, and thus to try to observe changes that the analysis and interpretation could explain. In other words, while it is fruitless to try and evaluate everything, it is conceivable that the major effects of NSD can be evaluated. Local evaluators were cautioned, however, that results cannot be attributed automatically to the selected variable elements without a specific analysis of the total chain of cause and effect.

The report recommended that the evaluation be organized through the teams responsible for NSD programmes. *Local observatories* should be established where relevant information would be collected and analysed for the evaluation of the relevant policy. This proposition is related to both methodological and practical considerations. The observatories enable the local actors to take over the evaluation process and integrate it within the management of their programmes. The local actors, therefore, not only collect the data but also choose which pieces of information are to be collected and how they are to be interpreted, even when statisticians or researchers contribute technical support. The recommended procedure asks that the local teams commit themselves to a self-evaluation process, provided the evaluation is made in accordance with the general methodological principles of a classical evaluation approach.

The working group set out to validate the use and practicality of the suggested approach. This was first tried in Romans (Drôme), with a study mainly centred on checking the availability of social policy information at a neighbourhood level and on the relevance of this information to the local programme.[5] It was then launched in Grande-Synthe (Nord) with methodological research on the approach as a whole. The work in Grande-Synthe undoubtedly extended the methodological reflection and experimentation. There, since the community had already set up thematic local observatories (for housing, employment and training, and other areas), it was possible to study the approach and its execution more deeply.

The local authorities of Grande-Synthe and the team responsible for the social development action decided that an evaluation of the first five years of NSD would be their priority action during 1987 and 1988. An institutional system was created based on some of the initial propositions of the working group: a 'guiding committee' meets with the local executives and some researchers to determine the object of the evaluation and discuss the priority objectives to be submitted to analysis. Thematic working parties collect and report on these pieces of information, which are then exchanged within the whole operation and presented at neighbourhood meetings. This is a unique experiment, as far as we know, since it considers the evaluation of a programme as its subject and tries to conciliate quantitative approaches and qualitative studies in fields like the image of the urban neighbourhood, patterns of settlement, the provision of equipment and services, and inter-partnership practices.[6]

It must be emphasized that these efforts require much time, more than initially planned, which explains the delay in the completion of the second

194

stage of activity of the General Commissariat for Planning working group. This group had underestimated the time needed to meet the methodological requirements, especially that the policy be evaluable, and for the development of an evaluation project by the local actors. In fact, we are faced with one of the limitations of Neighbourhood Social Development policy: its plasticity makes it difficult to evaluate *immediately*. Still, since these policies show an important departure from the classical forms of public intervention, such evaluations appear to be extremely beneficial. It would be a shame, indeed, if only impressionistic or reductive evaluations were made, when the issue at stake in setting up such policies is precisely to prove the efficiency of a contractual collaboration between the state, the local groups, and other actors interested in the development of a livable social space.

Some conclusions can already be drawn from the completed analyses. It is doubtful whether the social development policies have succeeded in transforming the living conditions of the neighbourhood residents as much as had been proposed. It is certain, however, that these policies have contributed, though unevenly, to positively changing the images of these neighbourhoods and to favouring new forms of public service at the local level (interpartnership, identification of local managers, etc.). By so doing, they prove the validity of a national intervention based not solely on providing assistance to the poor, which reinforces their stigmatization, but rather on empowerment of the local level to be responsible for the management of community development, and on resident participation.

NOTES

1. This article is based on various studies on NSD carried out by the author in 1984–88, partly as a rapporteur of a working group created by the General Commissariat for Planning (see *Les politiques sociales transversales, une méthodologie d'évaluation de leurs effets locaux*, report of the working group presided over by J.C. Ray, rapporteurs J.M. Dupuis and J.P. Tricart). The views expressed here were also presented in various seminars and other reports (see 'L'évaluation de la politique de développement social des quartiers', COMM, 32 (12/87)). The views expressed in this article are the author's and do not necessarily reflect the opinion of the Commission of the European Communities or the Community Member States.

2. This concept of social development is partly drawn from the programmes held in rural areas or in the Third World.

3. We can also consider the NSD policy as a 'laboratory of ideas and experiments' whose effects could also be felt in other fields of public policy. See La Documentation française (1986b).

4. This exhaustive analysis of attempts to evaluate NSD requires that we mention other works, such as the INSEE initiatives on the local information systems. In this respect, see our contribution to a report prepared for UNESCO, implemented under the responsibility of J.C. Ray (Ray *et al.*, 1988). See also the report of an administrative working group created by the General Commissariat for Planning and presided over by F. Lévy (1989).

5. Study implemented under the direction of M. Chevallier (1986).

6. A report on this self-evaluation experience was published in 1988 (*Auto-évaluation de l'opération DSQ*. Ville de Grande-Synthe, OMINOR, Lille: 1988).

REFERENCES

CHEVALLIER, M. (1986) *Test des instruments d'évaluation proposés par le groupe 'Évaluation des politiques sociales au niveau local' du Commissariat Général du Plan*. Lyon: Arcades.

La Documentation française (1986a) *Évaluer les politiques publiques*. Paris.

La Documentation française (1986b) *Les politiques sociales transversales, une méthodologie d'évaluation de leurs effets locaux*. Paris.

LÉVY, F. (1989) *Bilan—perspectives des contrats de plan de développement social des quartiers*. Paris: Rapport du groupe de travail présidé par La Documentation Française.

RAY, J.C., P. DICKES and J.P. TRICART (1988) *Méthodes d'évaluation des programmes de développement en France dans le domaine des politiques sociales*. Paris: UNESCO.

14 THE EVALUATION OF NEIGHBOURHOOD REHABILITATION PROGRAMMES: LESSONS FROM ISRAEL'S PROJECT RENEWAL[1]

Shimon E. Spiro

America's War on Poverty, Britain's Urban Programme, Israel's Project Renewal, and similar programmes reflect the confidence of planners and policymakers in their ability to create social change—redress inequities, reverse urban deterioration, and improve the life chances and living conditions of individuals and communities. Past experience, however, does not necessarily support such confidence. Ambitious social programmes are often not implemented as planned (Pressman and Wildavsky, 1973; Edwards, 1980). When implemented, their consequences may be very different from those intended (Coleman *et al.*, 1975). Plausible explanations are usually offered for past failures: inadequate financing or political support, lack of co-ordination between organizations, poor leadership, and so on. These explanations, although rarely based on systematic evaluation, reinforce confidence in the expected success of new programmes, which supposedly incorporate the lessons of past failures.

Growing awareness of the gap in public policy between intention and outcomes has spurred the meteoric growth of programme evaluation as an interdisciplinary field of practice. In the last two decades thousands of evaluations were conducted in the United States alone (Rossi and Wright, 1984), and the idea that every major new programme needs to be accompanied by an evaluation is now widely accepted.

With time and experience, however, evaluators have become increasingly aware of the limitations of current designs and methods (Cronbach *et al.*, 1980). These limitations are most prominent in the evaluation of large-scale, broadly aimed, and complex social programmes (Weiss and Rein, 1969), such as those attempting comprehensive urban rehabilitation. The American Model Cities and the British Urban Programme, for example, although accompanied by extensive research, were not evaluated systematically. The research focused mostly on the organizational and political aspects of the programmes (Frieden and Kaplan, 1975; Edwards and Batley, 1978; Higgins *et al.*, 1983). These studies, invaluable for understanding the rise and decline of urban programmes, provide useful insights into the politics of urban rehabilitation. But they do not attempt to assess the impact of the programmes on their target areas.

In the English Community Development Project every local programme was monitored by researchers from a nearby university, but their studies dealt more with an assessment of needs than with an evaluation of programme implementation and outcomes (Loney, 1983). With the exception of Scotland's GEAR (Glasgow Eastern Area Renewal) (Donnison and Middleton, 1987), few comprehensive urban rehabilitation programmes have been evaluated systematically, and only limited attention has been devoted to the organizational and methodological issues of such evaluations.

This chapter pulls together some of the experience gained in the evaluation of Israel's Project Renewal and offers lessons that may be applied to the evaluation of other large-scale, diversified, broadly aimed, and complex projects. The paper focuses on the organizational more than on the methodological aspects of evaluation. The chapter is based on the author's experience as director of the International Committee for the Evaluation of Project Renewal (ICEPR), and on the work of a number of scholars who did research on the evaluation of Project Renewal.

ISRAEL'S PROJECT RENEWAL

Project Renewal, a programme of comprehensive neighbourhood rehabilitation, was announced in 1977 as a joint effort on the part of the Israeli government and the Diaspora communities. The goal of the project was the social and physical rehabilitation of 160 distressed neighbourhoods throughout the country at a cost of U.S. $1.2 billion. The project reached its peak at the end of 1982. At that time 83 neighbourhoods with a total population of 600,000 were included in the programme. Project Renewal is unprecedented in its scope, given the size of Israel and the comprehensiveness and variety of the programmes and activities subsumed within the project.

The project was managed by an interorganizational committee (IOC), comprising senior officials from the relevant government ministries — housing, education, welfare, health, finance, and interior — and representatives of major non-government organizations. A team of officials at the Prime Minister's office (later moved to the Ministry of Housing) provided staff services. At the local level, the programme was directed by a local steering committee (LSC), chaired by the mayor and comprising representatives of the local community and municipal and central government agencies. Neighbourhood renewal programmes were developed incrementally: each LSC submitted annual budgets reflecting planned programmes to be approved by the IOC.

The specific programmes in a local renewal project varied among neighbourhoods. The LSCs were selected from among hundreds of possible programmes in such fields as housing (e.g. house enlargements, renovations of shared areas); environment (improvement of sidewalks, street lights, sewage); education (improvement of school amenities and equipment, extended school day); leisure (sports facilities, adult education classes); health (dental clinic); welfare (day centres for the elderly, drop-in centres for youth); and employment (training courses). Few of these programmes were new and innovative; most were taken off the shelf. Project Renewal made resources available for the expansion of programmes in all areas relevant to the wellbeing of the local population and to the development of the neighbourhood.

The goals of Project Renewal were restated in different ways on a number of occasions. It is possible to summarize the various statements by saying that Project Renewal was expected to achieve the following general goals (ICEPR, 1985):

- improve the quality of life of neighbourhood residents through upgrading the physical infrastructure, housing conditions, and the levels of social and cultural services;
- enhance opportunities for educational and occupational achievement for children, youth, and adults;
- increase the control residents have over their lives and their environment, encourage participation in neighbourhood affairs, and foster feelings of identification and belonging; and
- stabilize the neighbourhoods and reverse deterioration and selective out-migration by enhancing the image of the neighbourhoods.

Various stakeholders involved in the programme had other explicit or implicit goals. For example, some saw the project as a means of strengthening one level of government at the expense of others. Others saw the project as a testing ground for new technology.

These goals were to be pursued through the application of the following principles and constraints:

- local programmes are to be comprehensive and integrated, combining both physical and social aspects of neighbourhood improvement;
- authority for planning and management is to be decentralized, with neighbourhood-based institutions playing a major role in decision making;
- residents are to play an active and central role in the planning and implementation of the programmes;
- programmes are to be implemented through existing national and local agencies, avoiding the establishment of new bureaucracies;
- the contribution of world Jewry is to be realized through twinning Diaspora communities with individual renewal neighbourhoods; and
- within a limited predefined time, resources of sufficient magnitude are to be invested so as to create a meaningful impact on conditions in the neighbourhood.

The specific programmes that emerged from these goals and principles were put into operation incrementally through decisions and actions at the central and local level. Thus, a general goal such as 'the enhancement of educational opportunities' was translated in one locality into a special enrichment programme for gifted youngsters and elsewhere into auxiliary instruction for failing pupils. Thus the goals and operating principles of the programme were, at any point in time, fluid, ambiguous, and partly controversial. The consequences of this for the evaluation will be discussed below.

ORGANIZATION FOR EVALUATION

Project Renewal was actually started in 1979. In 1980 the heads of the project decided to appoint an international committee of experts to evaluate the project. The committee, consisting of five American and four Israeli academicians, first met in April 1981 and concluded its work in summer 1985. The available resources amounted to $700,000.

The committee was to be independent of the IOC and other agencies involved in Project Renewal. It was to define evaluation questions, initiate studies, and arrive at conclusions and recommendations without interference from project heads. At the same time, the committee was expected to maintain close contact with the heads of the programme and respond to their concerns. To ensure independence the management of ICEPR was separated from the management of the project. The committee had its own minuscule staff, operating out of a university.

EVALUATION FOR WHOM AND FOR WHAT?

ICEPR hoped to serve a number of different interests. The heads of Project Renewal needed evaluation as a basis for mid-course corrections and as a way of utilizing the experience of early project neighbourhoods when adding new ones.

Professionals and officials responsible for specific programmes needed experimental evidence for making decisions about the future of programmes and ways of improving them. The sponsors of Project Renewal in the government and the Jewish communities involved abroad needed to account for resources expended and wanted evidence concerning the conduct of the project and its effectiveness. Finally, students of policy and administration could apply the lessons derived from Project Renewal to other policies of social change in Israel and elsewhere.

Obviously, the evaluation of Project Renewal as it was organized could not respond to all of these interests. The evaluation turned out to be a summary account of the project's achievements and failures and of the lessons to be derived for posterity. As aptly put by one committee member, ICEPR's main achievement was to ensure that Project Renewal, unlike similar programmes elsewhere, would get a 'fair hearing' and not be judged a failure just because it was terminated prematurely when the interests of politicians and the public turned elsewhere.

The evaluation's limited contribution to the day-to-day operation of Project Renewal was a consequence of its methods and organization. The most crucial features of the evaluation were its separation from the daily administration of Project Renewal and its reliance on commissioned research. This paper will explore the consequence of these choices, but first we need to review the kinds of study commissioned as part of the evaluation.

TYPES OF STUDY

The committee embraced a broad view of evaluation, aspiring not only to assess the outcomes of the programme but to follow its implementation and to examine the relationships among the environmental conditions, the characteristics of programme implementation, and outcomes. In the absence of any widely known and accepted model of evaluation, the committee followed Cronbach et al.'s (1980) advice: 'It is better to launch a fleet of small explorations rather than invest all resources in one big study.' The committee launched four types of study.

Comprehensive evaluation

The largest study commissioned by ICEPR, *Integrated Evaluation in a Sample of Neighborhoods* (Alterman et al., 1985), was conducted between 1983 and 1985. The study was a variation of the field network evaluation (FNE) method (Nathan, 1982) developed at the Brookings Institute to evaluate the consequences of national policies through a series of local case studies. The studies are conducted by independent investigators who use a variety of formal and informal research tools and are linked to senior investigators who set the research agenda and perform a comparative analysis of the local studies. The American Community Development Block Grants programme was also studied in this manner (Dommel et al., 1982). The Project Renewal study of ten neighbourhoods, conducted by a team of researchers from the Neaman Institute at the Haifa Technion, differed from the original FNE method in that the members of the field network were junior rather than senior researchers, whose findings and reports were supplemented with data from a household survey (see below) and other sources. Unlike the American FNE studies, which focused mainly on the political and economic consequences of the national policies, this study tried to assess the impact of the programme on the lives of the residents. It attempted to evaluate Project Renewal from all possible perspectives: goals, implementation, and outcome. The goals of this study were close to the committee's conception of a comprehensive evaluation.

Anthropological studies

Anthropologists observing the interaction between renewal personnel, government agencies, and local residents can provide important insights into such issues as control and legitimacy and power and dependence. Looking at the process from the bottom up, they may be able to identify hidden agendas and unintended consequences. In short, they may discover what is really going on behind the official statements and statistics. Three local studies in three neighbourhoods were conducted for ICEPR. The field work took one year (from 1982 to 1983), and another year was required for the production of three reports and a short comparative statement (Hazan, 1983; Lavie, 1984; Marx, 1985; Shahak, 1985).

Household surveys

An attitude survey was administered to 2,500 respondents in 20 neighbourhoods to ascertain attitudes about various aspects of the neighbourhood and opinions about Project Renewal. The survey neighbourhoods included the 13 that were the object of the FNE and anthropological studies. The 20 neighbourhoods also included some that had only recently been added to the project, permitting a comparison between veteran and new project neighbourhoods. A replication in 1983 of an attitude survey conducted in the Tel Aviv neighbourhoods in 1977 made it possible to supplement the cross-sectional analysis of a country-wide sample with longitudinal comparisons in one town (Harpaz et al., 1983).

Evaluations of specific programmes

A significant aspect of Project Renewal was the great variety of programmes in such areas as housing, education, welfare, and recreation. Special evaluation studies were commissioned of some of the more widely adopted, controversial, and expensive programmes such as home enlargement (Lerman and Borukhov, 1985), external renovations (Ginsberg and Werczberger, 1984), work groups for delinquent youths (Gottlieb, 1985), and computer-aided instruction (Davis et al., 1986). In addition, the committee commissioned studies of special issues and a series of position papers. Official reports and statistics were also used quite extensively.

The multiplicity of studies undoubtedly helped the committee arrive at a balanced view of the project's achievements and problems. But the structure of the evaluation and the types of studies commissioned had some unintended consequences.

ISSUES IN EVALUATION

The approach to the evaluation of Project Renewal raises five issues in the evaluation of broadly based urban rehabilitation programmes. These issues are the ambiguity of goals and weakness of underlying theory, the turbulent environment of urban rehabilitation programmes, the inadequate database for evaluation, evaluation time versus action time, and the dependency relations between programme managers and evaluators.

Goal ambiguity

The goals of broadly based programmes are necessarily vague and fluid (Weiss and Rein, 1969). Project Renewal's organizational structure, with its multiple loci of decision making, may have reinforced goal ambiguity. While central bodies such as the IOC agreed on the overall goals of the project, dozens of local steering committees determined the actual programmes and in that process each of the participating organizations tried to enhance its share of the pie.

The absence of consistently defined goals does not preclude evaluation. On the contrary, the multiplicity of goals, principles, and programmes and the absence of explicit theories linking them create almost limitless opportunities for evaluation with questions and criteria deriving from the evaluators' interests and ideologies. Many evaluators enter the field positively inclined towards the programme and find no difficulty in identifying some successes among a host of activities (Wildavsky, 1987). For example, the project might not have resulted in a change in the neighbourhood's prestige, but it did raise satisfaction with the quality of services. The school enrichment programmes might not have led to a measurable change in achievement, but they did enhance the pupils' quality of life (ICEPR, 1985). The combination of indeterminate goals and evaluators committed to social action may create a positive bias—an emphasis on the glass being half full.

Evaluation in a turbulent environment

Project Renewal was not carried out in a laboratory but in the turbulent reality of Israel in the 1980s. The war with Lebanon, rampant inflation followed by stabilizing economic measures, a change of government, a wave of immigration from Ethiopia, and other major events overshadowed possible impacts of Project Renewal. Secular trends, such as the declining birth rate and a general rise in the standard of living, also brought significant social change. Because of these trends and events it is possible to offer alternative explanations for every outcome attributed to Project Renewal. Residential crowding in renewal areas declined in the 11 years between censuses by 30% (Hovav and Ben-Itzhak, 1986): is this a result of home enlargement loans and similar programmes sponsored by Project Renewal or of the trends mentioned above? Should the increase in the proportion of elementary school leavers pursuing academic secondary education in renewal areas be attributed to enhanced achievement levels encouraged by the project or to changes in placement policies?

It is difficult to answer these questions. Neighbourhoods were included in the programme on the basis of their level of distress and their potential for rehabilitation. It is impossible to find control neighbourhoods that are strictly comparable to the project neighbourhoods. Some researchers tried to resolve this problem by comparing changes in the project areas with national averages (Lerman and Borokhov, 1985; Hovav and Ben-Itzhak, 1986). There are, however, three competing (and contradictory) explanations of any differences between the trends in project areas and national trends:

- Since Project Renewal operates in deteriorating areas, it could be assumed that without intervention the gap between them and the national average would have increased. If this is the case, any comparison of project and national trends underestimates the true effects of the project.
- Since the project operates in neighbourhoods that were the lowest on some measure of wellbeing, it could be assumed, given the regression to the mean, that in repeated measurements these

neighbourhoods will be closer to the national mean. Thus, apparent relative improvements in their status may represent a statistical artifact (Campbell, 1969).

- Other welfare programmes may discriminate in favour of the renewal neighbourhoods and it may be impossible to differentiate between their effects and those of Project Renewal.

Not only is it difficult to assess the *impact* of Project Renewal, it is almost equally impossible to estimate the true *inputs* of a programme implemented by a large number of agencies. Any attempt to differentiate between the inputs of ongoing, regular programmes and Project Renewal is almost a mission impossible.

There are no easy solutions to these problems. ICEPR's emphasis on qualitative methods enabled us to peak into the 'black box' and try to arrive at some assessment of inputs and outcomes.

Weakness of the database

The assessment of implementation and outcome depends on an adequate database. This would include an ongoing collection and analysis of data on relevant social indicators (Land, 1983), such as local migration rates and the characteristics of in- and out-immigrants, the number of empty and abandoned flats, the incidence of delinquency and vandalism, and community participation in political and voluntary action. It is not enough that data on these indicators be available at the national level. It should be possible to relate them to neighbourhood boundaries. Similarly the database should encompass the kind of information usually collected for management information systems on expenditures, manpower, and activities.

The ongoing collection of such data should be the responsibility of the participating ministries, not only because of their role in programme implementation, but (mainly) because of their long-term responsibility for the development of policies and programmes. For example, the Ministry of Housing should collect data on empty flats and on home ownership; the Ministry of Education on achievement levels.

This did not happen in Project Renewal. The information available on social indicators or on performance measures is, at best, incomplete. Because the researchers serving the committee lacked a ready-made database, they had to devote a major part of their (and ICEPR's) resources to the collection of data, reducing the resources available for analysis. Furthermore, the separation of the evaluation from the management of the programme limited the ability of the evaluators to influence the activities of the ministries in this area.

Time and utility

The decision to have an independent committee of experts evaluate the project, based on studies commissioned from universities and institutes, tended to increase the time lag between policy making and evaluation. The

204

translation of policy issues into evaluative research typically proceeded in the following manner.

A member of the committee or one of the heads of Project Renewal would suggest a topic to be explored, which would be brought up in the earliest semi-annual meeting of the evaluation committee. The discussion often resulted in a Request for Proposals, distributed among potential researchers. Several months later proposals would come in, which would be discussed at the next meeting of the committee. If one of the proposals was accepted, changes would be negotiated and a contract discussed. Under favourable conditions the study would commence after a few additional months. A year might have passed between the time a question was raised and a study commenced. The time required for the completion of a study and the submission of a final report (or, at least, a useful interim report) might again be considerable. In short, the heads of Project Renewal had to rely on less formal processes to make mid-course corrections or to derive lessons from the experience of veteran renewal neighbourhoods when initiating projects in new neighbourhoods.

Furthermore, the research findings reflected the state of the project at the time the data was collected. It happened that data collected in 1983 were submitted in draft form in 1985 and published in 1986. By then many of the conclusions and recommendations were dated. As in the case of the U.S.A.'s Headstart programme (Datta, 1983), the public discussion of a programme may be affected by tentative findings that should have been revised much earlier.

The limits of independence

The evaluation literature assigns great importance to the organizational independence of evaluators (Scriven, 1977), but admits that this is a necessary, not a sufficient, condition for the prevention of bias. The evaluation of Project Renewal seemed to be organized to ensure maximum objectivity, with ICEPR acting as a buffer between the heads of the project and the researchers who performed the evaluation. It turned out that such an arrangement does not offer sufficient protection from bias.

Scholars interested in neighbourhood rehabilitation often enter the field with a positive bias towards the idea of government intervention. Once in the field, they tend to see themselves as part of the rehabilitation community and look to the local project staff for social recognition and emotional support. They are often dependent on project staff for access to information. This is especially true for members of an FNE network. It is less true for anthropologists, who rely more on the grass roots and tend to search for hidden meanings, implicit interests, and unintended consequences.

While the FNE approach may be prone to a positive bias, other research methods, such as opinion surveys, may have built-in negative biases. The low reliability of many questionnaires may attenuate the true effect of the programme (Rossi and Freeman, 1982). In short, the choice of methodology may strongly affect the outcome of the evaluation.

AN ALTERNATIVE APPROACH

We have discussed the problems encountered in the evaluation of broadly aimed and complex social programmes and how the organization and methodology of the Project Renewal evaluation affected these problems. It should be noted that in spite of all the problems, the evaluation provided some meaningful answers to questions about the extent to which project principles were adhered to and project goals were achieved (ICEPR, 1985). But would a different organizational structure for the evaluation have better served the needs of the various groups involved in Project Renewal? We shall suggest an approach that we believe will not only help evaluators derive lessons for the future, but also contribute to the daily operation of the programme.

For Project Renewal and similar programmes the evaluation should be strongly linked to the management of the programme. The headquarters of such a programme should include a strong team responsible for monitoring, experimentation, and evaluation. The main function of the team would be to motivate and assist participating agencies in collecting and analysing data on an ongoing basis. Data collected in the field should be transmitted to the centre, analysed, and fed back. The objective is not to reinforce central control, but, on the contrary, to strengthen the local steering committees and local agencies by supplying them with better information about their performance, needs, and resources relative to other areas. In Project Renewal an attempt to save on overheads left the IOC with inadequate resources for monitoring and resulted, paradoxically, in increased centralization. Since technical assistance to the localities was inadequate, the programmes and budgets they submitted were often mistrusted and overruled. Better central management of the information system might have resulted in greater local autonomy.

One of the functions of the central team would be to foster an experimental approach throughout the project. This cannot be done effectively unless specific programmes are monitored and evaluated properly. Few of the hundreds of specific programmes subsumed under Project Renewal have undergone such an evaluation (Adler and Dzuck, 1984). The experimentation should be carried out by the agencies operating the programmes, assisted and monitored by the central team. The results of such localized experiments would help the agencies better their welfare technologies and assist the central team in the overall evaluation of the programme.

In the proposed structure there remains a place for a high-powered committee of experts to serve as a steering committee for the monitoring and evaluation effort. This committee could, like ICEPR, initiate a few studies commissioned from independent scholars. The main evaluation and monitoring operation should, however, be more closely integrated into the project.

The Project Renewal evaluation shows that a broadly aimed and complex national neighbourhood rehabilitation programme is feasible and can achieve some of its goals. It remains to be seen whether such a programme can be structured as a 'self-evaluating organization' (Wildavsky, 1987), capable of creating knowledge useful for the navigation of the programme. Future evaluations should benefit from the experience of ICEPR and similar efforts.

NOTE

1. This paper was written while the author was an academic visitor at the London School of Economics. The author wishes to thank the Eileen Younghusband Foundation for its support.

REFERENCES

ADLER, H. and C. DZUCK (1984) *A Review of Educational Programs and their Evaluations.* Jerusalem: Institute for Innovation in Education, Hebrew University. In Hebrew.

ALTERMAN, R. and A. FRENKEL (1985) *The Outputs of Project Renewal: Services Delivered and Populations Benefited*: Vol. 3, Part II of *Comprehensive Evaluation of Israel's Project Renewal.* Research directors: R. Alterman, N. Carmon and M. Hill. The Samuel Neaman Institute for Advanced Studies in Science and Technology. Hebrew and English versions.

CAMPBELL, D.T. (1969) Reforms as experiments. *American Psychologist*, **24** (4), 409–423.

COLEMAN, J.S., S. KELLY and J. MOORE (1975) *Trends in School Segregation 1968–73.* Washington, DC: Urban Institute.

CRONBACH, L.J. *et al.* (1980) *Towards Reform of Program Evaluation.* San Francisco: Jossey Bass.

DATTA, L.E. (1983) A tale of two studies: Westinghouse–Ohio evaluation of Project Headstart and the Consortium for Longitudinal Studies report. *Studies in Educational Evaluation*, **8**, 271–280.

DAVIS, D., S. VINNER, T. FINKELSTEIN and R. REGER (1986) *Observations in School Computer Rooms.* Jerusalem: Research Institute for Innovation in Education.

DOMMEL, P.R. *et al.* (1982) *Decentralizing Urban Policy.* Washington, DC: Brookings Institute.

DONNISON, D. and A. MIDDLETON (1987) *Regenerating the Inner City: Glasgow's Experience.* London: Routledge & Kegan Paul.

EDWARDS, G.C. (1980) *Implementing Public Policy.* Washington, DC: Congressional Quarterly Press.

EDWARDS, J. and R. BATLEY (1978) *The Politics of Positive Discrimination.* London: Tavistock.

FRIEDEN, B.J. and M. KAPLAN (1975) *The Politics of Neglect.* Cambridge, MA: MIT Press.

GINSBERG, Y. and E. WERCZBERGER (1984) *The Renovation of Shared Areas in Project Renewal.* Tel Aviv University. In Hebrew.

GOTTLIEB, A. (1985) *Work Groups in Project Renewal.* Tel Aviv: Institute for Social Research, Tel Aviv University.

HARPAZ, CH., M. HADAD and M. FADIDA (1983) *The Influence of Project Renewal on Attitudes towards the Neighborhood.* The Center for Economic and Social Research, Tel Aviv Municipality. In Hebrew.

HAZAN, H. (1983) *Dora—A Paradoxical Community.* Beer Sheva: Institute for Desert Research, Ben Gurion University.

HIGGINS, J., N. DEAKIN and M. WICKS (1983) *Government and Urban Poverty.* Oxford: Blackwell.

HOVAV, H. and Y. BEN-ITZHAK (1986) *Changes in the Characteristics of the Population of Renewal Neighborhoods.* Jerusalem: Ministry of Housing. In Hebrew.

International Committee for the Evaluation of Project Renewal (ICEPR) (1985) *Summary of Findings and Recommendations.*

LAND, K.C. (1983) Social indicators. *Annual Review of Sociology*, **9**, 1–26.

LAVIE, E. (1984) *Project Renewal in One Neighborhood in Beer Sheva.* Beer Sheva:

SHIMON E. SPIRO

Institute for Desert Research, Ben Gurion University. In Hebrew.

LERMAN, R. and E. BORUKHOV (1985) *The Housing Initiatives of Project Renewal.* Jerusalem: Brookdale Institute.

LONEY, M. (1983) *Community against Government.* London: Heinemann.

MARX, E. (1985) An Evaluation of Project Renewal — Conclusions and Recommendations. Unpublished.

NATHAN, R. P. (1982) The methodology for field network evaluation. In: W. Williams *et al.* (eds) *Studying Implementation: Methodological and Administrative Issues.* Chatham House.

PRESSMAN, J. and A. WILDAVSKY (1973) *Implementation.* Berkeley, CA: University of California.

ROSSI, P.H. and H. FREEMAN (1982) *Evaluation.* Beverly Hills, CA: Sage.

ROSSI, P. H. and J. D. WRIGHT (1984) Evaluation Research — An Assessment. *Annual Review of Sociology,* **10**, 331–352.

SCRIVEN, M. (1977) Evaluation bias and its control. *Evaluation Studies Review Annual,* **1**, 119–139.

SHAHAK, O. (1985) *Powerlessness and Labeling as Components of Renewal.* Beer Sheva: Institute of Desert Research, Ben Gurion University. In Hebrew.

WEISS, R. S. and M. REIN (1969) The evaluation of broad-aim programs. *Annals of the American Academy of Social and Political Science,* **385** (Sept.), 20–38.

WILDAVSKY, A. (1987) The self evaluating organization. In: *Speaking Truth to Power,* 212–237. New Brunswick, NJ: Transaction.

15 DILEMMAS ABOUT CROSS-NATIONAL TRANSFERABILITY OF NEIGHBOURHOOD REGENERATION PROGRAMMES

Rachelle Alterman

An honest review of the twelve reports from nine countries in this book leads to the conclusion that it would be presumptuous, given the current state of research, to provide guidelines for the transfer of programme elements from one country to another.

THE STATE OF RESEARCH ABOUT TRANSFERABILITY

Systematic research into cross-national transferability of urban policies and institutions is as yet strikingly sparse. We define transferability as the likelihood that a particular policy, if applied in another country, would achieve the desired outcomes in the new setting. Transferability is more than just transplanting. It relates to the characteristics of the policies and their outcomes, as well as the characteristics of the originating and receiving countries.

Assessment of transferability involves a formidable research task. This may explain why few researchers have attempted to face squarely the question of transferability of urban policies. Notable exceptions can be found in a book edited by Masser and Williams (1986) which is devoted to research on the transferability of urban policies, and in a book edited by Hallett (1988) which attempts, albeit in an intuitive manner, to address questions of transferability of land and housing policies between the U.S.A. and several European countries. No research is known to us which systematically addresses the particular questions of transferability of neighbourhood regeneration programmes.

An indication of the preliminary state of cross-national transfer of ideas about neighbourhood regeneration can be found within this book itself. Perusal of the list of references at the end of each of the chapters shows that very few of the authors cite any literature outside their own countries. Partly, this absence reflects our definition of the authors' task: to provide an assessment of each country's policies rather than a comparative analysis. But if our book is a representative example of research into neighbourhood regeneration policies, then we must conclude that cross-national learning has probably not been a paramount factor in the formulation and assessment of each country's policies.

At the same time, we do find evidence in this book of some cross-national adoption of ideas, but without the benefit of systematic research into transferability. One example is Israel's adoption of certain elements from the Model Cities Program, a program originating in the U.S.A., one of the countries most dissimilar to Israel.[1] Israel's selection of this model was not based on a systematic evaluation of programmes world-wide, but rather on Model Cities' high visibility in the literature and the access of many Israeli policymakers to that literature. In Europe, where distances are short, there are probably many examples of *ad hoc* adoption of programme elements from other countries through informal contacts among policymakers.

A note on language

Comparative research is dependent, first and foremost, on the ability to speak the same language. However, although the authors in this book all write in English, one can easily discern differences in language, especially between North American English and what could be called Euro-English — a blend of British English with terms and constructions from Continental languages (Williams, 1989).[2]

International exchange requires more than an awareness of the commonplace differences between American and British English, such as 'renting' versus 'letting', 'apartments' versus 'flats', or 'high vacancy rates' instead of 'letting problems'. Our policy on editing has been to leave these routine differences in usage intact. International exchange requires an awareness that language differences sometimes point to more deep-seated differences in structures or perceptions. Two examples stand out in this book.

All the European authors in this book have used the British term 'housing estates' to denote a large housing area, initiated as a planned unit. Americans and Canadians do not recognize this term. They usually use the term 'neighbourhood' to denote a contiguous housing area, regardless of how it was initiated. This difference may, at times, be more than semantic. 'Neighbourhood' conjures up notions of identity and social relations, even though these might be a myth (see Chapter 3); whereas 'estate' connotes anonymity and refers to the physical and economic aspects of property (and conveys anachronistic and ironic connotations of nobility). While differences in direct meaning may be small, these difference in terms conjure up additional, indirect, meanings.

The second example goes still deeper. The European term 'social housing' is absent from American usage. Americans know the term 'public housing', but it denotes something quite different from social housing, referring to government-constructed housing that serves the very, very poor — perhaps 1% of the American population. Public housing separates out its occupants from the rest of the population physically, economically, and socially. By contrast, social housing in The Netherlands, Sweden, the F.R.G., or Israel, and to a lesser extent 'council housing' in the U.K., serves a much broader cross-section of the population. Indeed, in Sweden and The Netherlands, social housing predominates in large cities. Social housing involves some public support, perhaps only through preferred terms of mortgages, but does not necessarily involve direct construction by the government. Social housing may be initiated by the government, by housing associations, or

210

by private builders. So, social housing is generally free of the negative connotations of American public housing and, of late, British council housing.

The variables that condition transferability

The rigorous study of transferability of neighbourhood regeneration policies is a virtually unmanageable task. It should develop an understanding of the relationship between four sets of variables: contextual variables, programme characteristics, implementation characteristics, and types and degrees of outputs and outcomes:

Contextual variables. These pertain to differences among countries in factors such as political structure and ideology; economic structure; demographic make-up and housing demand; legal and institutional structure; geographic pattern of development; and definition and extent of the problem of distressed neighbourhoods. Analysis should point out those variables that are likely to condition a country's receptiveness to a particular public policy.

Programme characteristics. This is a finite set of variables by which neighbourhood regeneration programmes in different countries can be usefully characterized and compared. Such variables include programme goals, the degree of comprehensiveness, scale and time frame, degree and type of public intervention, and attitude to citizen involvement.

Implementation characteristics. A systematic identification of implementation characteristics is essential for understanding the linkage between programme characteristics, and outputs and outcomes achieved (Alterman, 1987–88). Research should identify differences among programmes on questions such as the institutional set-up for implementation, the division of labour between central and local government, the role and recruitment of personnel, the role of residents and the private sector, and the incorporation of ongoing planning and monitoring.

Outputs and outcomes. Outputs are those programme elements that have actually been delivered and have reached the target population. Outcomes are the changes achieved: physical, social, economic, or political (both desired and unanticipated).[3] The systematic assessment of transferability requires that a way be found to classify and measure the outputs delivered and outcomes achieved by regeneration programmes in various countries.

Any student of social research methods will be able to conclude that the research task of discovering the links among these four sets of variables is intractable. The number of variables is much larger than the number of countries that a single research project can reasonably investigate. The identification of controls for matching of countries would have to be superficial. And if hypothesized connections did seem to emerge, it would be almost impossible to sieve out spurious or intervening variables.

Therefore, the aim of this chapter is more modest: we highlight and review some of the similarities and differences among the neighbourhood regeneration programmes in the nine countries represented in this book to allow readers to consider which policies might be suitable for adoption in the complex context of their own country or city. In our review, we return to the four groups of variables discussed above.

SIMILARITIES AND DIFFERENCES AMONG COUNTRIES AND PROGRAMMES

Contextual variables

In this section we highlight only a few of the relevant contextual variables.

Political structure and ideology. The countries included in this book represent within the developed world a wide band of legal–institutional structures, political regimes, and ideologies: the U.S.A., with a predominantly private-sector economy and a corresponding low-intervention political ideology, where housing is almost exclusively a private-sector concern; Canada, with a similar economy and ideology but with a somewhat more positive attitude to government intervention; the U.K., formerly with a mixed economy but currently (under the Tories) promoting privatization and an intolerance of government intervention in housing and other spheres; continental Europe with a set of mixed economies that take a more positive attitude to government intervention, graded from the F.R.G. and France, where the private sector in housing is more dominant, to The Netherlands and Sweden where social housing is still the overriding norm; and Israel, with a mixed economy and a possible return to public-sector dominance in housing, after 15 years of a gradual trend of privatization. Finally, we included Hungary to represent the post-socialist countries of Central and Eastern Europe, where new political structures and ideologies are in a formative stage, and are likely to have a strong influence on housing and neighbourhood regeneration policies.[4]

Of all these countries, the role of political ideology in shaping neighbourhood regeneration policies is particularly striking in the U.K. Chapters 4 and 5 tell of a pageant of policies created and annulled with amazing frequency and willingness to veer sharply in response to ideological changes. In the other countries, political ideology has either been more stable (the U.S.A., Sweden, and The Netherlands), or its influence over public policies has been more subtle over time (France, the F.R.G., and Israel). The effect of the changing ideologies of post-socialist countries on housing and neighbourhood policies is not yet apparent in Gáspár and Birghoffer's report about Hungary (Chapter 12), perhaps because Hungary, more than other East European countries, underwent significant change in its economic structure prior to the autumn of 1989. Had we included a report from Poland, for example, the effect of ideological change on housing and neighbourhood policies would probably have been more apparent.

Demographics and demand for housing. All the countries in this book are developed countries. Most have a typically low internal growth rate that

212

reflects both a low birth rate (compared with developing countries), and a restrictive immigration policy relative to entry demand. Yet even the controlled intake of immigrants is a major issue in Sweden, the U.K., France, and the U.S.A. because many of the immigrants end up in distressed neighbourhoods. Two countries, the F.R.G. and Israel, committed to allowing large-scale immigration, experienced in 1990 a major influx of refugees because of the dramatic changes in Eastern Europe. According to Schmoll (Chapter 7) and Alterman (Chapter 10), the increased pressure for housing is likely to have major impacts, both positive and negative, on neighbourhoods in distress. There is also a danger that national urban and housing policies will return to the agenda (and perhaps the mistakes) of the 1950s and 1960s when acute housing shortages led to mass construction of public-sector housing.

Despite a low or negative natural growth rate and little in-migration, East European countries are now experiencing a high demand for housing which reflects many years' accumulated demand because of insufficient construction. In some ways, the needs of these countries are similar to the post-war needs of Western Europe, a period during which many of the neighbourhoods now in distress were built.

In countries such as the U.S.S.R., Poland, Romania, and to a lesser extent Hungary, people are sometimes asked to wait 10 to 14 years for housing in some cities. This continuing unmet demand explains why current housing policies in these countries, even after democratization, are likely to differ in many ways from the policies of the U.S.A., Canada, the U.K., or some other European countries. For one thing, the East European countries will probably continue to emphasize quantity of production rather than fine tuning of quality. The housing production agenda will determine priorities and policies for regenerating existing neighbourhoods in a way markedly different from that in Western countries (as emerges from a close reading of the report on Hungary). Israel's present housing crisis, because of the influx of East European immigrants, is leading once again to an emphasis on speed and quantity of construction as in the 1950s and 1960s. Despite the government's genuine attempts to ensure good planning and design, there is a danger that quality will be compromised.

Location. The distressed neighbourhoods in the continental European countries represented in this book, and in Israel, are mainly located in the outer areas of cities — the 'outer estates' or 'peripheral estates.' In Israel, the national neighbourhood programme also covers many new towns in their entirety. Only in the U.S.A. and Canada do neighbourhood programmes focus mostly on neighbourhoods within or near city centres. (The Canadian programme, however, was predominantly implemented in small, semi-rural towns.) In the U.K., many of the regeneration neighbourhoods are located in the inner city, which refers there to the ring of older housing around the city centre. Other U.K. neighbourhoods, constructed as council housing, adhere to the continental European paradigm. The greater emphasis of this book on outer estates is partly the result of the book's focus on post-war housing, which excludes areas of historic preservation. Given this bias, the

213

differences among countries in location of distressed neighbourhoods are attributable to the particular initiator or developer of the neighbourhood.

Neighbourhood initiator. Except in the U.S.A. and Canada, most neighbourhoods now targeted for regeneration are relatively new. Some were constructed in the immediate post-war years in the late 1940s and 1950s, but many originated in the 1960s and even the 1970s. In all continental European countries and in Israel (and to a lesser extent in the U.K.), most of these neighbourhoods were originally constructed through direct public initiative, either by local government (the U.K.), quasi-public housing associations (The Netherlands, the F.R.G., Sweden, France), or national government (Hungary, Israel, France).

By contrast, in the U.S.A. and Canada, almost all the now-distressed neighbourhoods (except the limited number of public housing projects) were built by private developers. This is partly true for the U.K.'s industrial cities as well. While the decline in private housing is a complicated process, there are existing theories that can help us to understand it (see Chapter 3). But what explains the decline of relatively new social housing built through government initiative with the best intentions and allocated to certain eligible populations?

Most of these distressed neighbourhoods were built in order to meet acute housing shortages of the time, emphasizing scale and speed. These estates were typically built on the outskirts of large cities and towns (in the F.R.G., France, The Netherlands, Sweden, and Hungary) where land assembly was easier, either because the land was already in public hands (as in Hungary, Israel, and often in The Netherlands and Sweden), or because special land-use tools were available in order to appropriate private land for housing on the peripheries of cities (as in France).[5] These large projects were in some cases hastily constructed, often using prefabrication techniques that had not yet been perfected. Usually, these massive projects exhibited a high degree of architectural uniformity (or experimentation with unusual architectural styles). Invariably, in their uniformity, they restricted consumer choice. The authors here report that even though these projects were under public control, public services such as transportation, education, sports and culture, and access to shopping were inadequate. An even worse level of public services is apparent in many East European countries, such as in Poland, where planners typically allocated land for services, but once the housing units were constructed residents were told that financial resources had run out.

The publicly initiated housing projects ran into problems almost from their conception. Technical and physical problems emerged; residents with more resources moved, in some cases even from estates intended for middle-class or mixed-class residents (in Sweden, The Netherlands, the F.R.G., and Israel), leaving behind the weaker population strata. Social problems such as delinquency and drug addiction often ensued.

This picture leads to the conclusion that large-scale direct government involvement in the design and construction of neighbourhoods has potentially a blighting hand, unless an effort is made to avoid the dangers of uniformity, poor services, isolation, and reduced consumer choice.

The irrelevance of ongoing planning controls. A consensus emerges from all the contributors, whether explicitly, or by implication:[6] planning controls – zoning, land use plans, building permits – have been chronically unsuccessful in preventing neighbourhood decline or in regenerating neighbourhoods. Traditionally, planning controls are better equipped to handle 'negative' decisions about what is not allowed, than 'positive' mandates about what should be done in order to create viable, long-term neighbourhoods. Secondly, despite new directions in planning theory and the greater sensitivity of recent planning laws to social and economic considerations, planning instruments still concentrate on physical aspects of infrastructure and design, and fall short when it comes to social or economic factors. Third, most regulative planning institutions are accustomed to dealing with proposed new development, rather than with upgrading existing development. Fourth, in most countries regulative planning is institutionally weaker than action-oriented development planning. Finally, in some countries the agencies in charge of regulative planning are notoriously slow in making decisions and are plagued by chronic bottlenecks. The obsolescence of housing standards is often reinforced by the time delays inherent in the planning system. Thus, in most of the countries here, neighbourhood regeneration did not emerge from the regular legal powers of the planning and permitting systems. Regeneration needed a specially designed programme.

Characteristics of regeneration programmes

Comprehensiveness. It was surprising to find that most of the European regeneration programmes described in this book are unisectoral and focus mostly or solely on the physical renovation of housing and infrastructure. This is true for Sweden, Hungary, Holland, the U.K., and the F.R.G. In these countries, if multi-sectoral programmes exist, they are experimental or local initiatives at a few select sites, and are only partially comprehensive. Examples here are the Gilliswijk project in The Netherlands; four projects in the F.R.G. (Kiel, Hamburg, and two in Berlin); and Middlesbrough and Newcastle in the U.K.

Comprehensive approaches, which link together social, educational, cultural, economic, and citizen-empowerment policies, have been institutionalized in only two countries, France and Israel, and have been encouraged in Canada. In France and Israel, where the particular programmes are packaged locally and vary in the spectrum they cover, national policy ensures a multi-sectoral approach. In Canada, although the national framework is multi-sectoral, the degree of comprehensiveness varies tremendously among cities and programmes. This diversity is probably a result of Canada's decentralized political structure and growing emphasis on provincial and local control. In the U.S.A., comprehensive programmes such as the Model Cities Program existed in the past and stressed mostly social services and economic development. The federal cutbacks of the 1980s, however, have almost dried up these programmes. Programmes in the U.S.A. today are more sporadic and limited in scope.

The dominance of physical-improvement programmes is enigmatic, especially in Western countries where extensive research into neighbourhood programmes carried out over the past two decades has shown that neighbourhood regeneration requires a co-ordinated social, economic, and educational approach. By contrast, the emphasis on physical improvement is not so surprising in Hungary and other East European countries, where housing is in short supply and physically inadequate, and the economy is struggling. In these countries, it is unlikely that scarce resources will be devoted in the near future to such 'luxury' items as enhancing community control, social interaction, and local cultural activities. Indeed, in the U.S.S.R., the community worker is virtually non-existent and sociologists are few.

Population relocation or stabilization. Some of the programmes described in this book, notably in Hungary, are unconcerned with whether renewal causes demographic change. In a few countries (notably the U.S.A. and U.K.), some programmes are explicitly designed to produce a population turnover through gentrification. In most countries, however, including the U.S.A. and the U.K., policymakers are aware of the negative lessons learned through urban renewal in the dislocation of residents. Most programmes in the 1980s explicitly tried to maintain the social fabric of the neighbourhood. This is especially true in the French and Israeli programmes. Partial exceptions are The Netherlands, where policymakers limited the influx of large families into the Gilliswijk district of Delft, and Sweden, where many 'problem families' were temporarily or permanently moved during renewal. Carlén and Cars (Chapter 9) state that the removal of problem families does not necessarily constitute a desired outcome since most evicted households simply relocate in neighbouring housing areas, displacing the problem rather than solving it.

Implementation characteristics

Most chapters in this book provide little information on the decision-making processes and institutional structures for implementing regeneration programmes (exceptions are Chapter 2 on Canada and Chapters 10 and 11 on Israel, and occasional references to this issue in the chapters by Wood, Schmoll, Priemus, and Tricart). It is difficult to judge whether this omission reflects a low level of institutionalization, or whether it merely reflects the professional bias of most of the authors toward the social sciences rather than the policy sciences. A few generalizations can, however, be made.

Levels of government. Every neighbourhood regeneration programme here relies on central government to some extent, most to a great extent. Differences can be seen in the kinds of mechanisms employed to achieve renewal, the stage at which the central government turns over the responsibility for implementation to local (or provincial, or state) authorities, and in the degree of control that remains at the central level.

216

In some of the countries here, central government involvement today is indirect. In the U.K., various incentives, such as improvement subsidies and loans, are provided by central government to encourage private owners and renters to improve their dwellings. The major role that local governments in the U.K. played in housing policy in the past has in recent years been drastically reduced, in favour of a privatization policy orchestrated by central government. In France, the effects of the landmark decentralization programme that began in 1982–83 are apparent in the degree of freedom allowed to local authorities and regions, yet the main goals, structure, and financing of the project are directed by central government. Hungary and Israel, to different degrees, show more direct central control over regeneration projects than the other countries. This involvement is likely to decline in Hungary with the progress of democratization, while it is likely to grow in Israel as a response to the urgent needs for housing new immigrants.

Control and administration is more dispersed in the three federal countries represented here. In the F.R.G., the states and municipalities have a significant degree of autonomy. Various incentives (including subsidy, rebates, and tax breaks) are employed by the federal and state governments to encourage privately owned housing companies to undertake renovation projects. Similarly, the provinces in Canada exert a considerable, and growing, degree of control over the actual planning and implementation of federally initiated programmes. In the U.S.A., the involvement of the federal government in housing and neighbourhood issues declined significantly in the 1980s as a result of Republican ideology about the role of the government. This has left local governments to search for various home-grown substitutes, such as 'linkage' fees requiring office and commercial builders to pay a contribution towards 'affordable' housing (Alterman, 1989). The result has been an exacerbation of urban problems, and a growing disparity among cities that reflects differences in local tax base and propensity for taking local initiative.

Scale of programme. Not surprisingly, the three comprehensive programmes are relatively large: Canada's Neighbourhood Improvement Program includes 479 areas in 322 municipalities; France's Neighbourhood Social Development programme covers 150 neighbourhoods nationwide; and Israel's Project Renewal (currently undergoing a yet unspecified process of gradual transformation in response to the challenges of immigrant absorption) has covered 90 neighbourhoods and, relative to the country's population size, is the largest of the three. Because comprehensive programmes require the co-ordinated effort of agencies not accustomed to working together, these programmes seem to depend on a relatively sophisticated form of institutionalization. Thus they merit their national status in Israel, France, and Canada. Unisectoral, physical regeneration programmes in some countries (especially in the U.K.) also cover a large number of neighbourhoods. These programmes usually do not require sophisticated organization on the national level.

Resident participation. Many of the authors link the success of regeneration programmes to resident participation. Surprisingly, public participation seems to be a relatively low priority in Sweden, perhaps because it is a tradi-tional part of daily life there and does not need a boost from neighbourhood regeneration programmes. Less surprising is the low priority placed on public participation in Hungary. In the U.S.A., public participation was a major goal of several of the federal programmes in the 1960s and 1970s. In France, public participation is an explicit goal of the Neighbourhood Social Development programme, which encourages the formation of co-operative groups of citizen representatives and local authorities to administer local programmes. In Israel, resident participation is an innovation explicitly introduced by Project Renewal.

Outputs and outcomes

Determining the outcomes of the numerous and wide-ranging programmes in this book is the most problematic aspect of this analysis and a major stumbling block to assessing transferability. The questions asked and the measures used are inconsistent among authors, programmes, and countries.

The role of evaluation. There is a near consensus among the authors con-cerning the insufficient attention paid by decision makers to independent, objective, and sustained evaluation that monitors the process and outcomes of programmes and uses the information to guide further decisions. This discontent is expressed even in the U.S.A., France, and Israel, where evalua-tion research has been relatively extensive and has studied 'live' neighbour-hood programmes. Tricart from France and Spiro from Israel, representing quite different countries, candidly discuss the dilemmas involved in produc-ing decision-relevant evaluations. Their similar conclusions point perhaps to universal issues.

Outputs. Outputs can be measured by money spent and populations reached by each programme. However, comparisons based on these cate-gories would be misleading because of differences in programme duration, costs, buying power, and economies of scale.

Outcomes. Comparative conclusions regarding outcomes are even more difficult, since evaluation measures differ. The Swedish and Dutch chapters prefer concrete indices, such as apartment vacancy rates and tenant out-migration. The American and Israeli papers refer to a broad range of indi-cators that assess both the implementation processes and the programmes' outcomes, including resident satisfaction. But even if the evaluation criteria were the same, it would be difficult to ascribe a causal relationship between regeneration programmes and the physical, social, or economic changes in a neighbourhood. Social and economic improvements, and even some physical improvements, may be caused by general trends rather than the regeneration programme, as Spiro notes for Israel and Kaplan for the U.S.A.

Several authors raise serious doubts about the outcomes achieved by regeneration programmes. Although many physical renovations have been made in the U.K., the absolute number of dwellings classified as unfit has

218

remained almost constant. In the F.R.G. and Sweden, technical problems in large-scale housing estates persist despite concerted efforts to solve them.

A programme's impact on social problems is even more difficult to judge. For example, improvement in the crime statistics in the Gilliswijk district in The Netherlands was found only on a limited scale and within a limited area. According to Priemus (Chapter 8) the longevity of this change is not guaranteed. Moreover, the problems in targeted areas frequently spill over to adjacent areas, as has been noted regarding high crime areas in the U.S.A. and areas with 'problem families' in Sweden.

THE GLOBAL CHALLENGE

Pessimistic as these conclusions might be, they stress the importance of continuing the task of cross-national exchange to enhance and build on what we know about how neighbourhoods in distress anywhere in the world can be regenerated. Although the 'grand research scheme' is unfeasible, and we cannot create an elegant model linking contextual variables, programme elements, implementation characteristics, and outputs and outcomes, cross-national learning is nevertheless both imperative and possible.

The kind of transnational exchange seen in this book is imperative because we are the 'haves'. If we, with our relatively tame housing problems, our stable population size, our capacity for furthering scientific knowledge, and our healthy economies (all relative to the 'have-not' countries), cannot improve our knowledge of how to pull urban neighbourhoods out of their cycle of decline, then we deny the promise of a better life to the majority of the world's population who must contend with much more obstinate problems.

We are at a threshold. The revolution in Eastern Europe challenges Western urbanists and social scientists to find a way to transfer neighbourhood regeneration policies to countries that are mid-way between the 'haves' and the 'have nots' and are still entrenched in industrial problems. Their urgent priorities preclude them from luxuriating in our post-industrial agenda. They will continue to place a higher emphasis on quantity of housing units than on optimal quality and design; and a higher priority on critical environmental issues such as polluted drinking water and air pollution than on the micro-environment of neighbourhoods. The disintegration of the Iron Curtain has revealed to us the enormity of the task of improving the life of the residents of these countries.

Transnational exchange is possible through a modest strategy of country-specific research rather than a grand strategy. There are no short cuts. Before we can undertake rigorous transnational research, we need to improve our theories in the social, behavioural, and policy sciences on questions that relate to both neighbourhood decline and to the operation and effectiveness of public regeneration programmes.

As Kaplan (Chapter 3) frankly admits, American scientists are not yet sure why some neighbourhoods decline and others do not. Country-specific research can benefit from findings from other countries that push the frontier of what we know about the behaviour of neighbourhoods. More country-specific research and evaluation of public policies — how they are formed, how they are implemented, and what results they achieve — can aid in the task of building theories which can then be tested for their cross-national applicability.[7] It is hoped that this book will contribute towards better transnational exchange and will provide useful information for the tasks of local research and policy making.

NOTES

My thanks go to David Shefer, a student at the Graduate Program in Urban and Regional Planning at the Technion, Haifa, for his assistance in parts of this chapter.

1. A comparison of the American Model Cities Program and Israel's Project Renewal is presented by Frieden and Kaplan (1987–88).

2. I first heard the concept of Euro-English from Richard Williams at conferences in 1988 and 1989.

3. For more comprehensive definitions of these concepts see Alterman *et al.* (1984).

4. The discussion of East European countries in this chapter relies on the author's study visits to Russia, Poland, and the G.D.R.

5. The particular tools in France were ZUP, ZAC, and ZAD. ZUP are 'zones à urbaniser en priorité', and were introduced in 1958. ZACs are 'zones d'aménagement concentré' and were introduced in 1967. ZAD are 'zones d'aménagement différé', and were introduced in 1962. All three tools are based on pre-emption and expropriation rights. ZUPs especially were used to construct large concentrations of housing, especially around Paris, and are today identified with neighbourhoods in distress. See Pearsall (1988) and Gohier (1988).

6. This conclusion is stated directly by Priemus on The Netherlands and by Alterman on Israel, and is implied by the other authors.

7. This author has attempted to apply existing implementation theory to the analysis and evaluation of the implementation process of Israel's Project Renewal, and then proceeded to draw conclusions about the transferability of the findings to other policy contexts. See Alterman (1988).

REFERENCES

ALTERMAN, R. (1987–88) Opening up the 'black box' in evaluating neighborhood programs: the implementation process in Israel's Project Renewal. *Policy Studies Journal*, **16** (2), 347–361.

ALTERMAN, R. (1988) Implementing decentralization for neighborhood regeneration: factors promoting or inhibiting success. *Journal of the American Planning Association*, **54** (4), 454–469.

ALTERMAN, R. (1989) *Evaluating Linkage, and Beyond*. Monograph published by the Lincoln Institute of Land Policy, Cambridge, MA. A somewhat abridged version has been published in *Washington University Journal of Urban and Contemporary Law*, 32, 3–39.

ALTERMAN, R., N. CARMON and M. HILL (1984) Integrated evaluation: a synthesis of approaches to the evaluation of broad-aim social programs. *Socioeconomic Planning Sciences*, **18** (6), 381–389.

FRIEDEN, B. J. and M. KAPLAN (1987–1988) Model Cities and Project Renewal: adjusting the strategy to the 1980s. *Policy Studies Journal*, **16** (2), 377–383.

GOHIER, J. (1988) Changes in trends and laws. In *Land Policy in France*. Paris: Association des Études Foncières.

HALLETT, G., ed. (1988) *Land and Housing Policies in Europe and the USA: A Comparative Analysis*. London: Routledge.

MASSER, I. and R. WILLIAMS, eds (1986) *Learning from Other Countries.* Norwich, U.K.: Geo Books.

PEARSALL, J. (1988) France. In: G. Hallett (ed.) *Land and Housing Policies in Europe and the USA: A Comparative Analysis*, pp. 76–98. London: Routledge.

WILLIAMS, R. (1989) Are we speaking the same language? Paper presented at the Annual Congress of AESOP — the Association of European Schools of Planning, Tours, France, November.

INDEX

223